Hollywood Films
in North Africa
and the Middle East

THE SUNY SERIES

HORIZONS OF CINEMA

MURRAY POMERANCE | EDITOR

Hollywood Films
in North Africa
and the Middle East

A History of Circulation

Nolwenn Mingant

SUNY
PRESS

Published by State University of New York Press, Albany

For information, contact State University of New York Press, Albany, NY
www.sunypress.edu

Library of Congress Cataloging-in-Publication Data

Name: Mingant, Nolwenn, author.
Title: Hollywood films in North Africa and the Middle East : a history of circulation / Nolwenn Mingant.
Description: Albany : SUNY Press, [2022] | Series: SUNY series, horizons of cinema | Includes bibliographical references and index.
Identifiers: LCCN 2021061293 (print) | LCCN 2021061294 (ebook) | ISBN 9781438488554 (hardcover : alk. paper) | ISBN 9781438488561 (ebook) | ISBN 9781438488547 (pbk. : alk. paper)
Subjects: LCSH: Motion pictures—Distribution—History. | Motion picture industry—United States—History. | Motion pictures, American—Africa, North. | Motion pictures, American—Middle East.
Classification: LCC PN1993.5.U6 M595 2022 (print) | LCC PN1993.5.U6 (ebook) | DDC 384/.809730904—dc23/eng/20220112
LC record available at https://lccn.loc.gov/2021061293
LC ebook record available at https://lccn.loc.gov/2021061294

10 9 8 7 6 5 4 3 2 1

To Vincent Pisani,

To Ezelius and Brune, my rainbow and sunshine

Contents

Illustrations

Figures

Tables

Acknowledgments

This book is the result of an intellectual and human journey, lived both through countless solitary and quiet hours in the depth of archival funds and through many lively and convivial conferences with colleagues from all over the world. This book would not have been possible without the friendship and emulation I found in two research projects I cocreated. The CinEcoSA conferences, organized with Joël Augros and Cecilia Tirtaine, were welcoming meetings points for academics from various points of the globe. In a friendly atmosphere, we exchanged about film marketing and public policy, sharing experiences, knowledge, and views. The MENA Cinema project, created with Abdelfettah Benchenna and Patricia Caillé, was also key to the journey toward this book. As a meeting point for academics from Europe, North Africa, the Middle East, and the US, all intent on opening a path of exploration on film industries in North Africa and the Middle East, the MENA Cinema conferences served as a compass to make sure I did not lose my way. I am grateful that our collaboration with Claude Forest morphed the project into the full-fledged research group HESCALE, dedicated to cinema in Africa and the Middle East and hosted at the Sorbonne Nouvelle University. My gratitude thus goes to my fellow organizers, who know what I owe them, but also to all the colleagues and friends who participated in these conferences and made these moments thought-provoking, challenging, and unique. I am also indebted to all my colleagues in international scientific fora, who shared their research and comments, during the annual conferences of the Association française d'etudes américaines (AFEA), the Société d'etudes et de recherches sur le cinéma anglophone (SERCIA), the European Network for Cinema and Media Studies (NECS), and the Society for Cinema and Media Studies (SCMS).

While academic emulation and support was essential, this book would not have been possible without the members of the film distribution community. I am deeply indebted to the film distributors and professionals who volunteered their time to be interviewed and shared their life and professional experience with me. A thousand thanks to Malek Ali-Yahia, Sherif Awad, Najib Benkiran, Gianluca Chakra, Andrew Cripps, Selim El-Azar, Joseph Fahim, Zertal Hachemi, Mario Haddad, Sr., Hamid Marrakchi, Pierre Mekary, Mohamed Layadi, Chris Marcich, Tarik Mounim, Hyam Saliby, Badar Salem, Mark Viane, and Antoine Zeind. My thanks also go to all the other film professionals from North Africa, the Middle East, and the US who provided candid accounts on conditions of anonymity.

Over the past dozen years, this project benefited from solid institutional support. In 2015, the Association française d'etudes américaines awarded me a travel grant to attend SCMS, an academic heaven for media industry scholars. The Conseil national des universités (CNU) granted me a sabbatical semester in 2018 to write the first draft of this book. My everlasting gratitude goes to the directors of my research centers for their unwavering support: Hélène Le Dantec-Lowry at the Sorbonne Nouvelle University and Georges Letissier at the University of Nantes. The original manuscript was also carefully reviewed by my *habilitation à diriger des recherches* (HDR) advisor, David Roche, who proved an infallible mentor, an astute advisor, and a friend. I am also grateful to the members of my HDR committee whose approval opened the way to professorship: Joël Augros, Frédéric Gimello-Mesplomb, Delphine Letort, Monica Michlin, and Anne Stéfani.

History books would not exist without the patient work of generations of archivists. Their contribution, though anonymous, is invaluable. I thus would like to thank not only a number of libraries and institutions who opened their doors to me, but also the librarians and archivists without whom this book would not exist. Many thanks to the Margaret Herrick Library in Los Angeles and the Bibliothèque du film at the French Cinémathèque, to the National Archives in Washington and the Diplomatic Archives in Nantes, and to the Pathé archives in Paris. I particularly would like to acknowledge the contribution of my colleague Morgan Corriou, who taught me how to navigate the world of archives.

Transforming this book project into a reality was possible through the patient and unwavering support of Murray Pomerance and James Peltz at State University of New York Press. Many thanks for their astute comments and frequent emails. I am also indebted to the anonymous reviewers whose insightful remarks helped me hone the original manuscript into a compelling volume. When the manuscript reached its final form, I was grateful to be able to count on Kaveh Askari and Patricia Caillé to cast a last look at some of the chapters and enable me to reference recent research.

On a more personal note, I would like to thank my parents, Danièle and Charles Mingant, whose tranquil confidence helped me go through the sometimes-difficult process of researching and writing this book. My sister, Frédérique Mingant, provided material help, intellectual stimulation, and comic relief. I am grateful to Vincent Pisani who has been my unfailing companion, come rain or shine. A dozen years dedicated to a research project is a lifetime, full of exhilaration but also low points. I am forever indebted to psychiatrist Elise Lelarge and relaxation therapist Magalie Michaud for helping me reinvent my life when it became necessary. As I write these lines, the world is grappling with a dreadful sanitary crisis. As we find ourselves confined and isolated, the necessity to rethink our lives has become imperative. What this project has taught me is that reinvention can only be possible through care, attention, and collaboration.

Introduction

IN OCTOBER 2001, THE *Los Angeles Times* ran an article entitled "Death to U.S., but Not Films." The journalists were puzzled by a paradox: while the US as a nation was largely unpopular in the Muslim world due to its foreign policy choices and military interventions, American films were loved by audiences in the region. In "societies where 'Death to America' is being chanted in the streets," they explained, people flocked to *Titanic* (1997) and *The Fast and the Furious* (2001). The article resolved the conundrum by attributing Hollywood's success to the myth-like universality of its films and their high production value, an argument traditionally developed by film historians. While the article did justice to the political value films can acquire, it failed to take into account the fact that American films had been present—and popular—in the Middle East long before US involvement in the region began. The journalists' surprise when noting that Middle Eastern people liked US films—as many other people around the world do—can also be linked to a general misconception equating the Arab world with antagonism towards everything American, a misconception partly fed by Hollywood itself in numerous "Arab-as-Enemy movies" and in "Kill-'em-all films," such as *True Lies* (1994) and *Rules of Engagement* (2000) (Shaheen 2008, xix). This book proposes to dispel this vision by bringing to light the very concrete relations, oppositions, and networks that have in fact intimately linked Hollywood to film professionals, state officials, and audiences in North Africa and the Middle East over the past century. Such a work of de-essentializing opens up access to the very complexity of these ties and provides lessons about transnational film exchanges.

While the press often refers to the region as the "Muslim world" and "the Arab world," these generic terms downplay the real-life intricacies

1

of an area comprising twenty-two Arab states, as well as non-Arab-states, each with its own political agenda (Shaheen 2009, 8). Indeed, in this book, not all the spectators under scrutiny will be Muslim, and not all the countries Arab. This study will concentrate on the presence and circulation of US films in the North Africa and Middle East region and cover nineteen countries in three geographical areas: North Africa (Algeria, Libya, Morocco, Tunisia), the Middle East (Egypt, Iran, Iraq, Israel, Jordan, Lebanon, Syria, Palestinian Authority), and the Gulf (Bahrain, Kuwait, Oman, Qatar, Saudi Arabia, United Arab Emirates, Yemen). Cinema was introduced in North Africa and in the Middle East at the same time as in the rest of the world. The French Lumière operators visited Algeria, Tunisia, and Egypt in 1896, both recording and showing film scenes (Armes 2006, 14; Shafik 2007, 10; Ginsberg and Lippard 2010, xxi). The first full-time movie theaters were opened in 1900 in Egypt and Palestine; 1908 in Algeria, Persia (present-day Iran), and Tunisia; 1909 in Mesopotamia (present-day Iraq) and Lebanon; 1910 in Syria; 1937 in Manama (Bahrain); and 1954 in Kuwait. By the early 1950s, cinema had spread all over the region, and countries such as Egypt and Iran had flourishing film industries. The North Africa and Middle East region has thus been present on the film map for more than a century now. From the early years of cinema, US films were largely present in the area. In 1926, they held 85% of the market share in the French colonies of the Maghreb, 55% of the Egyptian market, 40% of the Persian market, and 70% of the Syrian market. In 1930, they held 70% of the Palestinian market. In Iraq, 90% of films shown were American in 1937 (*Film Daily Year Book*, 1927, 1931, 1938). North African and Middle Eastern spectators' taste for Hollywood fare is thus not a novel phenomenon but has deep historical roots.

The encounter between US films and the Middle Eastern and North African audiences has been made possible through the agency of US, French, and local distributors, as well as state officials and informal players. Their strategies, collaborations, and confrontations are the topic of this book. The circulation of US films has also largely been shaped by the region's political history. The first US reels entered an area under European domination. European colonizers marked North Africa and the Middle East politically, socially, and geographically. Sealing the unraveling of the Ottoman Empire, the 1916 Sykes-Picot Agreement, reshaped country boundaries as two colonial empires were carved. France took control of Lebanon and Syria. Great Britain took control of Mesopotamia, Palestine, Transjordan, and Egypt (Thiollet 2009, 53). The British ruler had also established an informal protectorate on the Trucial States in the Persian Gulf in the 1820s and was an ally to the Saudi Arabian kingdom founded in 1927 (Piquet 2013, 39; Cloarec and Laurens 2007, 58–59). The Maghreb was dominated by France. Algeria officially became part of France in 1848 and was divided into three *départements*. Tunisia became a French protectorate in 1881 and Morocco in 1912 (Katan Bensamoun 2007, 379–81). Two other European powers held territories in the region: Italy in Libya and Spain in Northern Morocco. While, in cinematic terms, the region was characterized by a variety of audiences, accentuated by the social divisions imposed by the colonial order, US film distributors routinely wooed this fragmented audience and found market conditions very favorable.

After World War II, however, the political context radically changed. Nationalist movements gained strength and led their country to independence. Lebanon and Syria obtained independence in 1946, Morocco and Tunisia in 1956, and Algeria in 1962, after a bloody eight-year war. In the Middle East, countries whose independence from British rule had been officialized before World War II (Iraq in 1932, Egypt in 1937) experienced political turmoil as nationalist coups deposed British-supported monarchies: the Egyptian revolution of 1952, which brought Gamal Abdel Nasser to power, and the 14 July Revolution of 1958 in Iraq. The establishment of the state of Israel in 1948, leading to a protracted and violent political conflict with its Arab neighbors, strongly destabilized regional relations. In the context of the Cold War, anti-Western regimes allied with the USSR: Iraq after the 1968 Ba'athist coup, Libya after Muammar Gaddafi took power in 1969, and Syria after Hafez al-Assad's coup in 1971. Lebanon bore the brunt both of the Arab-Israeli conflict and the Cold War, finding itself engulfed in a bloody civil war between pro-Western Christian Maronites and anti-Western Palestinian forces from 1975 to 1990. Power balance in the region was further altered by the 1979 Islamic Revolution in Iran. The postwar North Africa and Middle East turned out to be a complex world for Hollywood film distributors to navigate, as countries experienced widespread political instability and US films became pawns in the larger political game of the Cold War.

While the circulation of US films was strongly destabilized by the region's political sea change from the 1950s to the late 1970s, technological evolutions provided additional challenges from the 1980s onwards with the advent of the VCR and the consequent spread of film piracy. In the past two decades, the development of formal and informal circulation paths, from DVDs and satellite television to Internet streaming and downloading, in fact became the major determinant of US film's presence, supersed-ing the influence of the political context. Although the 1991 Gulf War and the 2003 Iraq war and subsequent US military occupation revived anti-American feelings, US films have remained largely popular among North African and Middle Eastern audiences. Similarly, this presence and popularity does not seem to have been impacted by the major political movement of the past decade, the Arab Spring of 2011, which led to a transition toward democratic governance in Tunisia, but morphed into an Arab Winter, with the advent of civil wars in Syria, Libya, Yemen, and Iraq, and the tightening of state control in Egypt. While, in the postwar period, regime changes had a strong impact on US films distributed in movie theaters, the recent political turmoil had little impact on films now circulating largely through a variety of formal and informal paths.

Uncovering the rich, complex, and hitherto unexplored relation between Hollywood films, its distributors, and the North African and Middle Eastern film markets since the 1910s required gathering primary sources spanning over a century. For this project clearly focused on Hollywood distribution companies and their films, I first turned to US sources. The press articles gathered by the archivists of the Margaret Herrick library in Los Angeles provided information as far back as the 1930s for certain areas. Press clippings from the *Motion Picture Herald*, *Variety*, and *The Hollywood Reporter* conveyed how the North African and Middle Eastern markets were viewed at the time by US distributors. A second major source was the US State Department archives in Washington (NARA). I had access to the communications to and from US ambassadors in the region from 1910 to 1977. Compared to the press articles, the diplomatic telegrams provided an unvarnished description of the situa-tion. They also systematically analyzed the presence and circulation of US film both in the specific local political context and in relation to the larger US diplomatic aims. The industry perspective on the possibilities and challenges in each market was completed by a systematic reading of *Wid's Year Book* (1920–1921), the *Film Daily Year Book* (1922–1970), and the *International Motion Picture Almanac* (1964–2014). Given the colonial history of the region, French archival sources also proved invaluable for the first half of the twentieth century. I was additionally granted access to the Pathé archives in Paris, which furnished an overview of the dis-tribution strategy of one of the earliest key players of the international film world. The French diplomatic archives in Nantes then provided a sporadic but useful depiction of cinema in Morocco, Syria, and Lebanon. Most importantly this state source was very revealing about the vision of cinema within the colonial project, notably through the numerous censorship reports for Morocco. Finally, the French Cinémathèque library provided invaluable primary documents such as the *Middle East Motion Picture Almanac* (1947) and the *Annuaire du cinema pour le Moyen-Orient et l'Afrique du Nord* (1952).

The late 1970s and 1980s proved to be the most difficult period to document. However, I could rely on Margaret Herrick library press clippings as well as volumes written by film players and researchers in North Africa and the Middle East (Cheriaa 1978; Megherbi 1985; Nouri 1986). I also uncovered a series of publications from the Centre interarabe du cinéma et de la télévision at the French National Library. These local sources brought light on the place of cinema in the struggle for independence, as well as the way US cinema and distributors were considered by local film professionals and state officials. Researching the early twenty-first century posed another challenge. Information was accessible from varied sources: the US press, notably the short-lived magazine *Variety Arabia* (2011–2012), the local papers accessible online, such as UAE's *The National*, and the EuroMed Audiovisual II 2010s *Project of Statistical Data Collection on Film and Audiovisual Markets in 9 Mediterranean Countries*. Such information was, however, often factual. Figures do not tell the entire story. I thus set out to complete those sources by interviewing distributors of US films in the area. Their routinely operating in English and French, the two languages that I speak, made the interview process easier. The book thus draws on about two dozen interviews with film professionals: North African, Middle Eastern, and US film distributors, film policy executives, and exhibitors. Veteran film distributors such as Antoine Zeind in Egypt, Mario Haddad, Sr., in Lebanon, and Najib Benkiran in Morocco provided long-term accounts of the presence and circulation of Hollywood films in their countries, as well as a healthy balance to the book's perspective.

All through the project, I also reached out to professionals and academics from North Africa and the Middle East. In collaboration with Patricia Caillé and Abdelfettah Benchenna, I created MENA Cinema, a research project with the aim of igniting new academic interest in documenting the past and current history of film industries in the region. Through international conferences, professional roundtables, and panels at international academic organizations such as the Society for Cinema and Media Studies (SCMS), the MENA Cinema project created a momentum, bringing together confirmed and young academics, as well as film professionals, from all over North Africa and the Middle East, as well as Europe and the US. As the project drew to a close, the research group HESCALE, led by Caillé and Claude Forest and hosted at the Sorbonne Nouvelle University in Paris, was created to promote research on the history, economy, and sociology of film in Africa and the Levant. Four major publications, Benchenna, Caillé, and Mingant's *La circulation des films: Afrique du Nord et Moyen-Orient* (2016), Caillé and Forest's *Regarder des films en Afrique* (2017), Forest's *Produire des films: Afriques et Moyen Orient* (2018), and Caillé and Forest's *Pratiques et usages du film en Afriques francophones: Maroc, Tchad, Togo, Tunisie* (2019), are paving the way for what we hope will be a new and dynamic research field and a place of intercultural dialogue.

Drawing mostly on Western institutional and press sources, balanced by conversations with film professionals and academics from North Africa and the Middle East, this book is an effort in multicultural media studies, a field in which "multiculturalism means seeing world history and contemporary social life from the perspective of the radical equality of peoples in status, potential, and rights" (Shohat and Stam 1994, 6). As Shohat and Stam expand, "Multiculturalism decolonized representations not only in terms of cultural artifacts—literary canons, museum exhibits, film series—but also in terms of power relations between communities" (5). This book thus offers to bring to light the multifarious relations between Hollywood and North African and Middle Eastern film professionals, foregrounding the evolution of the circulation of US films depending on local political, economic, and cultural specificities and their evolutions. It proposes a very exhaustive exploration of the complex and multiple intercultural relations at play around the circulation of Hollywood films in North Africa and the Middle East over the past century. What it does not propose, however, is a definitive story. Access to local papers as well as film and diplomatic archives in North Africa and the Middle East would—and will—offer complementary, alternative, and challenging visions. This study thus purports to be one voice in larger conversations on cinema in North Africa and the Middle East, as well as on film industry and film distribution studies

Middle Eastern film studies has been gaining momentum under the impetus of Roy Armes (2001, 2011), Josef Gugler (2011) and, more recently, Terri Ginsberg and Chris Lippard (2010, 2020). This book will contribute to the field by proposing an economic perspective and a regional scope. Due to the highly charged political situation in many countries of the region, academic literature has mostly focused on the political resonances of North African and Middle Eastern cinema, with works such as Shohat's *Israeli Cinema: East/West and the Politics of Representation* (1989) and Khatib's *Lebanese Cinema: Imagining the Civil War and Beyond* (2008) Aesthetic and political analyses have also been the heart of encyclopedic efforts, especially Leaman's *Companion Encyclopedia of Middle Eastern and North African Film* (2001), Dönmez-Colin's *Cinema of North Africa and the Middle East* (2007), Ginsberg and Lippard's *Historical Dictionary of Middle Eastern Cinema* (2010), Gugler's *Film in the Middle East and North Africa: Creative Dissidence* (2011). I contend that bringing an industrial perspective in the conversation can be fruitful. Studies dedicated to the industrial issues of production, distribution, and exhibition do exist, but mostly date from the 1960s and 1970s. They were written at a time when cinema was seen as a means to develop a strong identity for newly independent nations. This activist approach can be particularly felt in Cheriaa's *Ecrans d'abondance, ou cinémas de libération en Afrique* (1978), and endured in Megherbi's *Le miroir aux alouettes: Lumière sur les ombres hollywoodiennes en Algérie et dans le monde* (1985) and Nouri's *À la recherche du cinéma irakien* (1986). Only the film industries in Iran (Issari 1989; Devictor 2004; Sadr 2006; Naficy 2011–2012) and, to a lesser extent, Morocco (Jaidi 1995; Dwyer 2004; Carter 2009) have continued to be the object of industry-centered documented research. For other countries, I gathered information in sporadic encyclopedic efforts (Sadoul 1966; Kamalipour and Mowlana1994) and in French academic Yves Thoraval's almost single-handed effort to document this industrial history (Thoraval 1996, 2000, 2003). This political economy approach places my work in line with that of a new generation of scholars such as Morgan Corriou and Kaveh Askari. Studying the industrial issue of distribution additionally invites a shift away from traditional national case studies and the adoption a regional perspective. While this book will examine national specificities, it will mostly be exploring the dynamic exchanges, collaborations, and competitions at play between the different film industries and markets. Through the history of the circulation of Hollywood films in North Africa and the Middle East, I thus also propose a history of the regional film market, which is another way of writing the history of cinema in North Africa and the Middle East.

Theoretically, the book is firmly grounded in the US tradition of film industry studies. Historical accounts developed from the 1980s onwards, such as Balio's 1985 *The American Film Industry* and Kerr's 1986 *The Hollywood Film Industry*, provided a useful framework to think Hollywood major distributors as players with their own traditional practices and helped in considering how these practices were applied to North

Africa and the Middle East over time. The political economy approach developed notably by Wasko was also a strong inspiration to conceptualize issues of balance and asymmetry of power. The book follows the tradition of giving prominence to the circulation of films through the Hollywood majors, since they have the most visible archival presence and their strategies can be traced over time, but it does refer to independent companies each time information was available. The book is not, however, simply about distribution by these companies, but about the circulation of US films. Lobato's *Shadow Economies of Cinema*, with its exploration of "alternative distribution networks" and "issues of access and agency" (Perren 2013, 168) has indeed been a strong influence. The story of film circulation in North Africa and the Middle East is as much a story of informal, secondhand, and alternative circulation as a story of official distribution. The shift in focus from distribution to circulation led to foregrounding the role of individual agents. I concur with Brannon Donoghue's assessment of "how invisible most of the international mid-level management and practices are to the academic community and general public" (2017, 11). This focus on a midlevel "view of industry operation" and "agency within industry operations" put this study in resonance with Havens, Lotz, and Tinic's (2009, 246) call for the development of critical media industry studies.

This book aims to contribute more specifically to the field of distribution studies, both through its ambitious methodological approach and its international scope. In "Rethinking Distribution for the Future of Media Industry Studies," Alisa Perren identifies four different "theoretical and methodological frameworks" used by scholars studying film distribution (Perren 2013, 166). A top-down political-economic approach scrutinizes the major media conglomerates and explores issues of corporate power. Cultural studies scholars, on the other hand, have developed a bottom-up approach "considering the cultural dimensions of distribution decisions" (166). Global media studies scholars have studied content flows over "local, regional, and global distribution networks" (166). Finally, media historians have studied nonprofit institution and organization participation in distribution processes. In this volume, I put all these different approaches to task. The perspective alternates from a top-down analysis of US distributor's strategies (chapter 1) to a bottom-up approach focusing on intercultural collaboration with local film players, as well as reception by varied audiences across the region (chapter 2). It often interrogates the role of states (chapter 3) and occasionally nonprofit associations (chapter 6) in shaping the paths of film circulation. The flows at the heart of the book are sometimes presented within national case studies (part 3) but, in the end, they always draw a larger portrait, uncovering changing regional dynamics (chapter 4), and unfolding global distribution networks that encompass not only North America, North Africa, and the Middle East, but also Europe and India. The book thus demonstrates how these theoretical approaches hitherto considered as separate can in fact dialogue and merge, providing a rich and all-encompassing framework.

The book contributes to distribution studies not only by this all-encompassing theoretical framework but also by its international scope, shifting away from a traditional North America–centered perspective to favor transnational phenomena. While Miller, Govil, McMurria, and Maxwell's political economy approach in *Global Hollywood* (2001) was a useful background to conceptualizing relations that have often been asymmetrical, I found more dynamic accounts in the small but strong literature dealing with the history of the international distribution of American films. Volumes dedicated to Canada (Jarvie 1992), Europe (Guback 1969; Ulf-Møller 2001; Trumpbour 2002), Latin America (De Usabel 1982), and the Motion Picture Export Association (Segrave 1997), although focusing on Hollywood distributors, also brought to light their everyday relations, negotiations, and confrontations with non-US state and film players. The dynamic exchanges between US and non-US players, the interactions between local, regional, and international are also at the heart of two books that take a more global approach. In her 1985 study *Exporting Entertainment: America in the World Film Market, 1907–1934*, Kristin Thompson identifies World War I as the turning point inaugurating the domination of Hollywood distribution networks worldwide. In *Hollywood à la conquête du monde* (Mingant 2010), I identified the economic and cultural strategies developed by Hollywood majors between the mid-1960s and early 2000s, and traced the origins of current global practices. Both books, however, made only passing allusions to North Africa and the Middle East, leaving it largely out of the US film distribution map. Selecting North Africa and the Middle East as the geographical scope for a study on the international distribution of Hollywood film could seem counterintuitive. News headlines these days focus on China and, to a lesser extent, India, while the North African and Middle Eastern market has always been at best peripheral (Mingant 2015b, 73). In 1965, the region represented 2.5% of foreign earnings.[1] In the late 2010s, it represented about 1.5% of global earnings. This area has consequently elicited low to no interest from US producers, distributors, and marketers, and remains largely unknown in Hollywood (Mingant 2010, 155–56). From a distribution studies perspective, however, exploring the circulation of US films in the Middle East and North Africa proves a fruitful field and will provide at least three avenues of reflections.

First, the book documents the insertion of cinema in power struggles that mobilize political, economic, and cultural arguments. Hollywood films have found themselves used both by the French and British during the colonial era, by nationalist movements during the struggle for and accession to independence, and by Gulf countries striving to develop post-oil economies in the early twenty-first century. Secondly, the book serves as a case study of interaction between the large variety of players that influence the circulation of films, including film professionals and lobbyists, state authorities and politicians, and consumers, from the different countries in North Africa and the Middle East, but also from the US, Europe, and Asia. Finally, it draws a portrait of the film landscape, or "filmscape," in which spectators from North Africa and the Middle East live their lives. Exchanges with Europe, especially France and Great Britain, and the US, should not obscure the rich exchanges with India— the Middle East has historically stood as a crossroads between East and West—as well as the century-old film history of the region—and especially in Egypt. By being attentive to the presence of Bollywood films, but also to the regional circulation of Egyptian films and, more recently, Syrian television series, the book aims at enlightening the multitude of influences, contacts, and exchanges that intersect in North Africa and the Middle East and provide a reflection on the filmscape US films are part of and contribute to. Examining such interactions is particularly vital at a time in which the film world involves connected agents that participate in formal and informal circulation all around the globe. Hollywood films have circulated in North Africa and the Middle East since the early twentieth century; they have been at the heart of heated political battles and have been handled by skilled US and local distributors who extended their reach over the whole region, and they have long inhabited the hearts of spectators who also enjoy Egyptian and Indian films. That early twenty-first century spectators in the Middle East should have flocked to *Titanic* and *The Fast and the Furious*, despite the context of contested US foreign policy, ultimately comes not as a surprise but as a testimony to a hundred years of common history between Hollywood and the North Africa and Middle East region.

The first part of the book traces the history of the circulation of US films from the early twentieth century to the early 1950s. Chapter

1 investigates the role played by French distributors in first introducing US films to North Africa and the Middle East, and the way they were superseded by Hollywood distributors in the 1920s; it also provides a history of the early exhibition sector in the region from the 1910s to the 1940s. Covering the first half of the twentieth century, chapter 2 offers unique insight into the ways language, social classes, and gender shaped spectatorship; it argues that two film cultures coexisted at the time: the *Gone with the Wind* culture and the cowboy culture. The exploration of this period is completed by chapter 3, which posits films as political objects used by the European colonizers, especially the French, to further their own ideological agendas.

Part 2 documents the slow collapse of the US companies' distribution system in North Africa and the Middle East faced with two successive challenges: the political sea change in the newly independent countries and the spread of VCR technology. Chapter 4 covers a period from the 1950s to the 1970s, a time when Hollywood films became a pawn in the move to decolonize the newly independent countries' economy and culture; it analyzes the way the Hollywood major's distribution structure, carefully built in the colonial era, started to unravel. Chapter 5 posits the 1980s as a turning point, as the introduction of new technologies and the subsequent development of piracy contributed to the decline of the film market in North Africa and the Middle East, and the final withdrawal of Hollywood companies from direct distribution, thus inaugurating the indirect distribution model still in effect today.

Part 3 maps the strong presence of US films in North Africa and the Middle East in the digital era. It provides a series of descriptive snapshots of the market in the first two decades of the twenty-first century. By focusing on countries closed to Hollywood films, such as Syria, Iran, or Iraq, chapter 6 discusses the differences between commercial distribution and unofficial circulation; it also foregrounds the efforts of individual entrepreneurs trying to revive the exhibition market in difficult political contexts. Chapter 7 is dedicated to North Africa and explores the complex relation between a derelict film sector and a flourishing informal market, offering reflections on the ensuing film culture. Chapter 8 follows the recent evolution of three historically flourishing markets—Egypt, Israel, and Lebanon—as they reach a state of maturity. Finally, chapter 9 offers a unique view into the future by examining the birth of the Gulf market in the early twenty-first century, as it positions to become a key market for Hollywood and change the cinematic center of gravity of the region.

Part I

Winning Hearts in the Colonial Era (1910s–1950s)

Entering the Market
(1910s–1940s)

IN THE FIRST DECADE OF THE twentieth century, the first movie theaters were opening their doors in Egypt, Algeria, and Persia. In the US, cinema was a fledgling industry, and US producers and distributors were focused on developing their home market. Competition was particularly strong, with French companies pioneering film distribution all over the world. Four years after opening its US office in 1904, Pathé had become the largest film provider in the country (Salmon 2014, 131; K. Thompson 1985, 4). The same year, Pathé, as well as another renowned French company, Méliès, became part of the Motion Picture Patents Company (MPPC), the association founded by Thomas Edison in the hope of organizing—or monopolizing—the US film market (Augros and Kitsopanidou 2009, 24–25). The structure of the US film industry stabilized in the mid-1920s around a small number of powerful companies: Universal, Fox (which became Twentieth Century Fox in 1935), First National (which was taken over by Warner Bros. in 1929), Loew's Inc. (which merged with MGM in 1924), Paramount-Famous Players-Lasky, Columbia, and RKO.[1] In the early years of US cinema, only Vitagraph had looked abroad for profit. It acted as a forerunner in international distribution when it opened direct distribution offices in Paris and London in 1906 (K. Thompson 1985, 3). Three years later, the MPPC had begun a "systematic push into foreign markets" (28), and by the 1910s, the international market represented from 20% to 40% of a film's revenue and complemented the grosses of films that had

already broken even on the home market (100). The basis of a powerful international distribution network was slowly being established. US
film distributors focused primarily on Western markets, using London
as a film distribution hub (34–43). North Africa and the Middle East
was a largely unknown territory, in the hands of French distributors. At
that time, a large portion of the Middle East was under Ottoman rule,
including part of today's Iraq (notably Baghdad), Syria (Alep, Damascus),
Lebanon (Beirut), Israel (Jerusalem), and Saudi Arabia (Medina, Mecca)
(Balanche 2014). Before, during, and after World War I, a strong battle of political influence over the Middle East was raging between the
British and the French authorities, and France had already established
its authority over most of North Africa. Although the region must at
first have appeared quite far away and nebulous to US film distributors,
it soon became one more commercial territory to conquer in their new
international expansion strategy.

Hollywood Films under the French Monopoly

The circulation of US films in North Africa and the Middle East in fact
predates the presence of US film distributors. While the Hollywood studios were still in their infancy, the nascent international film market was
dominated by the French Pathé, a company founded in 1896 to produce
and distribute phonographs, and that developed quickly after 1904, with
branch offices in New York, Berlin, Moscow, Brussels, and Vienna (Salmon
2014, 130). In 1907, at a time when films had become more profitable
than phonographs (Meusy 2009, 103), Pathé initiated a groundbreaking
practice: renting films instead of selling them (Salmon 2014, 162–63).
By the late 1910s, Pathé had opened ten additional foreign branches and
had deals with intermediaries in Latin America (Buenos Aires, Mexico,
Rio de Janeiro), Asia (Calcutta, Shanghai, Tokyo), Northern and Eastern
Europe (Helsinki, Berlin, Brussels, Warsaw, Vienna), and Africa (Alexandria) (Salmon 2014, 194). Important branch offices included a theater,
a laboratory, a film rental agency, and a phonograph agency (275). By
1912, Pathé could boast that,

> from Transvaal to Peru, from Borneo, Sumatra, Java to the
> far reaches of Siberia and Alaska, from Canada to the Tierra
> del Fuego, from China and Japan to Greenland, there is not
> one inch of earth on which man has set foot, where there is
> no Pathé representative. (quoted in Garçon 2006, 33)

In effect, Pathé monopolized the market (K. Thompson 1985, 5). By the mid-1910s, Gaumont, the other major French film distribution company at the time, also had a strong international presence, with branches in England, Argentina, Germany, Austria, Hungary, Romania, Russia, Italy, and Spain, as well as trading posts in Calcutta, Saigon, and Australia (D'Hugues and Muller 1986, 27–28).

For these companies, North Africa was a natural extension of the French market (Corriou 2011, 83). Algeria had been officially part of France since 1848; Tunisia and most of Morocco had become French protectorates in 1882 and 1912, respectively. In 1907, Pathé entered the area indirectly by signing a subdistribution contract for Algeria/North Africa with the company Omnia,[2] which opened the Omnia-Pathé movie theater in Tunis in 1908 (Meusy 2009, 103; Corriou 2011, 83). As the market became more lucrative in 1914, Pathé put an end to the concession contract and took over distribution (Corriou 2011, 105). By 1919, the two major French companies, as well as a few smaller ones, were firmly established in North Africa. The regional agencies in Algiers and subagencies in Tunis, functioned like similar offices in Bordeaux, Lille, Rennes, and Strasbourg (Corriou 2011, 105; Garçon 2006, 64; D'Hugues and Muller 1986, 27–28). Middle Eastern countries, in which France was influential, were also part of the French film companies' domain. Between 1911 and 1913, Pathé distributed directly in the Egyptian market before handing over operations to a local intermediary, Mr. Buccianti.[3] In 1924, Gaumont was apparently the only European distributor present in the French mandates of the Great Lebanon, which spanned present-day Lebanon and Syria.[4] Pathé's influence reached as far as Persia where, in 1912–1913, Pathé opened a movie theater in partnership with local Armenian entrepreneur Artashes Patmagrian (Thoraval 2000, 16; Sadr 2006, 10).

Several factors explain the domination of French companies in the North African and Middle Eastern markets in the early years of cinema. Although Charles Pathé himself attributed his company's international predominance merely to the fact that it had started expanding earlier than others, Thompson emphasized the importance of Pathé's strategic choices: establishing in "numerous small markets which could initially support only one film company," and financing further expansion with the profits generated there (K. Thompson 1985, 5). The existence of Pathé's phonograph distribution network, established as early as 1895, was also a strong basis from which to launch the film export business (Salmon 2014, 107). Film distribution was actually only one activity among others in Pathé's and Gaumont's expansion strategies. Both were vertically integrated, manufacturing film equipment and shooting, editing, and distributing films (Garçon 2006, 15, 24). Just as the Lumière operators had shot and shown their views, Gaumont's branches were both dedicated to selling Gaumont's film and news production, and to the shooting of newsreels (D'Hugues and Muller 1986, 28).

Another strategic function of the branches was the sale of projection equipment. Between September 1919 and August 1920, Pathé sold 49 items of projection equipment in Algeria, 11 in Tunisia, and 5 in Morocco (Corriou 2011, 98). A 1930 report by the US Department of Commerce reveals the extent of the French monopoly on film equipment in the territories under French influence: in Algeria's 50 cinemas, only 3 theaters had US-brand projectors, while all the others were French (Pathé, Gaumont) or German (Krupp) (US Department of Commerce 1930). In Egypt, Gaumont, Pathé, and Krupp-Ernemann provided all the projectors. The only projector in the whole region called "Arabia," that is, the Gulf countries, was a Pathé model. This domination was attributed both to the quality of the French equipment and to technological support: "An able demonstrator installed the machines when purchased" (US Department of Commerce 1930). When screens were used, they were also bought from Pathé and Gaumont. By creating a strong relationship with exhibitors and controlling both film and film equipment sale—that is, hardware and software—the two French majors had built a captive market. In fact, as the 1930 report noted, "All projectors and equipment of all kinds are purchased in Paris at the same time the films are contracted" (US Department of Commerce 1930). Pathé and Gaumont offered another valuable service: by the early 1920s they had turned into schedulers, providing ready-made film programs in their catalogs and thus saving exhibitors the annual trip to Paris to preview and select films (Garçon 2006, 64). In the late 1920s, for example, European companies provided the Egyptian markets with "complete program[s]" made of news weekly, short comedy, travel picture, and one feature film, or, alternatively, news weekly, short comedy, and two feature films (US Department of Commerce [c. 1928]). This practice, which was a form of blind bidding, epitomized monopolistic tendencies (Corriou 2011, 106–7). The force of the two French companies was thus to have established themselves as the only major interlocutor for North African exhibitors.

Although they monopolized distribution in the region, the major and smaller French companies did not deal in French films only. In the 1910s, pictures by Selznick, Griffith Productions, and Universal were respectively distributed in France by Select Distribution, Cosmograph, and Ciné-Location Eclipse (Garçon 2006, 66). After World War I, Gaumont strategically turned into a "multi-brand company," handling a film distribution slate comprising Hollywood films from Paramount Pictures, Famous Players, Jesse Lasky, C. B. de Mille, and Fairbanks Corporation (60). One can infer that, since they were included in the preestablished programs, US productions such as the films by Harold Lloyd, Goldwyn, Cosmopolitan, and Distinctive, acquired by Pathé Consortium Cinema in 1913, and Douglas Fairbank's *The Knickerbocker Buckaroo* (1919) and Will Hart's *Square Deal Sanderson* (1919), handled by Gaumont, traveled through the whole international network of the companies (D'Hugues and Muller 1986, 33).[5] Archival traces of this circulation exist: the Persian theater co-owned by Pathé and Patmagrian in the early 1910s was showing Charlie Chaplin films (Thoraval 2000, 16); in 1918, Famous Players-Lasky Films signed a deal with Gaumont for a zone covering Switzerland, Belgium, and Egypt (K. Thompson 1985, 73); in the early 1920s, Associated First National made a four-year deal with Gaumont for the distribution of four Jackie Coogan films—*Peck's Bad Boy* (1921), *My Boy* (1921), *Trouble* (1922), and *Daddy* (1923)—in a zone covering Egypt, Palestine, and Syria.[6] In effect, French companies were the first to introduce Hollywood films in North Africa and the Middle East.

Beside entry through Pathé and Gaumont, other distribution paths existed, such as the servicing of 1912 Syria through a British company in London (K. Thompson 1985, 33). At the time, US producers routinely sold British rights to London companies, offering the rights for the rest of the world as a bonus (31). This practice must have been quite marginal, as deals with French companies covering larger area must have appeared more efficient. Another route took Hollywood films east: in the early 1920s, "many of the fledgling early exhibitors in Iran either had ties to Russia or were Russian immigrants themselves" (Askari 2014, 106). Consequently, French and US serials were imported though Russia. Interestingly, one can surmise that a number of these films had, in fact, originally been introduced in Russia by Pathé, whose Russian branch was solid, before the Revolution forced its closure in 1921 (Salmon 2014, 341). The case of Iran also illustrates the situation of smaller markets, supplied with secondhand prints. These "junk prints" entered the territory in a disorganized fashion, from varied sources, including Russia, Iraq, Egypt, and Europe.[7] As for the British administered Aden Protectorate, almost the only market identified in the Gulf region at the time (Askari 2014, 100), it obtained its rare equipment and films from another part of the British Empire, India.[8] Film circulation in North Africa and the Middle East was, from the start, intertwined within global film dynamics.

Although the dominant and most systematically organized circuit of film distribution was in the hands of the French, local companies, often linked to the exhibition sector, were equally active in importing foreign films. Such was the case of Aurelio Fiorentino, owner of the Cinéma Palace and the Palace Théâtre in mid-1910s Tunisia (Corriou 2011, 105). Out of the seven film importers listed in the Great Lebanon area in the early 1920s, one was French (Gaumont) and six local (Cattan and Haddad, Jamil M. Baroody, Lutfallah Amme and Sons, Joseph Sarkis, Nicolas and Georges Bridi, M. Levy).[9] In the 1910s and early 1920s, a complex web of French and local distributors thus introduced US films to North African and Middle Eastern audiences, who soon acquired a taste for it. This early distribution of US films by non-US firms paved the way for the entry of US distributors from the mid-1920s onwards.

US Distributors Enter the Market

World War I marked a turning point in the US companies' attitude toward the international market. As early as 1916, subdistribution relationships with London-based companies were ended in order to establish control of the film distribution and revenues in and outside Europe (K. Thompson 1985, 64–73). Once the war was over and the political situation stabilized, all the major US companies entered the European markets, notably France, where Fox, United Artists, Paramount, Goldwyn, Export-Union-Film-Co., and Universal all opened offices between 1919 and 1922 (Garçon 2006, 67–68). The Paris subsidiaries had a structure modeled on local companies. In 1921, Paramount acted as a forerunner, swiftly constituting a large network including branches offices in mainland France (Marseille, Toulouse, Bordeaux, Lille, Lyon) (Garçon 2006, 68). Like its French counterparts, Paramount also controlled a number of movie theaters. By 1927, it had built a 1,900-seat movie theater in Paris, and was building a theater in Lyon and yet another in the Algerian city of Oran (Garçon 2006, 72). Incorporating their companies in France, modeling their distribution structure on the existing French ones, producing films in France,[10] the Hollywood distributors slowly became integrated into the French film industry fabric, and in 1932, they were among the firms behind the creation of the French union of film distributors (Chambre syndicale française des distributeurs de films) (Garçon 2006, 139).[11]

The entry of Hollywood distributors in North Africa was the logical corollary of their new French presence. Imitating the structure of Pathé

Table 1.1. First date of known presence of direct distribution branches of US film companies in North Africa and the Middle East (1920s–1940s)

	Algeria	Morocco	Tunisia	Egypt	Great Lebanon (Beirut)	Palestine	Iraq
Artistes Associés (UA)	1924				1938	1938	
Columbia				1933	1943	1938	
First National Pictures				1928			
Fox Films	1927			1922	1943		
MGM	1927*	1927*	1927*	1927*	1927*	1927*	1940
Paramount	1924	1927	1926	1924** 1929***	1940		
RKO				1940		1938	
Universal	1934			1924			
Warner Bros.	1926†			1934††		1936	

* as Gaumont-Metro-Goldwyn
** as Famous Players-Lasky
*** as Paramount
† as Vitagraph
†† as Warner Bros.-First National

Sources: Garçon 2006, 68; Vitalis 2000; *Film Daily Year Book* 1922–1923, 1924, 1926, 1927, 1929, 1934, 1936, 1940; "Political Rift Splits Palestine's Recovery," *Motion Picture Herald*, February 19, 1938; Telegram from Reisman, Vice-President RKO, to Cordell Hull, July 5, 1940, NARA RG 59, Country File, Egypt, 1940–1944, box 5781.n.

and Gaumont, they also opened offices in the French city of Algiers and a few subbranches in Tunisia and Morocco. As table 1.1 shows, the Société anonyme française des films Paramount had opened agencies in Algiers by 1924, Tunis by 1926, and Morocco by 1927. From the mid-1920s onwards, most companies would service North Africa from the Algiers office, as did United Artists and Fox Films. Warner Bros. films appear in the *Film Daily Year Book* of 1926 as distributed in Algiers by the Compagnie Vitagraph de France. It is likely that when Warner Bros. bought Vitagraph studio in 1925 (Finler 2003, 287), it also bought out its French subsidiary, including its North African office. Universal seems to have been the last to open an office in Algiers in 1934.

The attention the Hollywood companies were starting to give to the North African market is revealed by an episode pertaining to censorship in Tunisia. Between 1911 and 1925, censorship was in the hands of one local censorship officer (Corriou 2011, 174–75). In September 1925, Paramount officially complained to the resident superior about the erratic nature of the censor's decisions especially the fact he had sometimes banned a film "a few hours before the initial performance": according to the US consul report, his choices provoked "dismay and anger among the theatres and agents of US films and French films as well."[12] The decisions seem to have derived from individual political motivations: as a black person of "Martiniquian" descent, the censor favored "anti-American film rulings" in order to show his "dislike" for the treatement of African-Americans in the USA.[13] In order to avoid decisions they felt were arbitrary, US film distributors called to take the control of censorship out of the hands of a "unique censor," and to set up a committee that would include representatives of the public and of film importers.[14] A December 1925 decree subsequently created a preventive control commission constituted of the vice-president of the Municipality of Tunis, the chief of the Sûreté, an inspector of the Department of Education, a police commissioner, and a representative of the motion picture film agents of Tunis.[15] This episode testifies to the new involvement—and the new influence—of the US distributors in the Tunisian market in the mid-1920s. It also reveals the ambiguous relation that was settling in between US and French distributors. Here, a clear commonality of interests between otherwise rival companies existed, revealing the possibility of ad hoc alliances. In effect, in the second half of the 1920s, US and French companies both collaborated and competed, a phenomenon known as coopetition (Pardo 2007).

By that time, however, the French competitors were losing strength. Pathé's structure had been weakened by the war. Branches were closed in Germany, Austria-Hungary, and Romania. The Belgian branch, which comprised a distribution agency but also a production factory, was requisitioned in 1915. The Austrian production factory was requisitioned in 1917. World War I dealt a strong blow to a company whose financial equilibrium rested on international markets. Additionally faced with the growing competition from US, Swedish, and Italian films (Salmon 2014, 331, 335), Pathé had to reorganize. In 1916–17, it sold off its branches in countries torn by war (Berlin, Milan), revolution (Moscow), as well as its unprofitable branches (Barcelona, Stockholm) (Salmon 2014, 338–39, 343). By early 1921, the French company had only four foreign branches left: Copenhagen, Constantinople, Sydney, and Vienna (434). A year later, it decided to focus exclusively on the production and printing of reels, and put distribution in the hands of the 1920-created Pathé Consortium Cinéma (359, 434). Divorced from the original vertically-integrated company, Pathé Consortium had to rely on alliances with local distributors (414). In Algeria, Pathé Consortium was distributed by local exhibition circuit owner Joseph Seiberras.[16] In Egypt, it dealt with Poulain,[17] a French food company, which operated the US Cosmograph theaters in Cairo and Alexandria for advertising purposes (Meusy 2009, 194). Whereas the direct distribution system implemented by the original Pathé had guaranteed the swift movement of receipts to the Paris headquarters, the indirect distribution strategy implemented by Pathé Consortium proved dissatisfying, with receipts below expectations and impossible to check (Garçon 2006, 53). In 1922–1923, the struggling Pathé Consortium even considered allying with Gaumont.[18] Over the course of the 1920s, Pathé Consortium tried to regain strength. However, hampered by constant strife with Pathé-Cinéma, it never managed to reach the vertically integrated structure—and the dominant position—it was aiming for (Willems 1997, 98–101).

Gaumont also experienced difficulties after World War I. During the war, the dwindling market had led Gaumont to decrease its production (Douin 2015, 80). After the war, Gaumont consequently proved unable to supply enough in-house films to its large distribution and exhibition circuit, and it had to turn to US producers. In fact, Hollywood films had become very popular in France. In 1924, Gaumont sought to solve its supply problem by signing a joint venture with Metro Goldwyn Mayer: the Gaumont Metro Goldwyn (GMG). For the Hollywood company, this alliance was a means to enter the French market. It entailed buying into an already existing distribution and exhibition structure (Garçon 2006, 69–70), which spanned France as well as North Africa.[19] This takeover is visible in table 1.1: prior to 1927, MGM had no office in North Africa; by 1927, Gaumont Metro Goldwyn S. A. was listed with branches in Algeria, Morocco, and Tunis, as well as Egypt, Palestine, and Syria (Beirut) (*Film Daily Year Book* 1927). A 1925 contract also sealed the rental of the Gaumont theater circuit to MGM for five years (D'Hugues and Muller 1986, 78), including the Grand Cinema Gaumont in Sfax, Tunisia. Although Léon Gaumont and MGM Marcus Loew were both heading the company, Gaumont appeared to some as a mere puppet in the hands of the US company. Soon MGM films made up most of the distribution catalog (D'Hugues and Muller 1986, 78; Garçon 2006, 69; Douin 2015, 80), and the GMG monthly bulletin for exhibitors extensively covered Hollywood film projects and shooting, new releases, and the lives of Hollywood stars (Garçon 2006, 70). In 1925–1926, GMG distributed eighteen US films, two French films, and one Swedish (Garçon 2006, 82). The French circuit had clearly been taken over by the Hollywood major. In September 1928, the joint venture was ended. Gaumont briefly allied with Franco-Film-Aubert to create GFFA, but the company had to sell off or close down its foreign branches, such as the Alexandria office, to concentrate on exhibition. In 1934, the GFFA went into liquidation, and by 1938, Gaumont's heir, the Société Générale des Etablissements Gaumont was focusing exclusively on exhibition (D'Hugues and Muller 1986, 82–84; Douin 2015, 114). For MGM, on the other hand, the operation was a success.

Gaining strength on the hitherto French-dominated markets, the US distributors were bringing with them their own monopolistic practices. As they dominated the distribution of US films that had previously been distributed by French companies, the latter saw their catalogs reduced to French films only (Garçon 2006, 128). The fact that the US companies had taken over the distribution of Hollywood films must have been the coup de grâce to French firms already facing difficulties. Furthermore, the US distributors used dumping practices—since their films had already covered their costs in their home market—as well as two well-known arm-twisting practices: blind bidding (the sale of films unseen by exhibitors) and block booking (the grouped sale of films as opposed to the sale of individual films) (León y Barella 2012).[20] Combining monopolistic techniques and the guarantee of a regular and bountiful supply of quality products, the US distributors soon worked to depose Pathé and Gaumont as the key interlocutors on the French and North African market. By the late 1930s, the names Pathé Consortium Cinéma and Gaumont still occasionally appeared in the listing of distribution companies in North Africa, but they seem to have become minor players in markets dominated by US companies and local agents. In the late 1930s French protectorate of Morocco, the main competitor was not a French company, but Maroc-Films, a subsidiary of the Algerian company Isly-Film (*Film Daily Year Book* 1939). The Pathé and Gaumont era was over.

Over the course of the 1920s and 1930s, each US company devised its own strategy, and the landscape of the distribution of Hollywood films was a mosaic of main branch offices, secondary branch offices, majors' agents, and contracts with local distributors. As table 1.1 shows, MGM and Paramount had the most direct presence, with offices present early on in many markets. A smaller company such as United Artists serviced the market from a branded office in Algeria and through a deal with Ideal Motion Pictures in Egypt (*Film Daily Year Book* 1934). Films by independent companies like Republic Pictures and Monogram seem to have been distributed through smaller French companies or local agents.[21] As the US films were dominant in many markets, comprising up to 90% of imported films in some markets (table 1.2), once they had taken the distribution of their films into their own hands, US companies quickly became key players. By the early 1940s, Hollywood distributors had clearly established their presence in North Africa and the Middle East.

Table 1.2. Percentage of US films in the total number of films imported in North African and Middle Eastern countries (1927–1939)

	1927	1929–1931	1938–1939
North Africa	85	n/a	n/a
Egypt	55	70	76
Greater Lebanon	70	75	70
Iran	40	21.9	50
Iraq	n/a	n/a	90
Palestine	70	n/a	65

Sources: *Film Daily Year Book* 1927, 1928, 1929, 1938, 1939.

An Established US Film Distribution Structure

A Snapshot of the North African and Middle Eastern Market in the 1940s and 1950s

For local and foreign film distributors in the area, three elements characterized the film market at the time: an overall lack of screens, a geographic concentration in urban centers, and a specific seasonality linked to the climate. In the mid-1940s, the *Middle East Motion Picture Almanac* indeed noted the general lack of movie theaters over the region. With one cinema per every 100,000 inhabitants, the area was clearly underscreened (*Middle East Motion Picture Almanac* 1947, 84). The region was in fact marked by clear contrasts in terms of numbers of movie theaters (table 1.3) and attendance rates (table 1.4). At one end of the Middle Eastern spectrum stood Saudi Arabia, a country in which film exhibition was forbidden for religious reasons: just as paintings, photographs, and statues, films were viewed as sacrilegious, since they represented human face and form.[22] In the mid- to late 1930s, a handful of cinemas were set up in the Gulf: they were, however, owned and operated by North American oil companies, such as the Bahrain Petroleum Company and Aramco. As part of the corporate clubhouse, these theaters were open only to European company executives (Oruc 2020, 20). In contrast, by the late 1940s, three cinemagoing nations stood out: Egypt, Algeria, and Israel, the latter having been established in 1948. While Israel had a particularly strong attendance rate of 15 tickets per year per inhabitant in the 1950s, Egypt had the strongest overall attendance figure. North Africa appeared even more open to cinema. In 1939, the ratio of number of inhabitants for one seat was 78 in Algeria, 125 in Tunisia, and 197 in Morocco, as opposed to 212 in Egypt, 600 in Iran, and 711 in the Greater Lebanon mandate (Corriou 2011, 189). By 1950, Algeria had more movie theaters than Egypt. In the 1950s, Egypt had a 69 million attendance figure and 184 theaters, Algeria a 27 million attendance and 220 theaters, and Israel a 24 million attendance and 100 theaters. These leading markets were followed by three countries in the 8–9 million attendance bracket (Iran, Morocco, Tunisia), and the vibrant but small Lebanese market (1.3 million). Viewed from Hollywood, these figures placed the region among the less profitable markets; the number of Algerian theaters paled in the face of the 5,163 theaters of mainland France in 1950 (*Film Daily Year Book* 1950). At the time, the top three markets in the area were rather

Table 1.3. Number of movie theaters in North Africa and the Middle East (1925–1950)

	1927	1938	1946	1950
North Africa	60			
Algeria		150 (1932)		220
Morocco (French zone)		59		86
Morocco (Spanish zone)		16		18
Tangier	6	5		8
Tunisia	9	43 (1940)		45
Greater Lebanon	14			41
Lebanon			48	
Syria		39	41	
Palestine	12 (1928)	34	68	
Israel				100
Egypt	40	118 (1939)	198	184
Persia	4			
Iran		35	78	80
Iraq		17	57	54
Transjordan		1		
Jordan (1954)				4
Aden				6
Bahrain (1950s)		1 (1937)		4

Sources: *Film Daily Year Book* 1927, 1928, 1932, 1938, 1940, 1950, 1954; Sadoul 1962, 481, 490, 491; Leaman 2001, 359; *Middle East Motion Picture Almanac* 1946–1947, 85; Kamalipour 1994, 39; Thoraval 2000, 28.

comparable to Bulgaria (264 theaters), Eire (260), and Greece (170), while the mid-range markets were equivalent to Luxemburg (35) and Malta (29) (*Film Daily Year Book* 1950). Attendance figures also seem low compared to the peak of 1,635 million tickets sold in Great Britain in 1946—though that figure would tumble to 495 million in 1960 (Sadoul 1962, 368). Collectively, the region sold approximately 172 million tickets in the early 1950s. In his scrutiny of studio's ledgers and accounting reports, Askari noted that although Egypt, Syria, Lebanon, Iraq and Iran

Table 1.4. Movie attendance in North Africa and the Middle East in the 1950s

		Attendance figures	Number of tickets sold in relation to population
Algeria	1959	27,666,000	2.7 tickets/year for 100 inhabitants
Egypt	1955–1958	1955: 69,751,989	Cairo & Alexandria: 7 tickets / year/inhabitant
		1958: 77,500,00	Canal, Damiette, Suez districts: 3 tickets /year/inhabitant
			Kalioubyé (*sic*) district: 3 inhabitants out of 100 buy 1 ticket/year
Iran	1950	9,000,000	Less than 0.5 tickets/year/inhabitant (total population: 20 million)
Iraq	1949	20,000,000–25,000,000*	4–5 tickets/year/inhabitant (total population: 5 million)*
Israel	1954	24,750,000	15 tickets/year /inhabitant (total population: 1,650,000)
Lebanon	1950	1,300,000	6 tickets /year /inhabitant
Morocco	1954	Less than 8,000,000	Less than one ticket /year/ inhabitant (total population: 8 million)
Syria	1955	3,500,000	Less that 2 tickets /year / inhabitant
Tunisia	1946	8,500,000	2 tickets /year /inhabitant

Sources: Sadoul 1962, 482, 491, 493, 496, 498; 1966, 152, 164.

*Sadoul emphasized his doubts about these optimistic official statistics.

were usually listed as entries, the revenue column was often left blank. In the early 1950s, the Middle East represented about 4% of all foreign distribution revenues for United Artists (Askari, forthcoming). Although not a top market for Hollywood, the region still had potential. Its general openness to cinema and Hollywood films in particular made it a market worth operating in.

As in other countries, cinema was predominantly an urban leisure activity (Corriou 2011, 190). In 1951 Morocco, one third of the country's movie theaters were actually in Casablanca, and two-thirds of the movie theaters were concentrated over five cities: Casablanca, Fes, Rabat, Marrakesh, Meknes. In 1951 Algeria, 32% of the movie theaters were in Alger and Oran (Mingant 2017, 65). In 1949 Tunisia, 21 of the country's 50 movie theaters were in Tunis, and many movie theaters had been established along the Tunisian coast in seaside resorts such as La Goulette and Le Kram (UNESCO 1949). In 1947 Iran, 31 of the country's 78 cinemas were situated in Tehran (*Middle East Motion Picture Almanac* 1947, 43). In 1937 Palestine, the three key areas were Haifa, Jerusalem, and the Jewish settlement neighborhood of Tel Aviv, whereas more remote or poorer districts like Transjordan often had only one theater.[23] In Egypt, between 1955 and 1958, 84.8% of filmgoers were situated in Cairo and Alexandria (Sadoul 1966, 164). This discrepancy had a direct impact on attendance figures. As table 1.4 shows, attendance greatly varied in 1950s Egypt, from 7 tickets per year per inhabitant in Cairo and Alexandria to the fact that only 3 out of 100 inhabitants bought one ticket per year in the then undeveloped Qalyubia district (Sadoul 1966, 164). A 1943 report on Lebanon similarly noted that "theaters in the larger cities and town are patronized more than those in the smaller communities."[24]

The market was also characterized by a clear seasonality linked, as in other regions around the world, to weather conditions. The strong season for filmgoing started in late September-early October and ended in late April (*Middle East Motion Picture Almanac* 1947, 44; *Annuaire du cinéma* 1952, 241). In the summer, the hot weather made sitting in indoor movie theaters unbearable (*Annuaire du cinéma* 1952, 258)—in the summer, temperatures can reach 120°F in Baghdad; besides, it was also vacation time. In Tunisia, French civil servants tended to return to the mainland, while the local urban population moved to seaside resorts (Corriou 2011, 141). In Egypt, seaside resorts were also popular during summer vacation.[25] In Iran, most of the urban population spent their holidays in villages; in Lebanon, mountain resorts were the favorite choice (*Annuaire du cinéma* 1952, 261, 270). All over the region, attendance thus drastically fell in the summer (*Middle East Motion Picture Almanac* 1947, 43).[26] Exhibitors compensated by establishing open-air movie theaters. In late 1930s Egypt, the number of theaters seems to have remained stable, as a dozen indoor theaters closed down due to the excessive heat and the absence of air-conditioning, while a dozen open-air theaters opened (*Film Daily Year Book* 1937). Many open-air theaters of the region seem to have been linked to indoor theaters (Corriou 2011, 19). In 1950 Baghdad, there were 13 permanent, that is, indoor, theaters, 5 open-air theaters operated by indoor exhibitors, and 7 independent open-air theaters. In smaller towns, such as Kirkuk, Erbil, or Hillah, all the indoor theaters also operated an open-air theater, thus covering all seasons.[27] So, although the official number of theaters in the country was 82, one can assume that only about 41 theaters were functioning at any given moment. The type of films offered also changed during the lean summer season. Fully aware that attendance would be less important, exhibitors mostly offered reruns and B movies in indoor theaters, and new films in open-air theaters (*Annuaire du cinéma* 1952, 18, 261).[28] In the 1950s, exhibitors, eager to lengthen the film season and continue to distribute new films in the summer, introduced air-conditioning, as did the King Ghazi Cinema in Baghdad in 1950 (*Annuaire du cinéma* 1952, 241).[29] Lack of screen, geographical concentration on cities and temporal concentration on the winter-spring season thus formed the contours of the film market in North Africa and the Middle East.

Distribution Structure

By the 1940s, the well-established major US distributors serviced the market through an efficiently organized structure relying on two main branches: Algeria and Egypt (figure 1.1). As part of France, Algiers stood as the natural choice to centralize distribution over the North African area. The Hollywood companies established their offices in the busy commercial European district near the harbor, in the rue Michelet (Paramount), rue Sadi Carnot (20th Century Fox), *rue* Hoche (Universal), rue Charras (MGM), rue Dr. Trolard (Warner Bros.), and rue d'Isly (RKO), alongside the local distribution companies (*Film Daily Year Book* 1939). Since Algeria was French, the prints could be received from Paris, Marseille, or Lyon with no import duties or customs taxes.[30] These prints, which had already circulated in the mainland French market (Garçon 2006, 178), were then sent to transshipment offices in Casablanca and Tunis.[31] Transportation was probably operated by rail, as many agents were situated on boulevard de la Gare in Casablanca and avenue de Carthage in Tunis (*Film Daily Year Book* 1939). Prints from Algiers circulated easily, as no formalities, permits, and duties were required (*Film Daily Year Book* 1950).[32] By 1952, the Algiers officers imported 600 films per year. While three copies were usually enough to supply the North African cinemas, four or five copies could be circulated for successful films.[33]

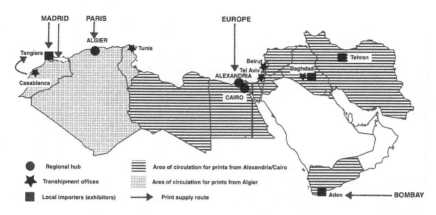

Figure 1.1. US major companies' distribution network in North Africa and the Middle East in the 1940s

The distribution hub for the Middle East was Egypt. Some Hollywood companies settled in Cairo, in streets that were located near the Nile River: Tewfik Street (Paramount, RKO, Columbia), Malaka Nazli Avenue (Warner Bros. First National), Malaka Farida Street (UA's subdistributor, Ideal Motion Pictures), Soliman Pacha Street (MGM). Universal, Twentieth Century Fox, and Republic Pictures had established in Alexandria, in Fouad Street, close to the harbor on the Mediterranean (*Film Daily Year Book* 1940). Local companies serviced independent US companies, such as Eagle Lion, Monogram, and Mascot from these two cities (*Middle East Motion Picture Almanac* 1947, 83). Prints imported from Europe were shown in Egypt, then reexported and circulated throughout a large area that could include Cyprus, Iran, Iraq, Lebanon, Libya (Benghazi, Cyrenaica, Tripolitania), Palestine, Sudan, Syria, and Transjordan.[34] In some cases, the Egyptian office was also responsible for distribution in Bahrain, Eritrea, Ethiopia, Kuwait, Somaliland, Aden, and Turkey (85–90). In 1946, the Egyptian branches of US companies imported 350 films (83). The distributors had percentage deals with all first-run cinemas, and some second-run movie theaters, but sold their films for a fixed—or flat—fee to other theaters (83). Distributors and exhibitors would usually sign a one-year contract for a group of 20 to 30 films.[35]

Two modes of distribution coexisted in some markets. This was the case of Iraq, where MGM and Twentieth Century Fox distributors had local branches, which depended on the Cairo office, while Paramount had given exclusivity to local agents F. Murad and E. Roumaya.[36] Most of the importers in the market were local exhibitors like Abdel Kerim El Hedery (Cinema Shatt-el-arab, Basra), Ismail Sherif (Cinema El Hamra, Baghdad), and Ezra Sawdiyee and A. Messayee (Cinema El-Rasheed, Baghdad) (*Middle East Motion Picture Almanac* 1947, 93–94). These importers would buy groups of pictures for a flat fee for a duration of five years (Khamarou [c. 1987], 78–79). Out of the 230 US films imported in Iraq in 1954, about 20% were sold on a rental basis—that is, a percentage deal—and 80% on an outright sale basis—that is, for a flat fee.[37] In smaller or more remote markets where no branch or agents was present, US films were exclusively imported by local exhibitors. In North Africa, this was the case for Tangier, where prints would be rented from distributors established in Spain (Madrid) or in French Morocco (Casablanca).[38] In the Middle East, two small markets were also managed by exhibitors. In Iran, "every cinema has formed a company which buys films in block and distributed them through the medium of its own cinemas" (*Middle East Motion Picture Almanac* 1947, 152). Rights to groups of films from 5 to 19 were licensed to these importers for a flat fee (*Annuaire du cinéma* 1952, 262).[39] In the mid-1940s, the main exhibitors-importers were thus Cinema Iran/Karavan Films (MGM, Paramount), Homa Cinema (Warner), Mayak Films (Universal), Metropol Cinema (Columbia), Mitra Film (United Artists, RKO, Eagle-Lion), and Tehran Cinema (20th Century Fox) (*Middle East Motion Picture Almanac* 1947, 93). In 1950 Aden, a market at a great distance from both European supply centers and US distribution hubs, the owners of the six movie theaters contracted their film prints through US, British, and Indian distributors in Bombay, and occasionally through Cairo.[40] By the 1940s, most of the countries in North Africa and the Middle East were part of Hollywood's international network. The US distributor's ability to oversee the circulation of their own films varied, however, from the tightly locked areas under the supervision of the Algerian and Egyptian branches, to the more faraway zones where presence was guaranteed through the intervention of local agents and importers. In spite of the Hollywood distributors' constant vigilance, some paths of circulation escaped their control.

Illegal Circulation

Illegal distribution started the instant the first print went into circulation. In the US, "film pioneers, including the Edison Company, had built their businesses on the practice of copying each other's films—that is, duping" (Decherny 2012, 19). These dupes "circulated rapidly and globally" (19). In 1933, MPPDA Frederick L. Herron wrote to the US Department of State that "it used to be quite a common thing in the old days of the silent film to have these stolen pictures, which we called 'pirated,' appear in numerous places in the world."[41] In North Africa and the Middle East, noncontractual showing of US films was perpetrated by exhibitors and took different forms. One was to import pirated prints. In the 1930s, Iraqi exhibitors showed films they had informally obtained from copies made by exhibitors in the US and passed on through London, Egypt, and Syria.[42] Exhibitors covered their tracks, for instance when the Royal Cinema of Baghdad released United Artists' *Sky Devils* (1932) under the title *The Western Front* in 1933.[43] Another illegal practice was "bicycling," the use of one print in several theaters. In January 1945, Twentieth Century Fox complained that Mr. Cohen, owner of Tangier's largest cinema, the Mauretania, did not respect his contract: instead of showing the prints rented first for two days in the Mauretania and then in his second-run cinema the Alcazar, he also circulated the prints over the following two weeks to cinemas owned by the two other Tangier exhibitors: Mr. Lenglet (the Rex) and Mr. Abitbol (the Paris).[44] In order to excuse the fact that the prints were sent back to Twentieth Century Fox's Casablanca office three to four weeks late, Mr. Cohen had evoked delays due to customs.[45] A third practice concerned markets situated at the very end of the circuit, where the prints were not to be returned to the Hollywood distributors' Egyptian branch but destroyed. Rather than getting rid of the print, the exhibitors simply continued to use them. MGM, for example, denounced such a practice in Aden in 1951.[46] In Iran, where films were sold for a flat fee to exhibitors who added Persian intertitles, exhibitors seem to have been particularly inventive in devising secondhand circulation circuits. Not only did they keep the prints intact at the end of the authorized three-year period (*Film Daily Year Book* 1949),[47] but they also developed a "booming business of piracy, reediting, provincial second-run circuits, repertory prestige screenings, and rapid motorcycle delivery to service multiple cinemas with a single print" (Askari 2016). In 1932, MGM's *Ben Hur* (1925) was thus illegally shown in Tehran.[48]

Controlling the fate of prints in markets situated toward the end of the circuit was, in fact, almost impossible. Iranian exhibitors, for instance, regularly obtained prints from Iraq,[49] as the following story suggests. In April 1944, RKO Near East licensed one print of *The North Star* (1943) and one print of *Days of Glory* (1944) to "Abdel Kerim Abdel

Jabbar El Khodeiri" in Baghdad—probably Basra's exhibitor Abdel Kerim El Hedery—until December 1947. In May 1951, however, these prints resurfaced in Iran: the Iraqi exhibitor had sublicensed the two prints to "Cogan-Abrahamovitch"—most probably Abraham Kogan, owner of Tehran Cinema in Tehran, who was showing them well beyond the time and geographical scope originally intended by the Hollywood distributor.[50] Little action could, however, be taken to stem such illegal journeys. While there was hardly a trace of such piracy in the French territories of North Africa where the copyright laws were similar to those in the mainland—notably the Berne Convention[51]—illegal distribution thrived in Middle Eastern markets (*Film Daily Year Book* 1928, 1938). The absence of any copyright law in Iran, Iraq, and Egypt made taking action impossible (*Film Daily Year Book* 1927).[52] Even when legislations existed, as in Palestine, it did not fully prevent illegal circulation (*Film Daily Year Book* 1933). Though the *Film Daily Year Book* of 1927 advised releasing films as soon as possible after the US release, US distributors seem to have mostly resorted to two initiatives: threatening infringing exhibitors with boycott[53] and filing sporadic court action (*Film Daily Year Book* 1937, 1938). Since fighting piracy was directly linked to the protection offered by the law, the improvement of the local legal situation was to some extent linked to more international copyright regulations, such as copyright negotiations between the US and Iraqi government, or the application to British-controlled Palestine of an agreement between the US and Great Britain in the early 1930s (*Film Daily Year Book* 1938).[54]

Illegal distribution of US film prints over North Africa and the Middle East from the 1920s to the 1950s was clearly an issue linked to the ability of the Hollywood distributors to operate tight management. It thrived in markets in which the majors sold rights for a flat fee to local exhibitors, in effect relinquishing all control.[55] This uncontrolled circulation tells a story much more complex than the mere divide between legal and illegal film distribution. One can interpret it through Lobato's concept of "piracy as access:" "piracy as an access route to media that is not otherwise available" (2012, 82). Most piracy cases did erupt in places where films were not officially distributed by Hollywood companies (United Artists was not servicing the Iraqi market when *Sky Devils* was illegally shown there),[56] or else officially distributed but in small quantity (in 1944 film supplies in Tangier had dwindled due to the war).[57] Through these uncontrolled circulation paths, distant markets were thus, in a sense, served. Additionally, Askari showed that sending used prints to these markets was inscribed in the US distributor's strategy to externalize the storage and disposal costs of prints. Rather than have the prints returned, they preferred local subdistributors and exhibitors to destroy them. That affidavits of destruction were sometimes fraudulent was a hazard of this disposal system (Askari forthcoming). In the end, just as Pathé had done in its evaluation of the US market in the 1900s, illegal distribution could also be read as a sign of market potential (Salmon 2014, 135). In a revealing twist of fate, an Iraqi "local exhibitor, who [was] known to have obtained motion picture film surreptitiously in 1932 [. . .] ha[d] since contracted with one of the largest US producers for the exclusive showing of their pictures." After all, his illegal activities had proved that he had all the qualities required.[58]

The history of the distribution of Hollywood films in North Africa and the Middle East thus paradoxically starts in another country. France held a pivotal role on several accounts. At the height of their power in the 1910s, French distributors first introduced US films to audiences in North Africa and the Middle East. A decade later, the US distributors entered the market by copying—and sometimes buying out—the existing French film distribution structures. While French distributors were supplanted in the market, France itself stood as a territorial pivot in the film prints' circulation between the US and the North Africa and Middle East region. Local entrepreneurs also held a central role in the circulation of US films, first of all as exhibitors. Outside their two distribution hubs, in Algeria and Egypt, US distributors also routinely collaborated with local distributors. North African and Middle Eastern distributors and exhibitors also played a key role in shaping circulation paths for US films. In the introduction to his study on cinema in Iran in the 1950s, Askari proposes to call this a "relay" system, emphasizing not only the "physical movement" of print from one relay point to the other but also the issues of agency, with agents ranging from the US executives with a top-down approach to the "decentered agency" of sub-distributors and exhibitors (Askari forthcoming). In the first half of the twentieth century, the circulation of US films in North Africa and the Middle East thus relied on a network of French, US, and local agents. Distributed by French and later US companies, shown legally or not, Hollywood films had, from the early years of cinema, largely circulated throughout the market. Although these films were proposed to spectators in all the region's movie theaters, they were experienced in a variety of different ways.

2

Hollywood Films and Their Audience

THOUGH CINEMA IS NOWADAYS recognized both as a work of art and a popular form of entertainment, it started out as a rather disreputable pastime. In North Africa and the Middle East, as in other regions of the world, films were first shown in cafés (Corriou 2011, 39; E. Thompson 2000, 205). The first actual movie theaters started to open at the turn of the century: 1900 in Egypt and Palestine, 1908 in Algeria, Persia, and Tunisia, 1909 in Mesopotamia and Lebanon, 1910 in Syria, 1937 in Manama (*Film Daily Year Book* 1954).[1] Well into the 1920s, however, cinema retained a bad reputation, and films played to an audience of working-class men (Corriou 2011, 162; E. Thompson 2000, 205).[2] Syrian theaters in the late 1910s showed "slapstick comedies, Wild West and detective dramas" to satisfy this clientele, but "were rarely frequented by the Syrian upper classes, firstly because they were not interested in such films, secondly because of the low class of the usual spectators, and thirdly because of the unsanitary and wretched theatres."[3] In late 1920s Iran, theaters were similarly reputed to be "dirty, improperly ventilated and uncomfortable."[4] A 1930 report describes movie theaters in the country thus:

> Most of the motion-picture theaters in Persia are large rect-angular halls equipped with benches and with chairs held together in rows by means of boards. Many of the halls have

been converted from other uses and are not especially adapted
to the exhibition of motion pictures. The lowest-priced seats
are near the screen, while the rest of the chairs, either of
hardwood or cane, afford a scale of prices depending on
how far they are removed from the front. Since there is no
slope to the aisles, the best seats are in the loges, which are
at the rear of the hall and raised above the level of the floor.
Some of the theaters have small balconies. There is usually
an orchestra of 2, 3, or 4 pieces, stationed behind a screen
at one corner of the stage. [. . .] Heating of the theaters is
effected by means of tin stoves, but in the winter it is generally cold notwithstanding, and most of the audience keep
on their overcoats during the performance. (US Department
of Commerce, 1930)

Going to the movies was also "a noisy experience," what with the
combination of the translator's voice, musical accompaniment, and the
conversations of "unruly spectators" (Naficy 2011a, 226). A journalist in
1927 Egypt reported visiting a theater with "two screens, showing two
different pictures at the same time," and noted that "dogs and babies
(were) allowed in all houses in Egypt [. . .] and smoking permitted" (*Film
Daily Year Book* 1927) The favorite Hollywood stars of this lively audience
were serial actresses Pearl White, Ruth Roland, and Edith Johnson, comic
actors Charlie Chaplin and Harold Lloyd, western actor Tom Mix, exotic
seducer Rudolph Valentino, and child actor Jackie Coogan (Thoraval
2003, 82; Corriou 2011, 142), as shows a 1925–1926 program leaflet for
the Régent Cinema in Algiers (figure 2.1 pages 40–41).[5]

By the end of the 1920s, however, exhibitors set out to move their
audience upscale by actively wooing women and children viewers (Corriou 2011, 153, 162; Naficy 2011a, 206).[6] The presence of families meant
more economic activity, but also a changed moviegoing experience. The
Beirut office of the consulate general noted this change with satisfaction:
"In 1922, all local theatres were exclusively interested in western and
detective dramas, but in 1923, out of seven movie picture theatres, two
were devoted to artistic films, and in 1924, the number showing the latter
was brought to five."[7] This new audience enjoyed French "artistic" films
such as Pathé's cloak-and-dagger *Les trois mousquetaires* (1921) and desert
adventure *L'Atlantide* (1921).[8] In Iran, movie theaters also upgraded their
facilities and increased ticket prices in order to attract a middle-class

clientele (Naficy 2011a, 206). Picture palaces appeared all over the region in the early 1930s, offering a new type of cinema experience, and by the 1930s, a stable exhibition sector was in place.

Not everyone could access cinemas, however. In the 1950 Aden Protectorate, out of a regional population of 5 million inhabitants, "less than 500,000 (would) ever have the occasion in their life to visit Aden," where the movie theaters were all situated.[9] In 1955 North Africa, where 75% of the population lived in the countryside, many would never have the opportunity to see a film (Rouissi 1983, 102).[10] Moviegoing habits and culture were, then, nonexistent in the remotest part of the region. A 1930 US Department of Commerce report notes that theaters in the Mesopotamia town of Basra were closed for over a year due to a lack of patronage: out of the 3 million inhabitants, nearly 2 million were "Bedouins pasturing their flocks in the deserts of cultivators living along riverbanks" (US Department of Commerce 1930). Economic reasons could also be an obstacle to filmgoing: in early 1950s Egypt, only factory workers and artisans could afford to go to the cinema (Sadoul 1966, 88). For those who could go to the cinema, US films became a staple entertainment. While Hollywood movies touched virtually all spectators in the region, they were, however, experienced differently as determinants such as national origin, language, class, and gender created a kaleidoscope of moviegoing experiences, tastes, and cultures.[11]

Film Audiences: A Mosaic of Cultures

The Language of Film

One of the first concrete elements that Hollywood distributors had to face was the sheer diversity of their potential audience in terms of national origin and cultural background. In the first half of the twentieth century, North Africa and the Middle East were characterized by the presence of a large and varied native and nonnative population. While French, British, Italian, and Spanish rule led to the presence of colonial administrative personnel, people had also immigrated from the Northern shores of the Mediterranean for economic and political reasons. Although this cultural mix became more acutely visible when talking movies arrived in the region in the late 1920s (Sadoul 1962, 486),[12] from the start, distributors and exhibitors had to devise ways to reach both local audiences and

OF 1-8-58 FROM W. H. ANDERSON, STATE DEP
BY
DATE
Régent
Cinéma
J. SEIBERRAS
directeur propriétaire

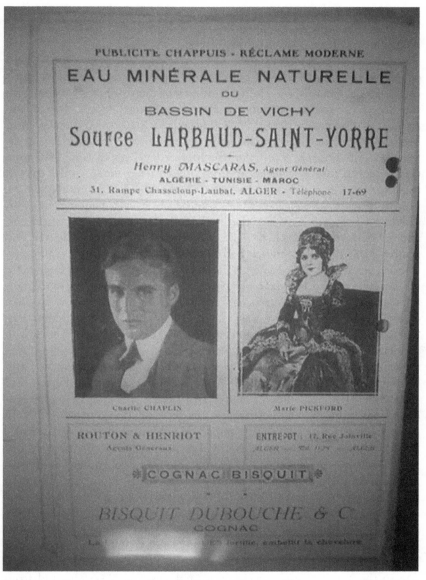

Figure 2.1. Program leaflet from the Régent Cinéma, Algiers, season 1925–1926. Source: Lewis W. Haskel, consul, Algiers, report submitted in reply to department's instructions, January 30, 1926, "Attitude towards American Films," June 2, 1926, NARA, Country File, Algeria, 1910–1929, M560, roll 154.

spectators coming from other countries and speaking different languages. The linguistic strategies adopted by distributors and exhibitors in Egypt, Palestine, and Iran epitomize this diversity.

Although some Hollywood films dubbed in French seem to have circulated in Alexandria and Cairo,[13] the most common practice in Egypt by the 1940s was to show Hollywood films in their original version, with side-screens providing written translations in French, Greek, Italian, and Arabic (K. Thompson 1985, 159; E. Thompson 2010, 187; *Film Daily Year Book* 1938). While the English dialogue would satisfy the British expatriates, and the Arabic translation the literate local population, exhibitors clearly had to cater to spectators from other backgrounds. In the days of the Ottoman Empire, France had developed a strong economic influence, especially in the areas of railroads, construction, and banking, but also a cultural presence through charity organizations, medical institutions, and schools where the local elite was taught in French (Cloarec and Laurens 2007, 16–17). French had become the language of the administration, army, and diplomacy, but also of business, art, and the news. It became the second language of Jewish, Greek, and Armenian immigrant populations (Bouquet, Pétriat, and Vermeren 2016, 13). Italian was also commonly spoken, as there was a large Italian community in Alexandria. In fact, the first subtitling system there had been invented by an Italian resident in 1912, and Italian companies were in charge of subtitling until the mid-1940s (Gamal 2009). The Greek Orthodox population had also been present since the era of the Ottoman Empire (Bouquet, Pétriat, and Vermeren 2016, 112). The cosmopolitanism of Cairo and Alexandria was one factor in the strong demand for foreign films (Leaman 2001, 17). In the provinces where the native population dominated, one can surmise the films were accompanied only by Arabic translations.[14]

Diversity also prevailed in Palestine. Zionist discourses had led Jewish people to migrate to Palestine as early as the 1880s, during the Ottoman era. The 1881 pogroms in Russia and Romania gave the impetus for the movement of immigration (Cloarec and Laurens 2007, 25). Between 1904 and 1914, a second wave of immigration, or *aliya*, occurred. About 40,000 people arrived in Palestine, mostly from Russia (Bouquet, Pétriat, and Vermeren 2016, 112, 161–62). Jewish people later arrived from Poland due to the adoption of discriminatory policies in 1924–1926, and from Germany after the Nazi Party came to power in 1933 (Perrin 2000, 154). The Jewish population increased from 84,000 in 1922 to 608,000 in 1946, when they constituted one third of the total population (205). After the creation of the state of Israel in 1948, immigration continued from Eastern Europe, but also from neighboring Arab countries (220). Although the official languages of this area under British mandate were English, Arabic, and Hebrew, many Jewish spectators coming from Europe spoke none of those languages (*Film Daily Year Book* 1938). Consequently, as in Egypt, written translation became the norm, and in the early 1950s, side screens routinely presented translations in Hebrew, Romanian, Yiddish, French, German, Bulgarian, and Polish (Sadoul 1962, 493).

The use of written translation was, indeed, a standard in the Middle East where Hollywood films circulated in their original version. In Iran, before Persian dubbing developed in the late 1940s, exhibitors did not use side screens, but inserted intertitles at frequent intervals during the film, a practice inherited from the silent cinema era (Issari 1989, 70–71). Intertitles routinely appeared in Farsi, French, and Russian (Naficy 2011a, 200). Mid-1920s advertising material circulated in English, Armenian, and French (205). The variety of languages that the English-language dialogues and advertising material were translated into in these countries testifies to the commercial desire to make Hollywood films accessible to all audiences, from the local population and lower-class European immigrants to the local and colonial elite. Interestingly, as the actual mix varied in each country, the responsibility for translation seems to have rested in the hands of exhibitors (*Film Daily Year Book* 1938).

Contrary to the territories under British influence, the population diversity in the French empire was silenced by the predominance of the colonizer's language. In Syria and Lebanon, which had been under French economic and cultural influence since the end of the nineteenth century (Cloarec and Laurens 2007, 16–17), and where the elite spoke French, US films were shown either in their original version with French subtitles or in the French-dubbed version (*Film Daily Year Book* 1938, 1939).[15] Arabic subtitles were added only in 1947, after the countries reached independence (Mingant 2019). In North Africa, audiences were exposed to French-dubbed Hollywood films coming directly from the mainland. In the French colonial area, although most of the population spoke Arabic, "French (was) the language of the talking films."[16] This linguistic strategy, which made commercial sense for Hollywood distributors, passed over the actual presence of a mix of local Arabic population, Spanish, Italian, and Maltese immigrants (Chevalier 1947, 22–24; Ferro 1994, 115). Spectators from the Northern shores of the Mediterranean, however, could still develop a culture of cinema in their own language by attending movie theaters offering films from their country of origin. In the Moroccan city of Fez, the Arc-en-Ciel thus showed neorealist Italian films, including *La Strada* (1954), *Bitter Rice* (1949), and *The Bicycle Thief* (1948) (Grouix and Halaoui 2013, 47).

Competition

The diverse audience of North Africa and the Middle East indeed had access to a variety of films beyond Hollywood. In the 1910s, when Pathé and Gaumont had the monopoly on distribution, French films dominated the screens. *Wid's Year Book* for 1920 and 1921 noted that Egyptian movie theaters proposed mostly French and Italian films, and "sometimes" an American one. In Persia, French movies were also dominant in the 1910s (Kamalipour and Mowlana 1994, 86). By the late 1920s, as the US distributors established their presence, French films came to be displaced at the box office. While competition could be linked to the economic structure of the market, it also derived from the local cultural mix. In 1930s Palestine, Russian films were particularly appreciated in Tel Aviv and Haifa by Jewish spectators who had come from Central and Eastern Europe.[17] All over the region, the country of origin of the films taking second place at the box office have cultural roots: the French influence in Egypt, Syria, and North Africa, the British influence in the Aden Protectorate, and the alliance with Germany in Iran (table 2.1). Before the 1930s, Hollywood mostly competed with European productions; the market shares in 1940 Iraq (table 2.1), however, reveal the development of a strong local competitor in Egypt.

Egyptian cinema developed after the Misr Bank established Studio Misr in 1934. The arrival of sound was "a decisive turning point for Egypt's film-making," since it "gave a unique chance to local production to use native language and music, and to develop film genres (such as comedy and the musical) which rely essentially on them" (Shafik 2001, 25). Egyptian films were quickly adopted by audiences who were illiterate, and thus unable to read the subtitles to foreign films, but also enthused at the use of their own language on film. By the mid-1940s, Egyptian cinema had made quick progress in Arabic-speaking countries (Thoraval 2003, 82). In 1947, "Iraq, which ha[d] become an extremely important market for Egyptian production, show[ed] Egyptian films almost exclusively whilst in Egypt out of approximately 200 cinemas one hundred and thirty [we]re devoted exclusively to Arabic pictures" (*Middle East Motion Picture Almanac* 1947, 85). Whereas in 1940, the average number of Egyptian films shown in Middle Eastern cinemas was 5%, seven years later it had skyrocketed to 45% (85). In fact, the statistics in table 2.1 do not fully

Table 2.1. Percentage of the market for films by country of origin in North Africa and the Middle East in the early 1940s

Country	Year	Country 1	Country 2	Others
Aden	1943	70% USA	20% England	10% Egypt & India
Algeria		n/a France	n/a USA	
Egypt	1938	76 % USA	10% France	7% England, 7% Egypt and Other
Iran	1940	60% USA	20% Germany	10% France
Iraq	1940	75% USA	15% Egypt	7% India, 2% Other (England, France, Turkey)
Morocco	1940	70% USA	30% French	
Palestine	1940	76.5% USA	15.7% France	7.8% Other (Russia, Poland, Egypt, England, Czech Republic, Italy)
Syria	1940	80% USA	ab. 20% France	
Tunisia	1940	60 % USA	30 % France	10% Other (England, Italy, Egypt)

Source: *Film Daily Year Book* 1938, 1940; C. Timberlake, "Motion Picture," Aden, Arabia, July 2, 1943, NARA RG 59, 1940–1944, Country File, Arabia, box 5786.

reflect the reality of the market. Based on the number of productions released, these figures do not measure the actual popularity of the films. In practice, an American or European film would be withdrawn from the screen after a week, but an Egyptian film would be shown for weeks and even months, as novelty or rerelease, even though the ticket prices were often higher (Sadoul 1962, 487; UNESCO 1949).[18] Though Egyptian competition did not present a commercial threat when it came to the established European audience, it had clearly won the hearts of local populations. By the mid-1940s, in the Egyptian provinces, "American films ha[d] completely disappeared from the cinemas except for serials which form[ed] the first part of the programs" (*Middle East Motion Picture Almanac* 1947, 87).

In the Eastern part of the region, another non-Western cinema was also competing for audience loyalty. Indian cinema gained a following in Aden as well as in Iran.[19] By 1950, a US diplomat in Aden pointed out that "the statement earlier reported by this Consulate to the effect that the populace prefers American films when they can get them are no longer true. Aden is composed of many racial and language groups and they prefer films in their own language and with a greater cultural affinity."[20] In Iran, Egyptian and Indian films were also preferred by a local population who considered them closer to their culture.[21] Egyptian cinema and, to a still limited extent, Indian cinema, were thus clearly competing with Hollywood for a large portion of its potential audience. In the second half of the 1940s, US distributors tried to respond to this new competition by dubbing a number of films into Arabic. As will be seen in chapter 4, however, this attempt was short-lived and proved unsustainable both for economic and political reasons. Hollywood films were thus part of a larger "filmscape" including films from local, Asian, and European countries. While a spectator's cultural background and linguistic abilities informally determined which films he or she felt closer to, the structuration of the exhibition sector accentuated and formalized a strict pattern of audience segmentation.

Movie Theaters: Segmented Moviegoing Spaces

Pictures Palaces and Second-Class Theaters

Before World War I, price differentiation was operated between seats within the same theaters, the seats closest to the screens being the less expensive ones. In her study on Tunisia, Corriou notes that differentiation between theaters was developed in the interwar years (2011, 150). By the 1930s, the commercial exhibition sector in all the North African and Middle Eastern countries where cinemas were open was structured around a hierarchy between first-, second-, and third-class theaters (Issari 1989, 64), formalized by differences in admission prices (table 2.2) (*Wid's Year Book* 1920–1921).

The discrepancy in admission prices corresponded to a difference in terms of comfort. At one end of the spectrum stood the "picture palace," a luxurious movie theater comparable to top cinemas in Europe and North America. The first movie theater equipped for sound in Tehran in 1931 was called the Palace Cinema: "It was a large and lavishly decorated hall seating twelve hundred people. It consisted of a ground level and two additional floors, which housed individual private theater boxes,

Table 2.2. Admission prices in first-, second-, and third-class theaters in five countries in North Africa and the Middle East (1930s–1950s)

Country	Year	First-class	Second-class	Third-class
Aden	1943	$0.35		$0.10–$0.20
Algeria	1939	8–15 francs	3–6 francs	1–3 francs
Iraq	1938	Boxes: $2.25 for 4 seats $0.40	$0.22	$0.15
Iran	1951	Box: 20 rials Seat: 12 rials	12/8/6 rials	
Morocco (Casablanca)	1951	150–300 francs	70–120 francs	

Note: The prices are not adjusted.

Source: *Film Daily Year Book* 1938; General Consul, Algiers, June 30, 1939, NARA RG 51, Country File, Algeria, box 1304; Amlegation Casablanca to DOS, December 28, 1951, NARA RG 59, 1950–1954, Country File, Morocco, box 5354; C. Timberlake, "Motion Picture," Aden, Arabia, July 2, 1943, NARA RG 59, 1940–1944, Country File, Arabia, box 5786.

each accommodating four individuals" (Naficy 2011a, 228). In Moroccan Fez, the Empire was built in 1931. Moroccan architect Rachid Haloui, who visited it as child, remembers feeling he was entering "a castle," and marveling at the marble floors, the stairs "as high as mountains," the rooms with mirrors and the huge hall with "an ocean of seats." He was awe-struck by the "monumentality of the place and the sense of mystery one felt there" (Grouix and Haloui 2013, 115–16, 356–57). In 1940, MGM opened its own theater in Egypt. It was "an Art Deco palace, with 1,500 leather seats and air conditioning in the heart of Cairo's theater district"; as Egyptian filmmaker Youssef Chahine noted, "You entered the Metro as if it were a temple" (E. Thompson 2010, 188). At the other end of the movie theater spectrum stood small neighborhood theaters and provincial halls. In the early 1950s, movie theaters outside of Tehran were still described as poorly furnished, dirty, and uncomfortable.[22] The situation in 1949 Aden is an extreme example of this:

> All theaters are equipped with only the necessities with as much as possible constructed locally in make-shift fashion. There is no interest in carpeting, change-makers, ticket-selling

machines, or special fire protection equipment. All theaters are constructed of stone with bare concrete floors and are equipped with only canvas or palm-leaf cord chairs and a screen attached to a solid wall with only the necessities for projecting an image on a white surface accompanied by any sort of sound. The public neither asks nor receives quality, comfort or efficiency.[23]

The state of theaters seems to have been so bad that Europeans in Aden preferred to view films in their clubs or in military facilities, and in 1951, MGM created the Aden Film Club to show films to subscribers.[24]

Another difference between first-class and other theaters was novelty and variety. First-class theaters were first-run, that is, they showed new films. Second- and third-class theaters showed reruns. One of Fez's neighborhood cinemas, the Apollo, showed films as rerun, second-time rerun, and even, as one spectator remembers, "35th-time re-run" (Grouix and Haloui 2013, 51). The offer was especially limited in the provinces. While people living in the largest urban centers could choose among different movie theaters, smaller cities usually had one or two theaters. In 1951 Morocco, half of the cities had only one theater (Mingant 2017, 65). In smaller cities, films were commercially shown in spaces that were, in fact, not solely dedicated to cinema. A list of Algerian movie theaters in 1951 includes community halls, town theaters, religious institutions, and military institutions (65). Not only were there fewer movie theaters in the smaller cities, but the shows were also less numerous, as can be seen in table 2.3. In Egypt, for example, movie theaters in large cities offered three to four shows a day, while in smaller cities there were two shows per day, and in villages, three to five shows a week (UNESCO 1949, 175).

Programs were also renewed at different rates. In the largest cities, where the overall potential audience was quite important, programs were changed once a week. In smaller urban centers, where the potential audience was less important, programs had to be changed more than once a week (UNESCO 1949, 170, 188). The content of programs also differed. In the largest cities, a show would comprise news, a short, and a feature film. In smaller cities, such as in Algeria and Egypt, a show could be constituted of two feature films of about one hour each, that is, lesser quality movies (UNESCO 1949, 170, 175).[25] The comfort and variety offered to a given spectator, and the ensuing movie experience,

Table 2.3. Number of shows per week in city and province theaters in five countries in North Africa and the Middle East (1940s–1950s)

Country	Year	City theaters	Province theaters
Algeria	1949	14	1–15
Egypt	1949	21–28	14
Iran	1951	21–28 & 1–2 matinees on Fridays	7–14
Lebanon	1943	31	14
Tunis	1949	23	3–15

Source: UNESCO 1949; AmEmbassy Tehran to DOS, August 18, 1951, NARA, RG 59, Country File, Iran, 1950–1954, box 5516; James T. Scott, "Motion Pictures (Syria and the Lebanon)," April 1943, NARA, RG 59, Country File, Lebanon, 1940–1944, T1178, roll 5.

were not simply predicated on whether he or she lived in a large city center, but also on stringent social determinants.

Social Hierarchies

Originally commercially motivated to maximize profit, price differentiation also created socially fragmented spaces of consumption along class as well as ethnic lines. As one US ambassador noted in 1951, segregated consumption was a tacitly accepted practice:

> There are no laws or regulation which restrict theater admission to Europeans or Moroccans. As a practical matter, however, Moroccans patronize chiefly those theaters located in the native sections; further, prices in the so-called European theaters are too high for most Moroccans and, in addition, managers of these theaters screen would-be patrons for cleanliness, thus eliminating many Moroccans. It is practical, therefore, to speak of European theaters and Moroccan theaters and this classification is commonly used by distributors and exhibitors.[26]

In her study on colonial-time Tunisia, Corriou concludes that the strong social hierarchy of movie theaters reproduced colonial hierarchies. As

Ferro notes, in the French colonies, "the colonized was both a class and a race" (1994, 188). In Tunisia, first-class theaters were patronized by Europeans as well as the native elite, who could afford more expensive tickets (Corriou 2011, 247–49). Second-class theaters were frequented by lower-class Tunisians as well as Maltese and Sicilians immigrants, who belonged to the working class (248). Tahar Cheriaa remembers the difference between the theaters of the "preponderants," that is, the colonial lobbies who dominated Tunisia's political and economic life, and the theaters of the "*bicots*," a racist term used to define a person from North Africa (Corriou 2011, 248). In some cities, spectators entered the cinema through two different doors depending on the admission price; in practice, this meant the Tunisian workers entered from a different door than the European executives (249). In large cities, a clear topography of movie theaters according to class and ethnicity could thus be drawn. In 1930s Tunis, smaller theaters were situated between the European center and the medina, while first-class cinemas had settled on the largest avenues of the European center (191–92). Interestingly, in Tunisia as well as Morocco, in smaller town where there was only one cinema, the audience was systematically mixed (249).[27]

The reproduction of social hierarchies by the commercial exhibition structure also prevailed in Middle Eastern markets. In 1930s Tehran, the first-class theaters were located in the new and modern avenues, while the second- and third-class theaters were located in the poorer areas (Naficy 2011a, 202). In 1930 Palestine, cinemas were differentiated according to the territory's population: more cosmopolitan cities such as Jerusalem and Haifa had only mixed theaters; the city of Acre, with a population constituted of both "Arabs" and "Christians,"[28] has one such mixed theater; in other cities, however, theaters were either exclusively "Arab" (Jaffa, Nablus, Tulkarem) or "Jewish" (Tel Aviv, Rishon-le-Tsion, Kfar Saba).[29] As for the first-run theaters, they were situated in Haifa, Jerusalem, and Tel Aviv.[30]

This social fragmentation of movie audiences also led to differentiation in the behavior of moviegoers. Attending a picture palace was an act of social standing. The audience at the premiere of *Gone with the Wind* (1939) in Cairo was elegant, "dressed in tuxedos and evening gowns," and a "social buzz" surrounded the event with a "distinguished guest list of top Egyptian, British, French and American officials" (E. Thompson 2010, 189). In Tunis, moviegoing was a time of socialization for elite women, who dressed up, observed the new fashion and enthused in both Arabic and French over the likes of Greta Garbo and Danielle

Darrieux (Corriou 2011, 262). It was an equally important leisure for French civil servants who also dressed up for the occasion (240). In Fez's chicest cinema, the ban on smoking was viewed as a mark of high standing (Grouix and Haloui 2013, 132). In small neighborhood cinemas, on the other hand, the audience was mostly male and very noisy (91). In Tunisia's most popular theaters, the floors were strewn with sunflower and squash seeds, smelled of urine and tobacco, and the brouhaha drowned out the soundtrack (Corriou 2011, 422). While on weekdays the audience was mostly masculine, families, and especially children, generally noisily enthusiastic spectators, attended during the weekend (419, 422).

A US diplomatic report in 1943 Aden epitomizes the overlapping of commercial segmentation, colonial hierarchy, and moviegoing experience. In the British protectorate, movie theaters were distinguished based on admission price and location in the city. European theaters charged $0.35 and were located in the port area of Steamer Point, the European residential district. Theaters catering to native and Indian audiences were situated in Crater, the old town of Aden, five miles away from Steamer Point, and charged from $0.10 to $0.20. Moviegoing for the European audience was a ritualized practice. Tuesdays and Thursdays were "social nights" when people wore evening clothes and invited friends for dinner before the film. During the show, "exhibitions of emotions [we]re restrained practically to the point of non-existence."[31] The movie experience in "native theaters," however, was a lively one, with viewers that were "very demonstrative, laughing heartily, shouting, clapping and freely expressing emotion."[32] By excluding their local employees from the corporate clubhouses in which films were shown, oil companies in the Gulf followed an even more formalized "segregation regime" (Oruc 2020, 23).

Gender Segregation

In some countries, the commercial structure also created segmentation along gender lines. Access to films for women had from the start been a complex issue. Movie theaters were both public spaces and dark rooms, consequently viewed as highly improper places for women (E. Thompson 2000, 204). In the Middle East, Muslim and Catholic authorities worried about the immorality both onscreen and in the movie halls (202–3, 207–8). In Saudi Arabia, movie theaters were never opened, as religious leaders objected to "the depiction of women in Western and even Egyptian films," but also to "references to Christianity and Judaism, alcoholic beverages, inappropriately attired women, kissing, sex, and excessive violence" (Kamalipour and Mowlana 1994, 253). Social conservatives were also concerned about the representation of gender relations presented in Western cinema (Mingant 2015a), which were considered utterly foreign to local mores.

From the exhibitors' point of view, however, women were a considerable potential audience. A 1930 report of the US Department of Commerce thus attributed the strong growth of the exhibition sector in Iran, notably the tripling of the number of cinemas in three months, partly to the "permission recently granted to women to enter public places, such as cafés, restaurants, and theaters" (US Department of Commerce 1930). Aware of this strong religious and social opposition but also of the need to enlarge their audience basis, Middle Eastern exhibitors set out to devise socially acceptable ways for women to become cinemagoers (Mingant 2015a). Since the presence of women in the public space was a central argument against female cinemagoing, the solution found by exhibitors was gender-segregated movie theaters. A 1935 decision in Baghdad instituted "for men only" and "for women only" matinees. This separation did not apply to evening shows at which girls were accompanied by their families, but to matinees that they usually attended alone and that were the opportunity to meet boys.[33] Such segregated showings existed in many Middle Eastern countries, from pre-1930s Iran to 1940s Jordan (Naficy 2011a, 264).[34] Thompson notes that "as early as 1928 the Victory [Nasr] theater in Damascus's Marja Square offered women's-only matinees every Wednesday afternoon. By the mid-1930s, there were women's-only showings in Beirut cinemas three or four times weekly" (E. Thompson 2000, 205). As Naficy points out about Iran, these early efforts institutionalized "women as regular and legitimate audience" (Naficy 2011a, 264). In September 1928, the Grand Cinema in Tehran thus inaugurated gender-segregated shows in order to enable "the respected ladies" to enjoy "the famous serial Copper Bullet" just as the men would (Issari 1989, 64).[35] Additionally, "screen translators apparently engaged in film censorship" (Naficy 2011a, 269). Noblewoman Sattareh Farman Farmanian remembers watching *Gone with the Wind* (1939) sitting in the "women's and children's section." When Rhett kisses Scarlett, the translator held "something up to cover the actor's faces so that the audience would not witness indecencies" (quoted in Naficy 2011a, 269). Though less common, gender-segregated cinemas also existed in North Africa, where they were specifically designed as a means to attract the female Muslim spectators (Corriou 2011, 161). By creating what they promoted as safe female spaces, exhibitors thus successfully adapted the new entertainment to the local social context, and enabled women to access the movie experience.

Not all female spectators were Muslim, however, and not all women experienced cinema in gender-segregated theaters. Clear intersectionality[36] can be observed, as a woman's origin and social class were equally determining factors. Women and girls of European origin did not chafe under any restriction, attending first-class mixed cinemas, either with their husbands or on their own (Mingant 2015a). A second category of women who could access these first-run cinemas was the native elite. In the late 1930s, middle-class women in Lebanon and Egypt attended the movies "in large numbers" and at "the same shows as men" (E. Thompson 2010, 198). A third category was constituted of native lower-class women, often of Muslim faith, who either did not go to the cinema at all or were restricted to attending second- and third-class movie theaters under the supervision of the men of the family. Though the cinemagoing experience could be different, female spectators in the region did not necessarily develop a separate film culture but shared the same film culture with men of the same class and ethnic origin. The social, class and ethnic segmentation resulting from the commercial structure of the exhibition sector created not only different spaces of consumption and moviegoing experiences, but also several film cultures.

Cultures of Hollywood Cinema

A study of the list of 236 Hollywood films released in Iraq in 1949 reveals the presence of a wide variety of genres. While musicals, westerns, and film noirs, staple Hollywood productions of the time, dominated, Iraqi audiences were also proposed dramas and comedies.[37] Films such as *The Harvey Girls* (1946), *Drums along the Mohawk* (1939), *Sleep my Love* (1948), but also *A Letter to Three Wives* (1949), *I Was a Male War Bride* (1949), and Laurel and Hardy's *The Big Noise* (1944) were all released in the country that year. Moreover, although most of the films were quite recent, with US releases from 1946 to 1949, some films were rather old, such as *Tarzan Escapes* (1936), *Cleopatra* (1934), and *Sign of the Cross* (1932). While this list gives us a valuable glimpse of the type of Hollywood films present in the country, it does not fully convey the fact that different audiences were offered different films: the segmentation of moviegoing spaces had led to the creation of two parallel cultures of Hollywood cinema.

The *Gone with the Wind Culture* versus the Cowboy Culture

Colonial and local elites lived in a film landscape that I propose to call the *Gone with the Wind* culture. The programs of picture palaces mostly consisted of A films from Hollywood. US diplomats recurrently remarked that "the more educated audience prefers a serious type of films, especially those based on known novels, or with historical connotations."[38] In Egypt, the "educated" enjoyed society dramas and musical comedies with subtitles in French (*Film Daily Year Book* 1938). Language, in fact, served as status symbol. As Thompson noted, "Egyptian and Lebanese elites performed their privileged status by attending *GWTW* at their city's most expensive and swankiest cinemas, the Metro and the Roxy, where lower-class spectators, and especially Arabic speakers, felt unwelcome" (E. Thompson 2010, 193). For the local elite, being able to attend a serious drama with many dialogues in English or French, such as "sophisticated drawing room stories where action is mostly psychological" (*Film Daily Year Book* 1938), was a sign that they were part of the "educated," that they had developed "a taste similar to that of the higher European classes" (*Film Daily Year Book* 1938). For the colonial elite, this meant that they shared the same culture as their fellow citizens of the mainland. In that sense, Moroccan Fez was, in cinematic terms, "a cultural extension of the French provinces" (Grouix and Haloui 2013, 110). Similarly, in Aden, the "European audiences [we]re typical English audiences and ha[d] the same tastes as the people in England."[39] A list of seven films advertised by Paramount in the *Middle East Motion Picture Almanac* of 1946–1947 shows quality pictures most probably distributed in first-class cinemas. They reflect a varied and up-to-date culture including musicals (*Blue Skies*, 1946), big-budget adventure films and epic westerns (*Unconquered*, 1947; *California*, 1947), historical comedies (*Monsieur Beaucaire*, 1946; *The Emperor's Waltz*, 1948), a Pearl White biopic (*Perils of Pauline*, 1947), and a film noir (*Desert Fury*, 1947). All were in Technicolor and featured stars such as Bing Crosby, Fred Astaire, Gary Cooper, Paulette Goddard, Berry Huttin, Ray Milland, Barbara Stanwyck, Bob Hope, and Joan Fontaine. Superproduction *Samson and Delilah* (1949), shown at first-run cinemas in Alexandria, fully represents the *Gone with the Wind* culture (figure 2.2).

On the other hand, I call the film landscape of the second- and third-class cinemas, in the cities and in the provinces, the cowboy culture. US diplomatic reports on these theaters are also unanimous: these theaters showed "Western pictures with plenty of riding or other adventures with plenty of action" (*Film Daily Year Book* 1938). In North Africa, these were

Figure 2.2. Advertising leaflet for the showing of *Samson and Delilah* (1949) in Alexandria first-run cinemas the Royal and the Mohamed Aly (1951). Source: Alexandria to DOS, January 16, 1951, NARA, RG 59, Country File, Egypt, 1950–54, box 5384.

called *"films mouvementés,"* that is, films with action, which comprised low-budget westerns, but also gangster films as well as visual comedies.[40] The preference for such genres was clearly linked to linguistic reasons: in Iran, "the lower classes prefer extravaganzas, sensational adventure, murders and musicals, partly because these not do require a long translation."[41] Subtitles would be of no help, as a large percentage of the audience could not read.[42] One report even adamantly stated about 1938 Iraq, "Films with long dialogues are not wanted" (*Film Daily Year Book* 1938). The linguistic reasons behind the preference for action, adventure, and visual humor films concerns not only the native population, but also the diverse population of lower-class European immigrants, who did not master French or English, as a 1942 report from Morocco noted:

> The natives who know enough French to be able to follow
> a dialogue or a commentary, as the film is projected, and to
> be interested in it, constitute only a very small minority in
> large urban centers, and are virtually inexistent elsewhere. The
> "Mediterraneans," whether naturalized or not, [. . .] also have
> difficulties with certain nuances and subtleties of the [French]
> language more often than you would think, and they do not
> always understand the meaning or even the basic sense.[43]

Out of the list of Hollywood films shown in 1949 Iraq, films belonging to the cowboy culture were most probably low-budget westerns (*Bad-man's Territory*, 1946) and western serials (*Black Arrow*, 1944), but also Zorro films (*The Mark of Zorro*, 1940), as well as comedies with Laurel and Hardy (*The Bullfighters*, 1945) and Abbot and Costello (*Buck Private Comes Home*, 1947). The program offered in a theater in Erbil, "a medium-sized town in northern Iraq having few inhabitants who speak any language other than Kurdish or Arabic" (table 2.4) confirms the mix of B movies offered to these spectators.[44] Low-budget adventure films and westerns, but also Tarzan stories were central to the film landscape of second- and third-class theaters. In 1949 Iraq, no less than five Tarzan films were actually distributed: *Tarzan Escapes* (1936), *Tarzan and the Green Goddess* (1938), *Tarzan Finds a Son* (1939), *Tarzan's Secret Treasure* (1941), and *Tarzan and the Huntress* (1947). Cowboys, Zorro, and Tarzan were thus the heroes of second- and third-class spectators' film mythology.

While Western reports on North Africa and the Middle East, whether from French or US diplomats, tended to judge these tastes with condescension (Corriou 2011, 151), opposing the "educated" to the "uneducated"

Table 2.4. Programming at a theater in Erbil (June 1952)

Tarzan and the Slave Girl (1950)
Aloma of the South Seas (1941)
Mighty Joe Young (1949)
Thief of Baghdad (1940)
Calamity Jane and Sam Bass (1949)
American Guerilla in the Philippines (1950)
Blood on the Moon (1948)

Source: AmEmbassy Baghdad to DOS, June 26, 1952, NARA, RG 59, Country File, Iraq, 1950–1954, box 5489.

according to the norms of the Western elites, what was at play was in fact the coexistence of parallel cultural universes. As table 2.5 shows, the *Gone with the Wind* culture of the colonial elite comprised A films from both Hollywood and France. It formed a Western cultural enclave disconnected from the local context. It was also a fantasy of high culture as it was supposedly practiced in the homeland, an imagination that largely passed over the fact that Tarzan and Zorro films, low-budget westerns and film noirs were widely popular in France too (Simsi 2000, 167). On the other hand, the cowboy culture came to be very much anchored in the local culture, especially rubbing shoulders with Egyptian—and sometimes Indian—cinema and becoming part of the same landscape for the native audience. As Corriou noted, Tunisian spectators jointly embraced Western and Egyptian films: in June 1947, the first issue of the *Al-Masrah wa al-Sinimâ* (Theater and Cinema) journal had two covers, one with Rita Hayworth and the other with Tunisian actress Hassiba Rochdi (Corriou 2011, 435). The cowboy culture thus represents a valuable example of cinematic syncretism. Although first-run movie theaters were the largest source of revenue for the Hollywood distributors (Issari 1989, 65), one can argue that the cowboy culture of second- and third-run theaters in the cities and provinces was, in fact, the most widespread.

Out-of-Sync Culture

Another element that differentiated the two cultures of Hollywood cinema was time. As table 2.4 shows, the films shown in Erbil in June 1952 were up to twelve years old. What we now call "windows" of distribution was formally organized within the exhibition structure. As can be seen on

Table 2.5. Movie theaters in Fez, Morocco (1940s–1950s)

Cinema	Type of films	Language	Geographical situation	Audience
Empire	A films (US)	French (dubbed)	European city	French colonial elite
Bijou	French films	French	European city	French colonial elite
Arc-en-Ciel	Westerns/B movies (US) Italian neorealist films	French (dubbed) Italian	European city	Spanish & Italian working-class communities
Apollo	Westerns/B movies (US) Egyptian films	French (dubbed) Egyptian Arabic	Between European city and medina	Moroccans
Boujeloud	Tarzan, Zorro/B Movies (US) Egyptian films	French (dubbed) Egyptian Arabic	Medina	Moroccans

Source: Grouix and Haloui 2013.

table 2.6, a Hollywood film in Cairo would be distributed first in a picture palace, such as the Palladium or the MGM theater, and would then be released as a rerun on to second- and third-class theaters such as the Oasis or the Mohamed Aly. The same window chronology existed for the distribution of Egyptian films. A given Hollywood film would thus reach second-class theater audiences later than first-class ones; *Gone with the Wind*, for example, which was released in 1939 in the USA, and 1941 in Cairo and Lebanon, appears on the list of films circulating in Iraq in 1949.

This time lag occurred even more in provincial theaters at the far end of the print circulation path such as Morocco, Iraq, or Aden.[45] In 1927 Aden, a local US diplomat complained that the pictures received were at

Table 2.6. Types of films present in Cairo movie theaters in 1947

Type of Picture	Name of the Theaters
American pictures (first- & second-run)	Cairo Palace, Diana, Kashmir, MGM (MGM films), Miami, Normandy, Odeon Theater, Opera, Palace, Palladium, Paradis, Regent, Rex, Roxy, St.-James
Arabic pictures (first-run)	Alf-Leila, Amira Ferial, Cleopatra, Cosmo, Dolly, El-Ittehad, Ferial, Kursaal, Lux, Majestic, Metropole, Rod El-Farag, Royal, Studio Misr
French pictures (first- & second-run)	Kursaal (open-air), Miami (open-air), Normandy Odeon
Italian pictures	Kursaal (open-air)
American pictures (second- & third-run), serials	Femina, Ideal, Oasis, Potiniere, Strand
Arabic pictures (second- to fourth-run), American pictures (reruns), serials	Ezebekia, El-Nil, Fantazio, Fleury, Fuad, Helouan, Honolulu, Misr, Mohamed Aly, National, Ramses, Rialto, Rio Palace, Saptieh, Sheharazad, Victoria
Arabic pictures (second- & third-run)	Al-Hilal, Isis, Olympia, Wahby

Source: *Middle East Motion Picture Almanac* 1947, 19–24.

least ten years old: "The romances were of 1912 to 1916, vintage, slow, crude and sloppy," and the comedies were "plain slapstick of the early days."[46] Not only were films rerun in lower-class theaters and sent years later to out-of-the-way theaters, but silent cinema continued to circulate long after its production had stopped. The transition to sound movie theaters took a number of years. All theaters were "wired for sound" in Palestine by 1935, Syria by 1936, Iraq and Morocco by 1938, and Egypt by 1939 (*Film Daily Year Book* 1935, 1936, 1938, 1939). In 1938 Iran, out of the country's 35 theaters, 3 small-town theaters were still not wired (*Film Daily Year Book* 1938). In early 1940s, silent Charlie Chaplin and Rin Tin Tin films were still shown in Tunis's Bagdad cinema (Corriou 2011, 240). In his study of the circulation of silent American serials in 1920s and 1930s Iran, Askari notes that, contrary to "markets in China and port cities in Latin America, where established exchange offices ensure rapid distribution," a long time gap existed between US and Iranian release, to the point that the silent serials enjoyed "prolonged popularity, which extended well into the early sound period" (2014, 105).

While European observers at the time might have felt that the cowboy culture was outdated and backward, it is, in fact, important to foreground the specificities of such a film culture. In his study of junk print circulation in Iran, Askari interestingly proposes to abandon "one-dimensional conceptions of media history, which too often depend on a narrative of development and progress"; he exposes the notion of "delayed film culture" as "the touristic fantasy that one (peripheral) place represents the past of another (central) place" (2014, 101–2), and contends that what was at stake is the way "elements of early cinema culture overlapped with 1920s modernity, [. . .] how mile markers of exhibition that were experienced elsewhere as continual sequence (the very premise of serialized stories) were often experienced in Tehran as simultaneity" (105), thus creating "a film culture out of synch" (99). The cowboy culture was such an out-of-sync film culture. Films from different nationalities and languages, as well as different time periods, merged to create this syncretic film culture.

An unexpected effect of the time lag was also to create new simultaneity effects, especially when it came to the popularity of stars. The list of films distributed in 1949 Iraq reveals the presence of seven films starring Tyrone Power, a particularly popular actor at the time (Grouix and Haloui 2013, 172) (table 2.7).[47] Although the films were released the same year in Iraq, their actual production date spanned one decade, from

Table 2.7. Films starring Tyrone Power distributed by Twentieth Century Fox in 1949 Iraq

Alexander's Ragtime Band (1938)
Jesse James (1939)
The Mark of Zorro (1940)
A Yank in the RAF (1941)
The Razor's Edge (1946)
Captain from Castile (1947)
The Luck of the Irish (1948)

Source: Foreign Service of the USA, Baghdad, to DOS, April 21, 1950, NARA, RG 59, Country File, Iraq, 1950–1954, box 5489.

1938 to 1948. In distribution terms, this made sense as Twentieth Century Fox, which had Power under contract from 1936 to 1954 (Finler 2003, 126), fully exploited the rights to the film through reruns. In terms of film culture, the simultaneous presence of Power's personas could have two consequences. First, the recurrent appearances of the actor on the screen must have played a part in maintaining his popularity. Secondly, as one can assume that the most recent films were distributed in first-run theaters and the oldest in second- and third-run theaters, this meant that spectators from different backgrounds could share a passion for the same star. In the context of this syncretic, out-of-synch culture, bridges thus existed between the separated spaces of film consumption. The temporality of production had been superseded by the temporality of reception.

Imagined Hollywood Cinema

A last characteristic of film culture in the region in the first half of the twentieth century was that the films themselves sometimes went through a process of transformation and reinvention. In her study of the reception of *Gone with the Wind* in Cairo and Beirut, Thompson stresses:

> Arabic-speaking audiences watched and understood the pictures as the studios intended—as texts written in what Miriam Hansen has called a "global vernacular," a flexible narrative code open to multiple interpretations. Moviegoers in Arab societies were as familiar with Hollywood's global vernacular as were other audiences around the world. (E. Thompson 2010, 185)

The popularity of American films, from *Samson and Delilah* to the ump-teenth rerun of *The Mark of Zorro*, confirms that audiences were familiar with Hollywood's codes and universe. However, while first-class theater audiences experienced film close to the form originally intended by the directors and producers, many spectators saw different versions for tech-nical, commercial, and political reasons.

Theaters that were situated in the provinces and especially toward the end of the print distribution circuit received films that were not only outdated, but also in damaged condition. The same print would first circulate in Europe before being sent to Egypt and later Syria (K. Thompson 1985, 33; *Film Daily Year Book* 1926). Aden and Iran, at the very end of the print circuit, seem to have particularly received such prints, but it was also the case in the provinces. In 1920s Egypt, independent exhibitors bought prints after they had toured the main picture palaces and showed them in the province villages (Askari 2014, 100). Askari points out that "accounts of the troubled and interrupted circulation of worn and incomplete prints depict the diverse kind of exhibition and reception of a considerable portion of the films screened throughout the region" (100). Travelers' accounts of mid-1930s Iran describe Hollywood talkies as films "whose dialogue and tunes are, because of faulty apparatus, a series of baffling squawks," thus making the accompanying written translation all the more necessary (Naficy 2011a, 200). But the language of the film could also be an issue for the audience. In 1940s Aden, although the films were in English and the audience mostly British subjects, the prints carried French subtitles, as they had been primarily circulated in Egypt, Syria, and other French-speaking areas of the Middle East.[48] In late 1940s Iran, the audience could also be frustrated by the awkward first attempts at Persian dubbing.[49] The bad quality of the prints, the sound system, and translation could all erase characteristics from the original film.

Transformations were sometimes even more profound as the films were recut. Sometimes, this was operated by the exhibitor. In the mid-1940s, Robert Lenté, owner of Fez's Rex cinema recut the fifteen chapters of Republic Pictures 1938 serial *The Lone Ranger* into four episodes to fit French exhibition standards (Grouix and Haloui 2013, 126–27). In Persia, dubbing directors also altered the film with a view to localize it. This strategy could be successful, as when Alexander Aghababian changed all the names of characters from Italian to Persian in *Le meravigliose avventure de Guerrin Meschino* (1952), but it could also prove annoying to audiences, as when one dubbing director chose a humorous option by postsynchronizing an Indian song over an American song by Jerry

Lewis in *The Patsy* (1964). As Issari notes, "The experiment did not work because the public, although accepting Jerry Lewis's talking in their language could not tolerate his singing in Hindustani!" (1989, 123). As the following chapter will show, scenes could also be cut at the request of censorship boards. Though few traces remain of these "scratched, warped, and heavily spliced prints" (Askari 2014, 113), the gap between the version of the same film experienced by a US spectator, an Algiers or Cairo first-class theater spectator, and an Aden second-run theater spectator cannot be overestimated.

In 1927, an American diplomat in Aden noted that the "native population appears to be better satisfied than the European with the films available, probably because they have not had the advantage of having seen better."[50] Putting aside the condescending tone, his remark was to the point: the spectators who were viewing Hollywood films in second- and third-run theaters, in small neighborhood cinemas or in the provinces, had no experience of US films other than B movies, reruns, and scratched prints. This does not mean, however, that they had no culture of Hollywood film, but rather that they had to develop a habit of filling the gaps—the cut shot, the unintelligible dialogue—with their own understanding of the film, their own knowledge of the genre codes, and, in the end, their own imagination of American cinema.

While a focus on distribution provides a narrative on how films came to be present in a territory and dominate a film market, the study of exhibition practices opens up a discussion on audiences and the way they experienced these films. The clues are dispersed but numerous: the exhibitors' translation strategies, the architecture of theaters, their geographical location within a given city, their price of admission, and their programming schedules. Because exhibitors adapted the cinema entertainment to the local social conventions, their choices provide us with a portrait of the society films circulated in. In the first half of the twentieth century, the North African and Middle Eastern audience was clearly strongly fragmented along national origin, class, and gender lines. The very diversity of spectatorial experiences thus uncovered invites rethinking of the notion of film culture. While traditional histories of Hollywood cinema provide a linear and US-centered narrative based on production stories and release dates, this chapter shows how the way films are actually experienced creates myriad alternative cultures of cinema. These different film cultures actually coexist, as the *Gone with the Wind* culture of the elite and the cowboy culture of the lower classes did in the colonial era Middle East and North Africa. They are also creating different temporal and geographical narratives. The out-of-sync culture formulated by Askari questions our linear vision and opens up new avenues for interpretation, as the case of Tyrone Power's popularity shows. They also invite a connected history focus, by looking at geographical affinities beyond national borders. European elites in the region lived in a film world intimately connected with the mainland, while local populations experienced US movies alongside Egyptian and Indian films. The focus on exhibition and audiences thus leads us to use the plural and not the singular, to identify film *cultures*, their local interactions and their transnational connections. Further on-the-ground research, especially oral history initiatives, would enrich this first vision of the variety of filmscapes that existed in the region. Film experience was about origin, class, and gender. It was about time and geography. In the end, it was also about imagination. In North Africa and the Middle East, as in other parts of the world, Hollywood films were in fact an imaginary space in which each spectator, within specific constraints, let his or her mind roam. Imaginations of Hollywood, however, could only develop within the strictly fenced area circumscribed by cautious and attentive colonial powers.

3

Hollywood Films as Political Objects

HE FILMSCAPE IN WHICH AUDIENCES of North Africa and the Middle East lived in the first half of the twentieth century was determined by commercial factors—the distributors' ability to establish a wide network, the structuration of the exhibition sector—but also the nature of political regimes. In the first half of the twentieth century, the political landscape in North Africa and the Middle East was characterized by widespread domination by foreign powers. International alliances and colonial zones of influences could be read in the nationality of films allowed for import. During the 1910s, Turkish films were dominant in Syria, a territory under Ottoman rule. German films were also strongly present due to the Sublime Porte's alliance with Berlin. These were, however, displaced by French and American films when France established its mandate in the early 1920s (Thoraval 2003, 82; E. Thompson 2000, 198). Similar political constraints can be observed in Libya, where the Italian occupation between 1911 and World War II was accompanied by the settlement of Italian immigrants. In major cities, cinemas were built mostly for the Italian audiences, and the films circulating in the country were "Italian drama, documentaries and news releases" (Leaman 2001, 407). In a region marked by strong European presence, and especially French and British colonial rule, Hollywood films soon became political objects to be observed, kept in check, and used for ideological purposes.

Enlisting Hollywood Films in the
Service of the Colonial Enterprise

Controlling Hollywood's Discourse

In the first decade of the twentieth century, when cinema was still a fledgling entertainment medium, authorities were mostly concerned with providing a legal framework in terms of exhibition hall hygiene and safety (Corriou 2011, 162). Early intervention regarding film content was dealt with on a local level by the police (Smyth 1979, 439; Douin 2001, 133). World War I marked a turning point, however, as states started to realize cinema's potential for visual propaganda (Goerg 2015, 73; Corriou 2011, 162, 167). The influence of cinema on the audience was becoming all the more important as movie-going grew as a popular leisure activity (Corriou 2011, 162). The arrival of sound in the late 1920s was a further element attracting authorities' attention: the national origin of the film was now clearly palpable through the language used (301). State policies consequently moved the focus from exhibition conditions to film content, from safety regulations to censorship.

In Egypt, state film censorship was first instituted under the joint authority of the Egyptian monarch and the British embassy in 1914, thus marking the move towards a centralized and bureaucratized process (Douin 2001, 133). Control of the entry of foreign films was established along a drastic line in 1921, as Great Britain established martial law over the country to smother national protest (133; *Film Daily Year Book* 1926). Film actually became a central discussion point of the British Colonial Office in the second half of the 1920s. It figured "prominently on the agenda at the first Colonial Office Conference" in 1927 (Smyth 1979, 437). By the late 1920s, officials were calling for an extension of the British film quota instituted by the Cinematograph Film Act of 1927 to the whole Empire (Jaikumar 2006, 4–5; Newman 2013, 81), and by 1930, the Colonial Films Committee recommended the organization of centralized censorship boards and committees in the colonies (Smyth 1979, 439). British representatives held key positions in those institutions. Among the seven members of the 1928 censorship body in Egypt, one was the representative of the European Public Safety Administration (Ali 2004, 61, 79). In a 1934 letter to MGM's manager in Alexandria, the director general of the European department within the Ministry of the Interior clearly stated that his mission was to "personally" represent the "European interests on the Censorship board."[1] In Palestine, censorship was mostly in the hands of British subjects. In 1932, the censorship board was composed of the "District Commissioner (chairman), officials of the Police, officials of the Department of Education, an officer of the Chief Secretariat, the Welfare Inspector (an English lady), a District officer, a British insurance agent, the wife of a British official, and an Arab journalist."[2] In the territories under French influence, the colonizer's stronghold was just as tight. The censorship committee established in Tunisia in 1925 comprised the public prosecutor or his representative, the vice-president of the Municipality of Tunis, the chief of the Sûreté (police), an inspector of the Department of Education, a police commissioner, and a representative of the film distribution agencies in Tunis (Corriou 2011, 636). In the Great Lebanon mandate, censorship was in the hands of a committee headed by the French high commissioner (*Film Daily Year Book* 1935).

Hollywood films that traveled to North Africa and the Middle East actually often went through a double process of censorship. The films examined by the Tunisian commission or by the Moroccan Protectorate's board of censors had already been censored by a French film committee for the mainland market (Corriou 2011, 302; *Film Daily Year Book* 1938, 1940). For films distributed in Morocco's Spanish zone, the censorship process had taken place beforehand in Spain (*Film Daily Year Book* 1938). Films reaching Aden from India and examined by a local commission composed of three British civil servants—the "Chief Censor, Aden, the Commissioner of Police and the Information Officer"—had already been censored by the Bombay Board of Censors.[3] While films arriving from India had already been toned down to accommodate colonial demands, films censored in mainland France were deemed potentially inappropriate to the North African audience. Although the Tunisian committee tended to routinely approve the French censorship decision, the protectorate authorities strongly defended the existence of a specific local commission "given the heterogeneity of the Tunisian society and the particularities of the governed population whose diverse sensibilities it intended to preserve" (Corriou 2011, 302–3, 299). The presence of specific censorship committees in the colonies was linked to the predominant view that the colonized audience was different from the mainland audience.

Both French and British colonizers considered native populations in the colonies as "children" (Goerg 2015, 67). Due to their alleged limited intellectual capacities, local populations were believed to be credulous and impressionable when it came to moving images (Corriou 2011, 250). According to Oliver Bell, president of the British Film Institute in 1942, African spectators should be "treated as 10-year-old white children" (quoted in Corriou 2011, 252). Local populations were thus to be both educated through selected films and protected from cinema's potentially nefarious influence. Authorities formulated films' harmful effects in no uncertain terms. The 1930 *Report of the Colonial Film Committee* emphasized the question of censorship as "of the first importance, as the display of unsuitable films is a very real danger" (quoted in Smyth 1979, 437). Two years later, Sir Hesketh Bell, former governor of Uganda and Northern Nigeria noted that the people of India and the Far East had already been spoiled by film but that action could still be taken "in our tropical African Empire" (quoted in Smyth 1979, 438). Censorship was thus guided by a strongly ideological—and imaginary—vision of what the local audience was like. In his study of the arrival of cinema in the Gulf region in the 1930s, Oruc shows how the colonial visions and decisions delineated "a reception theory of colonial difference" (2020, 26). Interestingly enough, a 1932 US diplomatic report sensed this hiatus, noting that the members of the Palestine board "[we]re inclined to place too much emphasis upon what they consider[ed] to be best for 'native' tastes."[4]

While paternalistic discourses justified the creation of specific committees, censorship criteria reveal the colonial authorities' systematic efforts to force Hollywood films into the ideological mold of the colonial enterprise. The main worry for British and French colonial authorities were that the "alien ideas and ideals" (Smyth 1979, 437) conveyed by Hollywood films would run counter to those officially promoted. A particular danger was the risk that American films would erode the respect for European colonizers, a respect vital to the colonial enterprise (438). A 1932 French report, for example, underlined that "foreign" (i.e., US) films "accustomed the colonial spectators to admire the industrial organization, the wealth, the well-being of other people [. . .] and to establish, in that regard, comparisons that were unfavorable to the guardian nations" (quoted in Goerg 2015, 77). Hence, "the massive import of foreign films in the colonies could put into peril the colonial policy of a great people" (quoted in Goerg 2015, 76). Consequently, it was the responsibility of the censorship committee to make sure that any harmful potential of Hollywood films was averted and that the films circulating were consonant with the authorities' discourse.

One guiding principle was that imported films should not show disrespect for British and French colonial authorities (Smyth 1979, 439; *Film Daily Year Book* 1928, 1938). In Great Lebanon, central criteria included the "prestige of the Army, respect due to foreign countries, and also public morals."[5] One Hollywood genre that particularly encountered difficulties on account of this criteria were French Foreign legion films. In 1926, *Beau Geste* was banned in North Africa for giving a false image of the French army (Jaidi 2001, 44). Produced by Paramount, directed by Herbert Brenon and starring Ronald Colman, the film follows the adventure of a young Englishman who joins the Foreign Legion, fights rebellious Arabs, and is faced with a particularly unpleasant commander. The film actually led France to lodge an official protest in Hollywood. Representation of the Foreign Legion in other films such as *Plastered in Paris* (1928) and *The Foreign Legion* (1928) kept this a burning issue (Vasey 1997, 57–58). In the 1930s, France produced its own colonial cinema, which presented a glorified image of the Legion as in *La bandera* (1935) (Orlando 2011, 2).

Censorship boards were not only vigilant in maintaining French and British images, but also systematically banned any films that could give an "unsavoury image of the white race" (Smyth 1979, 438): "Hence anything tending to lower the white man's prestige (was) eliminated" (*Film Daily Year Book* 1929). In 1935 Warner Bros.' western *Massacre* (1934) was banned in Palestine: the film was "an outrageous and probably grossly exaggerated picture of the inhuman manner in which the North American Indians were being economically and morally massacred with the tacit approval of the United States government."[6] Beside the morality of white men, the sanctity of white women also needed to be preserved. Crime pictures seem to have been especially problematic in this respect. A US diplomat noted in 1932 Palestine that due to "nights club scenes," "the Arab knows of only one class of women [. . .] and obtains a distorted view of western civilization."[7] Fox's adventure film *Fazil* (1928) clearly violated this taboo: this romance between a white woman and an Arab man, was deemed "objectionable" and the film was prohibited in the Great Lebanon. Interestingly, the original book itself had not been prohibited, but it was felt the film would reach a larger audience "whose emotions only the picture might arouse."[8] Again, preserving the image of white women was a key issue enaged with all over the British Empire, as demonstrated by Arora's 1995 study on India. The colonial enterprise subsumed geographical distances and cultural specificities into one ideological space, as reveals the transnational dynamics of censorship issues.

Censors were also careful to prevent circulation of films that could create social unrest, and religion was another taboo (*Film Daily Year Book* 1928, 1938). Cecil B. DeMille's *The Crusades* (1935) was banned in Tunisia in 1936 to avoid rousing dissensions between Christian and Muslim communities. In Palestine, where the situation was particularly tense between Muslim, Jewish, and Christian communities, colonial censorship was especially strict (*Film Daily Year Book* 1926).[9] Paternalistic censorship views in fact hid fears of the supposed "uncontrolled brutality" of the colonized populations (Corriou 2011, 252–53). Hence, any film exciting to violence was to be reproved. *Fazil*'s fault was not only to show a mixed love story, but also to feature conflict between Arabs and European troops.[10] In 1928 Syria, scenes showing attacks on police, revolution, or crimes were thus systematically cut (*Film Daily Year Book* 1928). Censors were particularly attentive as nationalist movements in the 1920s strongly contested the colonial presence. The 1920s was especially marked by the Rif War, which opposed inhabitants of the Moroccan mountains to the Spanish and French between 1921 and 1926, and the Great Syrian Revolt of 1925, which contested French rule (Katan Bensamoun and Chalak 2007, 207; Cloarec and Laurens 2007, 56). At such times, films depicting revolts were systematically banned.[11] MGM's *Rasputin and the Empress* (1932), subject to protest in London, and banned in Egypt and Palestine, encapsulates these colonial taboos. The story of a Russian monk and his relationship with the Czarina was considered "anti-monarchic, likely to cause anti-Christian feeling, and crude in its representation of the execution of the Royal family by the mob."[12] The use of mesmerism by a monk "would confirm in the eyes of a Moslem mob the worst allegations made against missionaries."[13] The film was particularly badly timed as anti-missionary unrest had irrupted in Egypt. In spite of MGM's appeal, the US diplomats sided with the censorship board—and the colonial vision of the native spectator—foregrounding that the film was "not the kind of picture which should be shown to ignorant and often fanatical Mohamedan audiences."[14]

In practice, these measures do not seem to have exceedingly hampered the distribution of Hollywood films. Apart from Palestine where censorship was reputed to be strict, reports for film professionals in the 1920s and 1930s tend to present censorship in the region as "lenient" and posing no real difficulty (*Film Daily Year Book* 1926, 1929, 1938). In 1938 Iraq, out of the 200 films examined by the censorship board, only seven were banned, including six from the USA (*Film Daily Year Book* 1939). In view of these figures, the *Film Daily Year Book* of 1939 concluded that the censorship in the country was "not strict." To Fox's agent denouncing the existence of anti-American discrimination by a commission apparently more lenient with French films, the consul remarked that *Fazil* had been the only American film banned by local authorities.[15] Given the fact that Hollywood films were already heavily controlled at the production stage through a process of self-imposed censorship implemented first through the noncompulsory guide known as the "Don'ts and Be Carefuls" in 1927, then through the compulsory Production Code in 1930, the films were already sanitized when they reached international markets. In fact, the development of state censorship boards in the second half of the 1920s could be seen as a positive evolution for the Hollywood distributors entering the market, since their criteria were easier to navigate than the arbitrary decisions of local police heads. Paramount's complaint against the lone censorship commissioner in Tunisia had been instrumental in the creation of a full-fledged board in 1925 (Corriou 2011, 174). The distrust against of Hollywood film content from state-instituted censorship boards did not prevent Hollywood distributors from operating and thriving in these markets. In the territories under French rule, the control of Hollywood films was not only about censorship, however. Additional legislation related to language extended the harnessing of Hollywood magic for the sake of colonization.

Controlling Hollywood's Language

France's influence over the region had not only been political but, as noted in chapter 2, cultural as well. The spread of the French language, through schools and missionary work, was a key part of the colonial enterprise. In the territories it directly controlled, France found Hollywood films a useful tool, as, in the 1930s and 1940s, the French parliament adopted a number of language-related film legislations. In 1932, a decree set up a quota on the importation of French-dubbed films in the mainland and made it compulsory to have the films dubbed in France (Cornu 2014, 57–59). Though the decree was originally aimed at protecting the mainland film industry, dubbing took on a more ideological connotation in the colonies as a privileged tool for the dissemination of the French language: "In 1931, seeking protection against US competition, Paris ordered French film distributors to market only French-language films in the colonies and asked US companies to dub their films into French" (E. Thompson 2000, 201). In North Africa and the Great Lebanon, the issue was less silencing English than foregrounding French, as demonstrated by the equal efforts to suppress the circulation of Italian- and Egyptian-language films in Tunisia after World War II (Corriou 2011, 371, 648): "Within France and in its African colonies, no other language was allowed to compete with French, a supposedly superior *universal* language" (Danan 1991, 612).

Hollywood films were all the more valuable to the spread of the French language that they circulated in all film spaces, from the picture palace to the second- and third-run theaters. While A films were an opportunity for local elites to improve their mastery of French, B movies did a more pioneering work. Laurel and Hardy, Tarzan, and Zorro films enabled French to penetrate the smaller mixed-language third-run cinemas. By watching dubbed films, the local population was "imperceptibly" taught the French language.[16] In 1942, the general resident in Morocco noted:

> The American film itself constitutes an element of national propaganda, as, more often than not, the Indigenous believes the films to be French, and, as he enjoys it, is first grateful to us, and attends more often—to see new programs where the same images and atmosphere are repeated, which binds him to us.[17]

Hollywood films had found themselves enmeshed in the colonial linguistic agenda and came to be used by the French authorities as a Trojan horse for acculturation. The advent of World War II further politicized Hollywood cinema, especially after the US entered the conflict in December 1941.

American Films as a Battlefield

The Changed Nature of Film

Initially fought on European soil, World War II soon spread to North Africa and the Middle East. After Italy unsuccessfully tried to extend its influence from Libya to Egypt in late 1940, Nazi Germany sent General Rommel and its Afrika Korps (Cloarec and Laurens 2007, 80). Great Britain, which defeated Rommel in Egypt in 1942, took control of the Great Lebanon away from Vichy France in 1941 and occupied Iran conjointly with the USSR the same year (79–81). North Africa was ruled by German-controlled Vichy government from the 1940 armistice to the landing of Allied troops in Algeria and Morocco in November 1942. Tunisia was occupied by the Germans. From November 1942 to May 1943, it became the ground of fierce battles between Allied and Axis forces (Bensamoun and Chalak 2007, 289–91). For distributors, the war meant disruption of commercial channels: it became impossible to obtain new films, but also to maintain communication between the US and the local offices. As battles raged, the film market was, in effect, frozen still.

Fighting was accompanied by intense propaganda activity, and Hollywood films became a pawn in a larger ideological game. Cinema came to be used as another battlefield, to the point that the geography of territorial conquest, the movement of advancing and retreating armies, could be drawn through observing the circulation of films. In late 1930s Iran, for example, German films were "the closest competitors of American films," representing about 30% of film shown, while 50% were American (*Film Daily Year Book* 1938). As World War II broke out, Iran remained neutral, although its preference leant toward Germany; but when the Allied forces invaded Iran in September 1941, German films were banned, and Russian and US films filled the gap (Issari 1989, 67). Film circulation was similarly conditioned by ideological objectives in Italian-occupied Libya. During the war, cinemas showed fascist Italian and German propaganda. As Allied forces entered the country in 1943, they used cinema "as an active tool of propaganda and intellectual and cultural domination" (Leaman 2001, 408). Propaganda was developed not through the commercial circuit, but through the mobile cinema units of the British Information Office and the American Cultural Center (408). Iran had similarly become a site of ideological struggle, mostly through the means of educational and propaganda material (Naficy 2011b, 4). Commercial distributors thus had to deal with a politically charged context in which films came to be judged only on the face of their nationality and propaganda value. Caught in a tug-of-war between Axis powers determined on evicting them from markets and US authorities seeking to use Hollywood films to promote the American ideology, film professionals strove to preserve their distribution network and commercial interests during the six years of conflict. Nowhere was this more clearly exemplified than in North Africa, a region under the control of German-occupied France and a strategic territory to conquer for the Allied forces.

Ideological Targeting and Commercial Survival in Vichy North Africa

The occupation of France by Germany in June 1940 and the establishment of the German-controlled Vichy government quickly led to the targeting of Hollywood companies and their films both for economic and ideological reasons. The new authorities first aimed at breaking the

American film dominance with a view to favor German film companies that had been strongly present on the French market before the war. By the late 1920s, German film interests had in fact been entrenched there through the sale of film equipment and had become Hollywood's main competitors (Garçon 2006, 82–84). After the armistice, Germany put French film distribution in the hands of two German companies: ACE and the August 1940–created Tobis Films (Garçon 2006, 167). In August 1940, the German Armistice Commission also banned 78 anti-German films: 15 French films, 6 English films, and 57 American films (160). A strong ideological bias was clearly at play. American distributors saw their Parisian offices requisitioned (United Artists, MGM) or sequestered (RKO), and by the fall of 1940, they had all left the occupied zone. United Artists, Warner Bros., and MGM continued to operate in the nonoccupied zone, which included North Africa (158). As shipments of new films had stopped, they had to survive on their backlog, distributing films that had entered France before the German occupation and were consequently quickly becoming outdated.[18]

The new authorities' measures, avowedly aimed at rationalizing the film market, also had ideological undertones. The suppression of the double bill on October 26, 1940, and the ban of all pre-1937 films in May 1941—with a final deadline set for August 31, 1941—can be interpreted as an economic decision favoring first-run houses and eliminating older movies from the market, with a view to improve audience satisfaction (Garçon 2006, 159, 169). US distributors, however, saw these measures as attempts by Vichy to "crowd out American films": in effect, the suppression of the double bill put an end to the possibility of releasing B movies, and the prohibited circulation of pre-1937 productions was deeply problematic at a time when no new American films could be shipped to France.[19] When the US entered the war in December 1941, Hollywood films definitively acquired the status of ideological symbols. As a consequence, they were fully banned in France, as of October 15, 1942 (172). By mid-November 1942, the Germans took control of the entire French territory and the US companies ceased their activity in France. The German occupier had managed to eliminate the US competitor from the mainland.

In North Africa, however, the control of the film market was not as tight. German occupation felt quite remote (Corriou 2011, 213), and the different measures came to be applied with distinct delay, if at all. The ban on pre-1937 films was postponed in North Africa from August to December 1, 1941 (212).[20] Decreed in mainland France in October 1940, the end of the double bill reached Tunisia only by December 1941, and the 1942 blanket ban of American films also fell flat in the three countries. The continued presence of Hollywood films was, in fact, strongly supported by local officials. Economic arguments were summoned: given the popularity of Hollywood films and notably B movies, a ban would lead to a strong decrease of the attendance and, consequently, a sharp fall in movie theaters' tax receipts.[21] Local authorities were also clearly moved by ideological motivations: as noted, French-dubbed Hollywood films were too valuable as a colonial propaganda tool, especially in the movie theaters attended by the native population.[22] Not only were the spectators learning French and being exposed to Western ideas, but their presence in the movie theaters also enabled the French propaganda newsreels shown before the film to reach a large audience.[23] Moroccan authorities thus called on the November 1940–created central Committee for the Organization of Cinema (COIC) to "adjust and adapt the decisions in order to take into account the peculiar situation in the Protectorate."[24] These ideological arguments did not go unheeded. The COIC, for example, decreed a six-month exemption for "class B" theaters in Tunisia in order to give spectators time to get used the replacement of Hollywood westerns and exoticas such as *White Eagle* (1932) and *The Jungle Princess* (1936) by French newsreels and documentaries. In the first six months of 1942, more than half of the Tunisian theaters were given this exemption (Corriou 2011, 259–60). As the full ban of US films reached North Africa in 1942—October 15 for Algeria and Tunisia and November 1 for Morocco—an exemption was given for the *film mouvementés*, that is, the action films destined for the first part of the double-bill program in class B movie theaters (Leonardi 2013, 128).[25] By the winter of 1942, the double bill was still in practice in the three North African markets (128). Contrary to mainland France, especially the occupied zone, American films were, in fact, never evicted from the North African screens, although their numbers decreased. On November 7, 1942, three Hollywood films were still shown in the first part of a double bill in Algiers: one action film, *My Son Is a Criminal* (1939), and two westerns, *Whistlin' Dan* (1932) and *The Lone Ranger* (1938) (129). The following day, Operation Torch started, and Allied troops landed in Algeria (Algiers, Oran) and Morocco (Casablanca, Safi, Kénitra). While late 1942 German occupation in the South of France and Tunisia still hampered the operations of Hollywood companies, one can consider that the majors' distribution structure in North Africa was not destroyed by the war and the companies were poised to resume business as soon as military action ended. Meanwhile, the US was also planning to use Hollywood films for its own propaganda purposes.

Hollywood Films in the Service of the US

During World War II, cinema came to be considered a valuable ideological weapon by the US authorities, which established the Office of War Information (OWI) in June 1942 with the mission to develop educational and information programs, that is, propaganda. Hollywood was much involved in the war effort, with artists joining the army, organizing shows to collect war bonds and entertain the troops, and making propaganda films for the OWI (Mingant 2002, 29–33). In her 2013 PhD dissertation, *Les films du débarquement*, Leonardi additionally brought to light an innovative propaganda campaign devised for France and Italy, and first tested in North Africa. Conceived a few months before the November 1942 Torch landing in French North Africa, the operation proposed, for the first time ever, to send US films to liberated regions immediately after the arrival of US soldiers. This would enable enable rapid countering of the French and German propaganda that, the US authorities supposed, had dominated the screens (Leonardi 2013, 110–11). This implied an unprecedented collaboration between a federal agency (the Psychological Warfare Branch, which was the OWI's foreign operations arm), the film industry (the Hollywood majors), and the military (the Allied Forces Headquarters, led by General Eisenhower) (Leonardi 2013, 79, 107). The Hollywood studios willingly collaborated with the Psychological Warfare Branch, providing copies of their films with French subtitles. By collaborating with the state, as they had been doing since the beginning of the conflict, they nurtured their relationship with the partner who had supported them in international negotiations in the 1930s and whose support would be vital in reconquering the international markets after the war. This collaboration would also bring immediate benefits for the concrete operations of film distribution in North Africa. It would enable the distribution companies to reestablish communication with their local offices. In late November 1942, for example, the US office of MGM was allowed to communicate with its Algiers office through the Navy.[26] In early 1943, the communications between the New York and Algiers branches seem to have passed through the OWI.[27] Such contacts were vital for the Hollywood majors to be informed of the local situation and to be able to control offices that had hitherto been managed from France. Collaboration with the US government was also seen as a way to solve the supply issue, since shipments had stopped in 1940.[28] The films selected for the program were to be transported by military means but distributed by the majors' local agencies (Leonardi 2013, 126).

With the Hollywood studios' full cooperation, the OWI's Control Office constituted a list of films selected on ideological criteria. Forbidden content included class differences, gangsters, poverty, Oakies, as well as any content ridiculing the US and the Allies or presenting the US as hubristic (Leonardi 2013, 114–15). The key purpose was to promote a positive image of the US. Some of the selected films (*Foreign Correspondent*, 1940; *Flight Command*, 1940; *Commandos Strike at Dawn*, 1942) did have an openly ideological dimension, justifying and glorifying the US involvement in the war. Most, however, were escapist fare. While a number may have been chosen for want of a better choice, these films were all "typical of the way the U.S. want[ed] the rest of the world to see it" (*Hollywood Reporter*, March 2, 1943; quoted in Leonardi 2013, 122). The OWI shipment thus comprised many comedies (*Andy Hardy Meets Debutante*, 1940) and musicals (*Strike up the Band*, 1940; *You Were Never Lovelier*, 1942), as well as westerns (*Virginia City*, 1940), horror films (*Cat People*, 1942), and animation (*Dumbo*, 1941) (Leonardi 2013, 125).

According to Leonardi, however, the collaboration did not go smoothly, as institutional and commercial players soon worked at cross-purposes. While the OWI was aiming for a swift circulation of the selected films, the distribution companies prioritized the reestablishment of their prewar modes of operations. Before distributing the films shipped by the OWI, the local agencies thus took the time to negotiate the best release dates and distribution agreements, and plan their distribution campaigns, in what the *Hollywood Reporter* called a "business as usual" attitude.[29] Only after Robert Riskin, head of the Cinema Bureau of the OWI Overseas Branch, threatened to put film distribution into the hands of the military did the distributors agree to put aside these commercial considerations. The films arrived in North Africa in January 1943 for first-run distribution, but started to circulate extensively only in the summer of 1943 (Leonardi 2013, 133). In spite of the OWI's call to order, the US companies continued to focus on their own commercial objectives, insisting, for example, in the fall of 1943, for the right to transfer to the US the revenues earned but temporarily blocked in North Africa (135–36).

As the Hollywood distributors reestablished their operations, they could count on an addition to their usual audience: British and American troops.[30] In liberated Tunisia, this presence was one factor in the rebirth of local cultural life. US entertainers such as Bing Crosby or Josephine

Baker presented shows to the troops in Tunis. In the summer of 1943, movie theaters reopened their doors, showing English-language films, with and without French subtitles (Corriou 2011, 222–23). World War II foregrounded the complexities of propaganda, as German-inspired anti-American measures clashed with colonial France priorities, and ideologically motivated US agencies formed an uneasy partnership with commercially minded US distributors. In the end, the local Hollywood distribution offices managed to weather the storm in North Africa, as well as in the Middle East, and as war ended on May 8, 1945, they were ready to return to their prewar business routine. Changed economic and political circumstances were to thwart these plans.

Economic and Political Tensions in the Aftermath of the War

Luxury versus Necessity

While the US emerged from the war as the world's strongest economic power, many countries' economies, especially in Europe and the Middle East/North Africa region, were fragile. Currency reserves became a key issue of economic survival that directly hit the commercial sector. The currency situation in Iraq exemplifies how US film distributors were impacted. After World War II, Iraq was strongly dependent on the British economic health and policy: it was part of the sterling area, benefitted from direct financial support from Great Britain, and was signatory to an Anglo-Iraqi hard currency agreement (US Department of Commerce 1949a).[31] In effect, "the British Commercial Councilor with the British Secretary of the Foreign Exchange Control Committee" was "de facto controller of foreign exchange transactions in Iraq."[32] In Great Britain, the government was facing a strong balance of payments crisis and leading an all-out battle to stem the outflow of US dollars, notably when it came to film revenues (Puttnam 1997, 208). In that context, dollar allocations for the import of US films into Iraq were denied to distributors in 1947–1948 and 1948–1949: no new Hollywood film could enter the country.[33] A first round of negotiations between the US embassy and the Iraqi government led to the opening up of a $200,000 allocation for the import of American films for the 1947–1948 quota year.[34] When the problem erupted again and no allocation was given for the following year, intense negotiations ensued in early 1950 between M. Healy, MPAA manager for the Middle and Far East, and the Iraqi government.[35] Debates over the exact dollar allocation were accompanied by an atmosphere of mounting restrictions, as the Iraqi government negotiated for a plan imposing that each Hollywood major sell to more than one distributor in the country, a demand contrary to the usual practices.[36] By May 1950, the MPAA representative expressed the "hopelessness of our trying to continue business in Iraq": "It is bad enough trying to adjust business to unavoidable economic and financial difficulties, but to be made use of for other less creditable aims is more than we are able to cope with."[37] In his views, the impossibility of importing new films and obtaining revenues would inevitably lead to "our companies being forced out of Iraq."[38] By May 1950, a $200,000 allocation had been earmarked for the import of American films by eight firms authorized by the state, and Hollywood films started entering the country again.[39] In June 1950, about $82,400 dollars were still blocked on local bank accounts.[40]

The dollar allocation issue reveals a clash of priorities between US distributors intent on reopening their export markets and British authorities in charge of devising an economic recovery strategy. As the American Embassy in Baghdad noted in early 1949, "The British Secretary of the Foreign Exchange Committee opined that in view of the limited amount of foreign exchange available to Iraq for essential requirements, it was difficult to see how an adequate dollar allocation could be established for the import of cinema films."[41] In Great Britain, Scottish member of Parliament Robert Boothby had summarized the core issue by stating, "If I am compelled to choose between Bogart and bacon, I am bound to choose bacon at the present time" (quoted in Puttnam 1997, 208).

The same debate over whether Hollywood films were luxury items or basic necessities erupted in postwar Iran. American films could enter the Iranian market without restriction, but were classified as category 3 imports, that is, luxury goods. Hence, the payments had to be authorized by the Foreign Exchange Commission and obtained at the free market exchange rate (*Film Daily Year Book* 1952).[42] In November 1953, films were moved from category 3 to category 2, that is, semi-essential goods.[43] Films were moved the category 1, that is, essential goods, by 1956, a group for which import certificates were lower (*Film Daily Year Book* 1956),[44] and by 1958, "while import and exchange controls [were] still in effect in Iran, they [were] liberally administered and United State film companies [were] encountering no difficulty in the importation of their films or the remittances of foreign exchange" (*Film Daily Year Book* 1958). The currency crisis had passed.

Currency availability issues plagued the whole region, proving a major impediment to the resumption of Hollywood distributors' activities. In effect, it prolonged the closure of these markets by preventing the import of the new films and the remittances of earned revenues. While in Iran, the issue was solved by the late 1950s; in a number of countries, it took on a more political hue. As chapter 4 will show, blocked earnings and dollar allocation came to be used as a major leverage tool well into the 1960s as Egypt and the newly independent countries of North Africa renegotiated their relations to Hollywood distributors. The luxury versus necessity debate was symptomatic of the changed context of the postwar era, as political tensions mounted.

Unwelcome Hollywood Genres

The threat of social unrest was another issue that interfered with the return to "business as usual" for film distributors. The rise of nationalist Arab discourses and the beginning of the Cold War led to high tensions, as colonial authorities experienced widespread fear of revolutionary ideas. While Syria and Lebanon gained independence in 1946, France was determined to keep control of the three North African territories, and local boards tightened political censorship (Corriou 2011, 381). Fear of unrest also led the monarchies in Iran and Iraq to become more stringent toward films (Sadr 2006, 66–67). In Iraq, the pro-British Hashemite monarchy repressed a popular uprising known as the intifada in 1952 (Cloarec and Laurens 2007, 123). In Iran, the Pahlavi dynasty was weakened by Prime Minister Mohammed Mossadegh in 1952, leading to a brief exile of the shah in Italy. The shah was, however, reinstated the following year through a CIA-supported coup (Corm 2007, 91). Consequently, revolution became a taboo topic for movies, as show the banning of French Revolution dramas *Tale of Two Cities* (1935) and *Marie-Antoinette* (1938) in early 1955 Iraq.[45]

One Hollywood genre in particular met the ire of censors: westerns. A study of the reports of the Moroccan censorship committees in Rabat and Oujda from the mid-1940s to the mid-1950s[46] reveal that westerns epitomized the colonial authorities' taboos: the plots were routinely based on armed confrontation between cowboys and natives, and included scenes showing Native Americans attacking white people such as in *The Great Sioux Uprising* (1953), *Pony Express* (1953), and *Cattle Queen of Montana* (1954). Westerns featuring treacherous white characters were detrimental to the prestige of the white man as they went counter to the benevolent and paternalistic image supporting the French and British colonial enterprise. Ford's *Fort Apache* (1948) and Sirk's *Taza Son of Cochise* (1954) were, for example, strongly reproved by the boards. Quotes deemed derogatory for the whites were systematically cut. The subcensorship committee for the Moroccan Oujda region had two sentences taken out of John Wayne's *Hondo* (1953), notably one in which a Native American chief said, "I don't have any more son; the white men have killed them all." The board also cut out the sentence, "The Indians have risen up against the whites because the whites have broken the agreement between the two peoples." As the head of the board emphasized, "The cutting of these sentences was motivated by the reaction of the Muslim audience who had clapped on hearing them, or showed discontent."[47] Beside the 1850s–1880s Indian Wars, another favorite topic of western filmmakers grated on colonial sensitivities: the fight for independence and admission into the United States of the territories of California (*The Man behind the Gun*, 1953) and Texas (*The Man from the Alamo*, 1953). Censorship boards feared such films would both heat the imagination of young native men and give them concrete ideas on how to rebel.[48] Exotic adventure films, often variations of western plots in Asian and African locales, were also met by bans and cuts, such as *Sundown* (1941) in Tunisia (Corriou 2011, 380) and *Jungle Drums of Africa* in Iraq (1953).[49] Another genre not deemed suitable for the region was the postwar avatar of the gangster film: film noir. Out of the 17 films banned in Iraq on January 22, 1955, 5 were westerns/adventure films and 5 were film noirs. The two genres were particularly unacceptable to colonial authorities who had become "unusually sensitive to films portraying violence of any sort—crime, riots, rebellion, civil war."[50] Lang's *Big Heat* (1953) and *Clash by Nigh* (1952), and Wyler's *Detective Story* (1951) were among the films banned in 1955 Iraq.[51] Censorship authorities in Iraq insisted that "there was no intention of discriminating against US films [. . .] but unfortunately, there seemed to be a considerable number of films from the US that were presently objectionable."[52] There was a clear discrepancy between the predominant genres in postwar Hollywood and the objectives of colonial authorities. When Hollywood producers followed the fast rhythm of popular success, French and British personnel were striving to keep the long note of colonial ideology. Due to this phenomenon of desynchronization, Hollywood films were not seen any more as tools to be put in the service of the colonial project, but potential threats to be controlled and muted.

Interestingly, the colonial and local authorities were not alone in their criticism of the ideological content of Hollywood films. During the war, the US embassy in Egypt had warned that "the unrestricted export of American pictures [had] done considerable damage to American prestige," and castigated "producers who, motivated by the profits, [would] export any film regardless of what impression it create[d] abroad."[53] US embassies themselves occasionally protested the circulation of Hollywood films they deemed controversial and detrimental to US prestige. In 1951, the US embassy in Tehran disapproved of the release of prison drama *Deep Valley* (1947), a film in which the "mistreatment of prisoners by police" was all the more foregrounded as "for the most part the Persian translations only covered what was said by the prisoners and not the police."[54] The same year, the US embassy in Tehran called for the withdrawal of two pro-Russian World War II films, *The North Star* (1943) and *Days of Glory* (1944), feeling the showing of these films was "damaging to US prestige and [. . .] counteracting effectiveness of Embassy's information program."[55] In the postwar era, the advent of the Cold War entailed new allies and new objectives in the Middle East, and widened the gap between US political interests and Hollywood's commercial priorities.

Hollywood distributors do not seem to have been overly worried by the tightened censorship of the postwar era, as not all films and companies were equally touched.[56] The targeting of westerns and film noirs as undesirable genres meant that B movies were more likely to be cut and banned than A films. Politically, it is no coincidence that these stricter censorship measures touched the Hollywood genres that were the most popular, especially in the numerous second- and third-run houses. Economically, this meant that independent studios (Republic) and companies producing many B movies in the 1950s (RKO, Universal, Warner Bros.) were more hampered than companies distributing prestige films. As the B movies were already amortized on other markets, and probably yielding much less return than A films shown in first-run theaters, censorship, a fact that the Hollywood distributors had always adapted to, must have seemed a marginal issue as compared to the more vital currency problem.

Hollywood film distributors' relationship with local, colonial, and US authorities around the time of World War II in North Africa and the Middle East brings to light another dimension that observers of film industries need to pay attention to: film policies. In *Reconceptualising Film Policies*, Tirtaine and I noted that the traditional film policy paradigm rested both on rhetorical and practical lines. The rhetoric used to justify state intervention operates in a tension between economic (supporting the national film industry) and ideological arguments (defending national identity). The practical operations of film policies oscillate between protection-oriented measures (subsidies) and control (censorship) (Mingant and Tirtaine 2018, 13–14). In the first half of the twentieth century, film policies in North Africa and the Middle East were clearly ideologically motivated and leaned primarily on control through a strictly applied censorship. However, the situation presents specific characteristics that are worth underlining and that contribute to our understanding of film policies. While policies are usually devised at the national level, the colonial situation presents the case of policies applied to one territory but created in another. As the case of censorship shows, colonial film policies were predicated both on a two-layered system (mainland censorship and local censorship) and a transnational system, as censorship rules were similarly applied to all the countries within a given colonial empire. France colonial censorship rules were also applied to its sub-Saharan territories. British rules in the Middle East were directly inspired by colonial policies in India. World War II additionally presents the rare case of a triple-layered system with Germany controlling France that controlled North Africa. In that case, analyzing film policies required identifying layered ideological priorities that sometimes clashed, as the case of the suppression of the double bill showed.

Two other lines of reflection on the relations between state and film stand out here. Traditional means of controlling cinema were visible in North Africa and the Middle East at the time: the use of censorship by the French and the British to keep a firm hand on the ideas circulating, the selection of certain films for propaganda purposes by the OWI. The use of US cinema by the French colonial authorities points, however, to an original situation, in which a nation repurposes films from another nation in order to advance its own ideological agenda. How native audiences received US films appropriated by France, what kind of interpretative strategies they put in place would be rich fields of exploration. Finally, this chapter contributes to an ongoing reflection on the discrepancy between state policies and the film industry itself. In the World War II North Africa and Middle East, film distributors and US state officials formed an uneasy alliance. Soon the divergence between each partner's interests came to light. Propaganda and commerce could only go hand in hand to a certain point. The rift between the US nation's foreign policy objectives and the US distributors' commercial plans in fact continued to enlarge in the decades after World War II.

While the Hollywood distributors had routinely adjusted to the colonial authorities' demands, World War II led to a strongly heightened politicizing of cinema. Silent Hollywood films had been an entertainment widely enjoyed in North Africa and the Middle East. Sound had made them more distinctly western, but World War II led to their being clearly identified as US. The economic and political tensions that slowly became apparent in the aftermath of the war foreshadowed the revolution that was soon to sweep over the region and make business conditions for distributors of American nationality increasingly difficult.

Part II

Losing Ground in a Changing Market

Political Independence and VCRs (1950s–1990s)

4

Political Upheavals

The Slow Disintegration of the Majors' Distribution Structure (1950s–1970s)

I N DECEMBER 1979, JACK VALENTI, the head of the MPAA-MPEA, the
association representing the interests of the major Hollywood studios,
declared, "We are doing business all over the Middle East where
governments are allowing us to do business on a fair or competitive
basis, or under conditions we think are palatable."[1] Ten years later, the
US majors had closed all their offices in North Africa and the Middle
East. The new political conditions that were to spell the end of the
established Hollywood distribution system in the area became visible as
early as the 1950s. The French colonial empire unraveled as independence
was gained by Syria and Lebanon in 1946, Morocco and Tunisia in 1956,
and Algeria in 1962. In the Middle East, countries that had obtained
independence from British rule before World War II (Iraq in 1932, Egypt
in 1937) experienced coups as the pan-Arabist ideology developed; and
a new state was created in 1948: Israel. Accession to independence and
revolutions marked the beginning of a new era for the region, an era of
political upheavals in which business conditions became definitely less
"palatable" to the Hollywood majors, leading to a slow disintegration of
their distribution organization.

Pan-Arabist Momentum and
Anti-Americanism in the Middle East

In the Middle East, the fate of the Hollywood distributors and their films after World War II must be viewed in the context of US foreign policy choices. The US government's interest for the Middle East developed during World War II as oil supply became a national security issue (Little 2008, 48). After the war, the Middle East became one of the battlegrounds on which the Cold War was fought. In 1955, the US signed an "anti-Soviet mutual defense agreement," the Baghdad Pact, with Turkey, Iraq, Pakistan, Iran, and the United Kingdom (129–130). Two years later, the Eisenhower Doctrine guaranteed that the US would provide economic aid and military protection to any anti-Soviet country in the Middle East (132).[2] With the European colonizers' influence waning, US involvement steadily grew. It did so, however, in the context of the expansion of the pan-Arab nationalist ideology, epitomized in March 1945 by the creation of the Arab League, a group founded by Egypt, Iraq, Transjordan, Lebanon, Saudi Arabia, and Syria, and later joined by Yemen (May 1945), Libya (1953), Morocco and Tunisia (1958), Kuwait (1961), Algeria (1962), and Bahrain, Oman, Qatar, and the United Arab Emirates (1971) (Cloarec and Laurens 2007, 86). Pan-Arabism aimed to unite all Arab countries and modernize the Arab world in an original way that would not imitate the West (63). In the 1950s and 1960s, this often meant adhering to socialist principles and opposing Western involvement in the Arab world as well (Sela 2002, 160–66). From 1952 to 1970, Egypt symbolized the triumph of Arab nationalism under the leadership of Gamal Abdel Nasser, who showed his independence by constantly playing the US and the Soviet Union against each other. Starting in the late 1950s, a wave of nationalist revolutions took place—the 14 July Revolution in 1958 Iraq, and the Baath Party coups in Syria in 1963 and Iraq in 1968—shifting the political balance in the region toward leftist ideologies and away from the US. The US decision to support Israel, recognizing the new state a few minutes after it was born on May 15, 1948, was also instrumental in drawing a wedge between the US and Arab nations. The Hollywood majors found themselves unwillingly caught in these ideological battles that jeopardized the circulation of US films, their established distribution networks, and their very presence in the region.

New Regimes, New Rules

One area in which the influence of nationalist ideologies first became visible for US distributors was the translation strategies for their films. A

central tenet of the Arab nationalism theory developed by thinker Sati'
al-Husri in 1920s Iraq was the unifying dimension of the Arabic language
(Cloarec and Laurens 2007, 62). Hence, as Arab countries were gaining
independence, new rules were decreed about the language in which foreign
films were allowed to circulate. In Egypt, two circulars in April 1939 and
1940 made it compulsory to insert Arabic subtitles on film prints.[3] Postponed due to the war, the presence of Arabic subtitles was finally made
into a law on June 15, 1946 (*Middle East Motion Picture Almanac* 1947,
18). In Iraq, a similar requirement was decreed in late 1939.[4] Syria and
Lebanon, also influenced by the development of pan-Arabist discourses,
made Arabic subtitles compulsory in 1947 (UNESCO 1949, 191).[5] So did
Libya in 1960 (*Film Daily Year Book* 1961). The importance of language
in the new nationalistic context was also visible in the growing popularity
of Egyptian films in the region since the 1930s.

Hollywood majors decided to respond by dubbing their own films
into Arabic (Mingant 2019). Between 1946 and 1951, the Hollywood
majors distributed seven dubbed films, including several British coproductions: *Arabian Nights* (1942), *Caravan* (1946), *Jungle Book* (1942), *Samson
and Delilah* (1949), *Sinbad, the Sailor* (1947), *Snow White and the Seven
Dwarves* (1937), and *The Thief of Bagdad* (1940). The popular success of
these dubbed films generated a political backlash. This was particularly
the case with *The Thief of Bagdad*, which had been dubbed in Egypt's
Misr Studio. On February 29, 1948, Egyptian film pioneer Yusuf Wahbi
led a strike by technicians and artists against the exhibition of the film's
dubbed version. Prophesizing that Arabic-dubbed Hollywood films would
represent too strong a competition, Wahbi warned that dubbing was
"the first nail in the coffin of the Egyptian film industry" (Vitalis 2000,
276).[6] Following the 1948 protest, King Farouk's pro-pan-Arab government opened negotiations with the US distributors to limit the entry
of Arabic-dubbed versions. The Ministry of Social Affairs proposed to
permit the dubbing of three entertainment films a year. Keenly aware of
the commercial potential of Arabic-dubbed versions, the local heads of
majors' distributing agencies made a counterproposal: each of the eight
Hollywood companies should have one authorization a year. They insisted
that American films would not compete with but complement the presence
of Egyptian films, and that they would be dubbed in Egyptian studios
(Mingant 2019). Their arguments went unheeded, however, and soon
the Egyptian market became heavily protected. The number of dubbed
pictures was limited to three per year; the films would be selected by the
Ministry of Social Affairs for a one-year circulation period. Furthermore,
a quota was instituted, which made it compulsory for theaters dedicated

to European films to show Egyptian films at least four weeks per year (*Annuaire du cinéma* 1952, 241; US Department of Commerce 1949b). US distributors had no solution but to accept this "gentleman's agreement."[7] Faced with opposition from the Egyptian government, on economic and ideological grounds, the Hollywood distributors stopped dubbing their films into Arabic. Not only had the quota made the practice unviable, but the fact that Egypt was the distribution center for the rest of the Middle East also meant that Egyptian legislations conditioned the rest of the distribution chain. In effect, Egypt had "established the norm for film translation in the entire Arab world" (Gamal 2009, 8).

Regaining control of their countries, Arab authorities also started to devote acute attention to the content of US films. A first taste of obstacles to distribution that would soon be encountered was given to Paramount as *Samson and Delilah* was subjected to cuts in Egypt in 1951, banned in Syria in 1952, and narrowly escaped prohibition in Lebanon in 1950.[8] Official criteria for banning films were decreed in the early 1960s by the Arab League Israel Boycott Office, which established censorship rules related to film content and listed prohibited productions. Films identified as "anti-Arab and pro-Israel propaganda" were systematically banned in the Arab world.[9] The list of American film prohibited in Arab League countries as of 1963 (table 4.1) shows the extent to which these new censorship rules could hamper the circulation of Hollywood films. Were considered as pro-Israel propaganda films that dealt with the Nazi elimination of Jewish people during World War II (*Judgment at Nuremberg*, 1961), but also historical epics "glorifying the Jewish people" such as *The Prodigal* (1955). Were considered "anti-Arab propaganda" two specific types of films: colonial films (*The Lives of a Bengal Lancer*, 1935; *Beau Geste*, 1939) and *Arabian Nights*–inspired adventure films (*The Thief of Damascus*, 1952).[10] Foreign Legion film *The Three Musketeers* (1933) was banned for "bring[ing] French power and greatness in Algeria into prominence and distort[ing] facts."[11] As for Orientalist fantasies, they were banned for "contain[ing] matters harmful to Arab dignity" (*The Adventures of Hajji Baba*, 1954), "injur[ing] certain aspects of the social life and Arab nationalism" (*Song of Scheherazade*, 1947), or being "injurious to Islam and its Caliphs" (*The Trumpet of Baghdad*).[12] The representation of certain Arab countries was particularly pinpointed: Algeria (*Prisoners of the Casbah*, 1953), Syria (*Sirocco*, 1951), and Libya (*Pirates of Tripoli*, 1955).[13]

The new censorship rules directly touched the US distributors. Orientalist big-budget films and biblical productions in Technicolor and Cinemascope, which were a major genre in 1950s and early 1960s

Table 4.1. US films banned in Arab League countries in 1963

Distribution companies are indicated for each film.

Born to Be Loved (1959, Universal)
The Veils of Bagdad (1953, Universal)
David and Bathsheba (1951, 20th Century Fox)
The Three Musketeers (1933, MGM/Mascot pictures)
The Black Knight (1954, Columbia)
Merry Andrew (1958, MGM)
Wind across the Everglades (1958, Warner Bros.)
The Great Dictator (1940, Chaplin)
Ben Hur (1959, MGM)
Land of the Bible (unidentified, 20th Century Fox)
Solomon and Sheba (1959, United Artists)
Little Egypt, a.k.a. Chicago Masquerade (1951, Universal)
Road to Zanzibar (1941, Paramount)
Princess of the Nile (1954, 20th Century Fox)
West of Zanzibar (1954, Paramount)
Bengazi (1955, RKO)
El Alamein (1953, Columbia)
Abbot and Costello in the Foreign Legion (1950, Universal)
The Golden Horde (1951, Universal)
The Desert Legion (1953, Universal)
Saadia (1953, MGM)
Ali Baba Goes to Town (1937, 20th Century Fox)
The Desert Hawk (1950, Universal)
The Adventures of Hajji Baba (1954, 20th Century Fox)
Song of Scheberazade (1947, Universal)
The Sword of Victory (unidentified, Columbia)
The Juggler (1953, Columbia)
The Prodigal (1955, MGM)
Pirates of Tripoli (1955, Columbia)

Pampa and the Alarming City (unidentified, United Artists)
Mudlark (1950, 20th Century Fox)
Arabian Nights (1942, Universal)
The Lives of a Bengal Lancer (1935, Paramount)
Beau Hunks (1931, Classic Film)
Vigilante (1941, Columbia)
Casbah (1948, Universal)
Beau Geste (1939, Paramount)
The Sultan's Daughter (1943, Monogram)
The Foreign Legion (1928, Universal)
Prisoners of the Casbah (1953, Columbia)
Tripoli (1950, Paramount)
Sirocco (1951, Columbia)
The Thief of Damascus (1952, Columbia)
The Ten Commandments (1956, Paramount)
Samson and Delilah (1949, Paramount)
King Richard and the Crusaders (1954, Warner Bros)
The Story of Ruth (1960, 20th Century Fox)
Never Love a Stranger (1958, Allied Artists)
Operation Eichmann (1961, Allied Artists)
Judgement at Nuremberg (1961, United Artists)
Hand in Hand (1961, Columbia)
Two Weeks in Another Town (1962, Columbia)
The Inspector (1962, 20th Century Fox)
The Crimes of Adolf Hitler (1961, MGM)
The Journey (1959, MGM)
Good Morning, Miss Dove (1955, 20th Century Fox)
Kismet (1955, MGM)
The Trumpet of Baghdad (unidentified, Columbia)

Source: Airgram from AmEmbassy, Baghdad, to DOS, June 6, 1963, NARA, RG 59, INCO MP, 1963, box 3545.

Hollywood, feature prominently in the list of banned films, with exot-icas such as *The Veils of Bagdad* (1953) and *Arabian Nights* (1942), and Bible-related epics such as *Ben Hur* (1959) and *Solomon and Sheba* (1959). Banned films, in fact, covered the whole spectrum of US productions, and quite a number of B movies distributed both by major studios and independent companies were also prohibited, such as Universal's *Desert Hawk* (1950), RKO's *Bengazi* (1955), and Monogram's *Sultan's Daughter* (1943). Although some of the films listed were made in the late 1930s and early 1940s, the list was far from being outdated, but reflected the fact that these films were still circulating in second- and third-run movie theaters.

Not only did the Arab League boycott focus on film content, but it also targeted specific actresses, actors, and directors who had been vocal in their support to the creation of the state of Israel. This gave a polit-ical coloring to Hollywood films that were predominantly entertaining in nature. As early as June 1948, Egyptian censors demanded the ban of films with Danny Kaye and Mickey Rooney due to reports that they collected funds for "Zionists,"[14] and in January 1949, films with certain actors were semi-officially censored in the country (US Department of Commerce 1949b). By 1964, the Israel Boycott Office of the Arab League officially decreed the prohibition in its member countries of

> all Israelite films; all foreign films which support the existence of Israel; all film which feature well-known actors or actresses who have either participated in one form or another in pro-paganda for Israel, or who have played in film [. . .] or who [. . .] have given entertainment parties in the interests of Israel and have not given similar parties to the Arabs.[15]

The document (table 4.2) was to be completed over the years.[16] Although the blacklist also included artists from France (Juliette Greco, Pascale Audret, Philippe Clair, Olivier Hussenot, Francis Lax, Jack Riberolles, Maurice Sarfati), Sweden (Catherine Berg) and Greece (Nikos Koukou-los), most of the names were those of famous US actors and actresses, whose films figured at the top of the US companies' distribution list.[17] *Life with Father* (1947), *Giant* (1956), and *Cat on a Hot Tin Roof* (1958) were thus banned due to the presence of Elizabeth Taylor.[18] The actress was welcome again in Egypt only after the 1978 Camp David Agreement marked the peace between Egypt and Israel. When she visited the 1979 Cairo Film Festival, none of her post-1962 films, including *Cleopatra*, had

Table 4.2. US talent blacklisted by the Arab League's Israel Boycott
Office (1960s–1980s)

Harry Belafonte	Jack Benny
Eddie Cantor, born Edward Israel Iskowitz	Jeff Chandler
Scott Finch	Carl Foreman
George Jessel	Danny Kaye
Jerry Lewis	Viveca Lindfors
Paul Newman	Edgar G. Robinson
Phil Silvers	Frank Sinatra
Elizabeth Taylor	Shelley Winters
Joanne Woodward	

Source: Letter from AmEmbassy, Baghdad, to DOS, November 15, 1960, NARA, RG 59,
1960–1963, Country file, Iraq, box 2830; Airgram from AmEmbassy, Baghdad, to DOS,
June 6, 1963. NARA, RG 59, INCO MP, 1963, box 3454; "Arab Film Rally of '64 reported:
UNESCO volume replete with typos, repeats 'Blacklist' vis-à-vis Israel," *Variety*, June 29,
1966; Airgram from AmEmbassy, Beirut, to DOS, October 16, 1972, NARA, INCO Motion
Pictures, 1970–1973, box 1310; Telegram from AmEmbassy, Manama, Bahrain, to SecState,
August 25, 1976, NARA RG 59, ADD, 1976MANAMA01234; Telegram from AmEmbassy,
Manama, to SecState, March 1, 1977, NARA, RG 59, ADD, 1977MNAMA00498; "Arabs
End Ban of Actors from TV 'Death of Princess,'" *Variety*, May 19, 1982; "Syria Bans Seven
Films with Links to Jews," *New York Times*, October 20, 1983.

been legally shown in the country.[19] The boycott continued in the other
Arab League countries, which also started banning Egyptian films.[20] By
1979, the blacklist included two hundred actors and filmmakers.[21]

It is hard to evaluate the exact impact of these new censorship rules
on the US distributors' everyday operations. Accounts of the blacklist
could be quite dismissive, from a *Variety* journalist judging the boycott
of US actors and actresses for their pro-Israel activities "a masterpiece
of ridiculous reasons,"[22] to MPEA executive Griffith Johnsons noting the
decrease of the boycott issue in late 1970s Egypt: "It hasn't been enough
of a problem for us to pay close attention to."[23] Behind the façade,
however, the distributors cannot but have been worried as these new
rules meant increased hassle. A journalist warily noted about the strict
censorship in the late 1970s that, "if things continue the way they're
going, about the only kind of film that can be shown in Iraqi cinemas
will be Disney's."[24] By targeting Foreign Legion films, Judeo-Christian
epics, and Orientalist exoticas, the new censorship rules demonstrated that
the colonial era was ended. It brought to light the strong discrepancy
between Hollywood's traditional genres and the new political context

in the Arab world. By targeting politically committed A-list talent, the Arab countries showed that US foreign policy discourses on the Middle East would impact film distribution. With the new nationalistic rules, the Arab nations were sending a strong signal to the US distributors: as political considerations took center stage, the business conditions in the Arab world were to change radically.

Fragmentation of the Distribution Structure

Nowhere was this better exemplified than in the Arab League headquarters and the center of pan-Arab ideology: Cairo. Egypt had been the heart the majors' distribution infrastructure, the strategic center supplying the entire Middle East with US films. The arrival of Gamal Abdel Nasser at the head of the country in 1952 was a turning point for the film ecosystem in the region (Thoraval 2000, 145). The new government adopted an interventionist approach toward the film sector in order to encourage a cinema that would be both national and nationalistic. State involvement started with the production and distribution al-Nil Society in 1953 and culminated with the nationalization of the historical Misr Studio in 1960 and its reorganization into the General Film Organization in 1963 (Shafik 2001, 28). Film laboratories and movie theaters were also nationalized (Thoraval 2000, 145). This was accompanied by measures aiming at shielding local cinema from foreign competition: an increased screen quota for national products in 1956 and a new import tax in 1957. This strong state intervention was not wholly welcome in local film industry circles. The nationalization, and the consequent ban of Egyptian films by some Arab countries (145), primarily struck Egyptian, but also Syrian, Lebanese, and Jordanian producers working in Egypt, who soon fled the country and settled in Lebanon, where they found a more economically liberal climate (Shafik 2001, 28). Egyptian distributors also saw their activity strongly curtailed, as they were "no longer at liberty to acquire foreign product and conduct free enterprise foreign sales in the Arab world."[25] The Hollywood distributors also felt the brunt of this new nationalistic approach. As Vitalis notes:

> The real problem for the American firms was the continuing obstacles put in the way of securing the necessary import licenses, which minimally suggested rent seeking on the part of customs agents, although some firms believed the impediments were more deliberate and systematic. (Vitalis 2000, 285)

In the mid-1950s, the majors were also embroiled in remittance negotia-tions; as discussed in chapter 3, after the war, the dollar had become a rare currency and a number of countries, including Egypt, placed limitation on the revenues that were allowed to leave the country to be converted into dollars. The Hollywood majors found themselves constantly nego-tiating the actual amounts authorized (*Film Daily Year Book* 1959, 1962).

Though the US distributors were not directly concerned by all the new measures, the core issue was that, in a few years, strong state intervention had radically transformed the Egyptian business environ-ment. The context had not only become uncertain, as new legislations were constantly unfolding, but also clearly unfavorable to the presence of private Western companies. The majors started looking toward a more welcoming environment as early as 1956.[26] The *Film Daily Year Book* records the creation of a Columbia Pictures of Lebanon office in 1956 and a Paramount Films of Lebanon in 1959, both situated in Beirut. By late 1959, separation of operations between Egypt and Lebanon was increasingly apparent: Twentieth Century Fox had two different offices; Universal had an office in Egypt and a distributor in Lebanon; United Artists relied on two different distributors (*Film Daily Year Book* 1959). As the Egyptian offices became strictly nationally oriented branches, regional responsibilities moved into the hands of the Lebanese office (*Film Daily Year Book* 1965).[27] By 1966, Beirut had become the new hub for the Hollywood majors, directly supervising distribution over Lebanon, Syria, Iraq, Egypt, Jordan, Iran, Turkey, Cyprus, Kuwait, Bahrain, Sudan, Eritrea, Ethiopia, Somalia, Libya, and Saudi Arabia (Sadoul 1966, 171–72).

The anti-Israel atmosphere that developed after 1948, as constant tensions pitched the new state against its Arab neighbors, also partici-pated in the demise of the distribution system that had formerly been centralized in Egypt. In the mid-1950s, the US majors' employees in Egypt bore the brunt of the "intensification of anti-Jewish policy" in the region, especially in the context of the 1956 Suez crisis.[28] MGM's Cairo manager and assistant manager, respectively Tunisian and Spanish of Jewish faith, conveyed to the embassy their fear of being deported.[29] By late 1956, "Jewish representatives of various nationalities ha[d] left town," notably Oscar Lax, Fox's American Middle East supervisor.[30] Anti-Zionism affected the US distributors' staff in Egypt, but also their entire regional structure. Hitherto, Palestine and Transjordan had been serviced through Egypt. In 1948, the Israel Boycott Office of the Arab League, based in Damascus (Weiss 2017, 2), decreed that a company could not function both in Israel and in the Arab countries. Servicing Israel from the Egyptian head office was not legally possible anymore. The majors had no choice but to promptly comply. MGM Picture Co. Israel separated from MGM of Egypt as early as 1949, as did Twentieth Century Fox the following year (*Film Daily Year Book* 1949, 1950). In order to achieve swift and smooth reorganization, the distributors either turned their local branches into full-fledged offices, promoting the local managers, such as Warner Bros.' Richard Laufer, or chose to put Israeli distribution in the hands of a local company, as Universal did with David Mallah (*Film Daily Year Book*, 1946–1947, 1950, 1952). Although compliance seems to have been quick, this issue remained sensitive well into the 1960s. Around 1962, United Artists opened a branded distribution office in Israel (*Film Daily Year Book* 1962). However, the company "sold its Tel Aviv branch in 1964 under pressure of boycott threat" by the Arab countries. As the Tel Aviv office continued to operate under United Artists' name, the company was summoned by the 1970 Arab boycott conference in Baghdad to put an end to the situation and produce documents attesting that it was not operating in Israel, to which UA complied.[31] Egyptian distributor Antoine Zeind clearly remembers UA being boycotted in Egypt for three years at the end of the 1960s (Zeind interview of 2013).

The fragmentation of the Hollywood distribution system was further accentuated by the nationalist demands of the newly independent Syria. While the majors considered Lebanon and Syria as one unit, even after the end of the French Mandate in 1946, Syria was adamant on gaining recognition as a separate market. In 1947, Syria established its own censorship structure and decreed that all companies with offices in Beirut must open offices in Syria before January 1, 1948.[32] By pressuring for the opening of local offices, the authorities aimed at putting Syrian trade into local hands.[33] Feeling they were in a position of strength, maybe all the more so as Syria was plagued with political instability until 1952 (Cloarec and Laurens 2007, 107), many Hollywood distributors violated the law. By 1954, only Columbia and Universal had full-fledged agencies in Syria; Twentieth Century Fox had a representative in Aleppo, and MGM, Warner Bros, and Paramount were still operating from Beirut.[34] The US distributors were clearly annoyed by the demands of the small Syrian territory, considering that the censorship fees were too high "in view of the limitations of the Syrian market,"[35] and that the new arrangement was cumbersome, causing delays and additional expenses.[36]

Under the double assault of nationalist regimes in Egypt and Syria, and the imposed severance of the Israel branch, the Hollywood majors' distribution system was compromised. The forced move to Beirut and fragmentation into multiple local offices implied more expenses and less efficiency. Faced with political events beyond their sphere of control, the US majors adopted a pragmatic attitude, adapting their structure, sometimes promptly, sometimes reluctantly. In the late 1960s, however, Hollywood films became increasingly amalgamated with the US foreign policy and the majors' pragmatism became powerless in the face of growing anti-Americanism.

Collateral Damage of the US Foreign Policy

In June 1967, Israel won a surprise victory over its Arab neighbors in what came to be known as the Six-Day War. In order to protest against US support to Israel, the Arab countries decided to break diplomatic relationships (Cloarec and Laurens 2007, 142). A symbol of the US, Hollywood films fell as collateral damage to the larger foreign policy stakes. Egypt froze the remittances of US majors and placed a ban on the import of American films until November 1967.[37] Syria and Iraq immediately blocked the entry of US films and operation of Hollywood distributors. Iraq boycotted US films and companies from 1967 onwards.[38] Algeria, who had joined the Arab League five years before, also prohibited the entry of US films for two months.[39] The 1967 film boycott intervened at a time when relationships between the Hollywood distributors and the new Arab regimes were already tense. It marked the final step in the deterioration of the US majors' position in the region.

Two years after the start of the US film boycott, the Syrian regime nationalized the film distribution sector, including imports (Shafik 2007, 20). The decision was ideologically motivated, aiming both to take control of this economic sector and to monitor the content of imported films.[40] In 1971, Syria lifted the boycott on US films and declared itself open to negotiations with the Hollywood distributors.[41] Although films by American independent companies started entering the country again in 1972, no negotiations with the majors occurred.[42] Considering that collaboration with state distribution agencies meant less control of the market and smaller remittances, one can hypothesize that the majors were not keen on opening negotiations. The Syrian General Cinema Agency was for example adamant to refuse any block-booking practice on the part of the foreign distributors.[43] The small size of the market and the strongly state-controlled context were not the only deterrents explaining the majors' lack of enthusiasm: the country also faced political unrest. Syria's attack on Israel in 1973, its support of the Palestinian Liberation

Organization (PLO), a group considered as terrorist by Washington,[44] and its close link to the USSR pointed to continued tensions with the US (Little 2008, 287; Kennedy-Day in Leaman 2001, 390). The new economic and political conditions in Syria in the early 1970s acted as strong deterrents for the US distributors. A similar pattern is visible in Iraq. After the start of the 1967 film boycott, Iraqi authorities decided to control imports in order to reduce the ideological influence of US cinema, which had hitherto made up to 60% of imported films. In the absence of American cinema, Iraqi spectators were offered productions from Italy, Yugoslavia, Egypt, and Lebanon (Khamarou [c. 1987], 83–86). In April 1973, film imports were put into the hands of the Iraqi Ministry of Information (Khamarou [c. 1987], 87; Cluny 1978, 397). The Hollywood majors, however, refused to enter into negotiations with the state agency (Khamarou [c. 1987], 88). In effect, 1967 marked the end of direct film distribution on the Syrian and Iraqi markets, as the interventionist, monopolistic, and ideological views of the two states became incompatible with the free market vision of the Hollywood majors.

In the late 1970s, anti-American sentiment was also directed at US films in the non-Arab state of Iran. From the 1930s onwards, the Iranian political context had been extremely favorable to cinema. The Shah's Western-inspired modernization program had weakened traditional entertainment and pastimes—ta'zieh gatherings, coffee houses—thus paving the way for the development of other forms of mass entertainment, especially cinema-going. Interestingly, when the authorities banned the wearing of a veil for women, they counted on the new medium to help enforce the ruling, as "no woman wearing the chador was allowed in any cinema" (Issari 1989, 71). After World War II, the US became a strong proponent of the country's modernization. With Arab nations leaning to the left, Iran's importance as a pro-Western ally grew, and the US offered both open and covert support, with the coup against National Front Prime Minister Mossadegh in 1953, the development of the tightly controlled White Revolution in 1963, and the crackdown against Islamic protesters in 1964 (Little 2008, 217–19). The Iranian market had come belatedly to the Hollywood majors' attention. Although by the end of World War II, US films represented 70% of the market (*Middle East Motion Picture Almanac* 1947, 43), it skyrocketed mostly from the 1950s onward, especially as films started to be dubbed in Persian (Mingant 2019). The US distributors recognized the opportunity and, from the late 1950s onwards, ended their indirect distribution contracts to open their own offices. Columbia established in Tehran in 1956, MGM in 1959,

United Artists in 1961, Twentieth Century Fox in 1964 (*Film Daily Year Book* 1957, 1960, 1962, 1965). By the late 1960s, Iran had become "an important market for American motion picture films."[45] Interest for the market—and its strong potential—is visible in the Hollywood majors' decision to lobby for an increased ticket price. Under the impetus of Charles G. Bludhorn, the chairman of Paramount's parent company Gulf and Western Industries, who emphasized that OPEC countries had quadrupled the price of oil in 1974, the MPAA called for a 40% increase of ticket prices and a reduction of box office taxes. After negotiations failed, Warner Bros., United Artists, Twentieth Century Fox, Paramount, and Universal launched a boycott at the end of March 1975. Only Columbia had not participated in the boycott, wary of endangering its position in the country.[46] In September 1975, Iranian authorities decided that film distribution was to be placed exclusively in the hands of native companies. Although the boycott was still in place, US companies swiftly complied, creating the Film Importers Association, which Paramount did not join.[47] In May 1976, when the Iranian government gave in and increased movie-house admission prices by 35%, the Hollywood distributors were ready to start business again (Naficy 2011b, 423–25).

The symbolic value of US films under the Westernized Shah regime had benefited the Hollywood distributors, but turned out to be their undoing as the Islamic Revolution erupted in 1978. As early as June 1963, Ayatollah Khomeini had denounced the Shah as an American puppet and condemned US-backed initiatives, including "secular education, women's rights, and land reform as affronts to Islamic tradition" (Little 2008, 220). Condemnations of manifestations of Westernization were an essential part of the discourse held as anti-Pahlavi protest developed. Ayatollah Khomeini maintained that "cinema and other manifestations of Westernization (theater, dancing, mixed-sex swimming) 'rape the youth of our country and stifle in them the spirit of virtue and bravery'" (Naficy 2012a, 5)." During the 1978 demonstrations, the "torching of the movie houses," such as the Rex Cinema in Abadan, on August 19, 1978, seen as symbols of the Pahlavi era, became "a new revolutionary tactic" (Naficy 2012a, 1–2, 15). In major cities such as Tabriz, martial law was decreed and cinemas closed down (a,21). During the revolution, half of the country's movie theaters were burnt down or closed, leaving only 270 theaters open in the country (Devictor 2004, 12, 114). The film sector was suspended. In January 1979, at the time when the Shah fled the country, the majors decreed a moratorium on sending film to Iran as an "economic precaution."[48] By November, the MPEA signaled it had "no exact knowledge of what is going on in Iran in relation to the film industry"; although no new films had been shipped for about a year, "they [were] probably sitting around the company offices."[49] One might surmise that the films were in the hands of the Foundation for the Disinherited that had confiscated film reels belonging to foreign companies. Between 1979 and 1980, 27 American films were distributed in the country, including *Modern Times* (1936), *The Great Escape* (1963), and *Three Days of the Condor* (1975), far behind the 69 films from the USSR and 38 from Italy (Devictor 2004, 28, 35). In July 1979, import restrictions were decreed against foreign "karate," "antirevolutionary," and "imperialistic movies," a decision that was aimed first at Japanese films deemed too violent, as well as Turkish and Indian films, "due to their banality," and secondly at American films, as "the political relationship between the two countries deteriorated" (Naficy 2012a, 24–25). The banning of American films, however, was mostly a symbolic gesture, as the US majors had already long fled the markets and stopped providing new films.[50]

In the late 1970s, one more market closed its doors to Hollywood films. In 1969, Colonel Muammar al-Qaddafi overthrew the pro-Western Libyan monarchy established in 1951. Combining elements of nationalism, pan-Arab socialism, and Islamic revival, the new regime was characterized by a strong rejection of the West (Little 2008, 207–9, 213). In 1979, the film sector was nationalized and put in the hands of the General Company for Cinema (Leaman 2001, 411). Although by December 1979, the MPEA had "come close to an agreement with the Libyan Cinema Organization which could result in the distribution of American films in that country,"[51] the breaking up of diplomatic relationship by the US in May 1980 spelled the end of the presence of American films in the country.

From the 1950s to the early 1980s, cinema was one political arena in which Middle Eastern countries fought their battles against the former colonizers, the new state of Israel, and the US power. For the American film distributors, this translated into the proliferation of constraints that rendered business increasingly difficult, less profitable, and sometimes impossible. The disappearance of the Hollywood distributors and their films from a number of markets resulted from a dual movement: on the one hand, the state authorities temporarily excluded American films for ideological reasons; on the other hand, the majors withdrew due to unprofitable or unstable business conditions. By 1980, the size of the Middle Eastern market had radically shrunk. In North Africa, as in the Middle East, calls for independence were the order of the day in the aftermath of World War II, and the same nationalistic demands were jeopardizing the US film distribution structure that had thrived in the French colonial context.

The Decolonization of Film Distribution in North Africa

The three North African countries gained independence a dozen years after the end of the war. As the French and Spanish protectorates were ended in Tunisia and Morocco, a regime of nationalist and socialist inspiration was established in the former and a monarchy in the latter. In Algeria, a bloody war opposed French and Algerian partisans between 1954 and 1962. Once independence was reached, socialist regimes governed the country. Although the three North African countries had different types of leadership, they shared the same determination to turn over the leaf of the colonial era. Cinema became part of the nation-building effort.[52] In Algeria, film "formed a vital part of the liberation struggle": Algerian cinema was, indeed, founded in 1957 by the Group Farid, led by French pro-independence activist René Vautier (Armes 2011, 294). In the 1960s, the role of state-produced films was to glorify the liberation struggle and embed the war in Third World fights, with films such as *Such a Young Peace* (1965) and *The Dawn of the Damned* (1965) (Armes 2001, 446). Cinema was also a priority for the Tunisian government as an instrument of propaganda and education (Martin 2011, 272).[53] In 1957, a semigovernmental organization was founded, the Société anonyme tunisienne de production et d'expansion cinématographique (SATPEC). Operational in 1960, the SATPEC set to oversee the development of national production.[54] The importance of film was also visible through the creation of the Carthage Film Festival in 1966 and the reopening of the Tunisian Cinemathèque in 1973 (Martin 2011, 272). The new nation's preoccupation with cinema also had regional resonances: Tunisia's aim was to create an Arab film industry that would compete with Egyptian films in the region.[55] As for Morocco, it based the development of its national film industry on the Centre cinématographique marocain (CCM), a state agency created before the independence in 1944. Although, in the three North African countries, the first measures were centered on production, authorities soon realized that the development of a true national voice could only be achieved if control was regained over cinema's entire economic structure.

Denouncing Western Influence

In a June 1962 press conference, Moulay Ahmed El Alaoui, the minister of Information and Tourism, exposed "how dependent Morocco was on foreign suppliers, distributors and theatre owners."[56] Out of 2,263 films shown in 1961, 40.3% were American and 12.2% were French. Out of the 173 movie theaters in the southern zone of Morocco, only 82 were owned by nationals. Out of the 41 distribution companies, only 16 were Moroccans. Production, distribution and exhibition were clearly in foreign hands.[57] In Tunisia, Western films similarly dominated cinema programs—American films represented 41.7% of releases and French films 25.6% (Sadoul 1966, 156)—and distribution was predominantly in the hands of American and French companies.[58] Although dissatisfaction simmered in Morocco and Tunisia, the strongest denunciation of Western dominance was probably developed in socialist Algeria. A 1969 press article from the newspaper *El Moudjahid* thus listed the arguments in favor of the national monopolization of film distribution:

> (1) through forced package deals, the profit-motivated dis-
> tributors have exploited Algeria by pawning off old and sec-
> ond-rate films; (2) the "parasitic" distributors have engaged
> in price-gouging, thus draining the national economy; (3) the
> great majority of these films are of low cultural content, hence
> threaten to corrupt the mentality of the masses for whom they
> are destined; (4) to allow the bourgeois middlemen to continue
> to exploit this developing country would be contrary to the
> socialist option; (5) the distributor will not give up without
> a struggle but, with the help of our socialist and third-world
> brothers, "we shall overcome."[59]

Opposition to Western dominance of the film sector was both economic and cultural. Economically, the Western distributors exploited Algeria by selling films at a high price and adopting arm-twisting practices, such as "forced package deals" or block booking. Culturally, the films were considered of low quality and guilty of corrupting the spectators.[60] Interestingly, the final arguments place Algeria within the context of liberation struggles, calling for solidarity with other Third World nations, but also with oppressed minorities around the world, with a direct allusion to the civil rights movement in the US and their anthem "We Shall Overcome." The anti-capitalist stand was also an anti-Western fight. In a 1970 speech at the Mostra Internazionale d'Arte Cinematografica in Venice, Ahmed Rachedi, head of the Algerian state-run agency ONCIC denounced the Western distributors who still considered Algeria as a part of the French market: no dialogue was possible as long as they used "typically colonialist dialectics."[61] The distribution sector thus became the primary focus of political attention and several strategies were devised to decolonize the cinema structure.

Three Roads to Film Independence

In his 1978 book *Ecrans d'abondance, ou cinéma de libération en Afrique?*, Tahar Cheriaa, head of the Tunisian Federation of Cine-Clubs and head of cinema services in the Ministry of Cultural Affairs,[62] summarized the three roads open to the newly independent nations to reform their film distribution sector. A first way was the "Africanization" of the cinema structure (Cheriaa 1978, 88). This was chosen by Moroccan policymakers who decided to put film distribution in Moroccan hands. In early December 1963, a new legislation ordered the separation of production and distribution activities.[63] The Ministry of Information also informed the US agents of the Hollywood majors in Casablanca that they must hand over the distribution of their films to Moroccan companies as of January 1, 1964.[64] Cheriaa was not favorable to this solution, pointing out the risk that pseudo-national companies would be born, which would continue to favor Western distributors (89). Carter, indeed, notes that the moroccanized distribution companies "were thus considered to be more 'middle men' than independents in their own rights" (Carter 2009, 55). American films still amounted to 33.8% of the 485 films imported in 1970 and 1971, and French films to 20%.[65]

A second policy, according to Cheriaa, would be the "reformist way," a "strategy of erosion" (*stratégie du grignotage*) in which the state should strive to progressively invert the balance of power, pushing the dominant players into making concessions, "until the party which was initially the most powerful finds no interest any more in managing directly the little power it still has . . . and ends up by definitively giving in" (Cheriaa 1978, 96–97). This was the way chosen by Tunisia, which kept gnawing at the Western companies' domineering presence throughout the 1960s: a 1960 film legislation instituted an entry tax of 25 millimes (6 cents of the time) per meter for new films and a 10 millimes (2.4 cents) tax for reissues more than two years old (*Film Daily Year Book* 1962); a May 1964 decree instituted the compulsory programming of one Tunisian short each quarter;[66] and in 1969, the state-run SATPEC was granted a monopoly on film import (Bachy 1978, 33). Again, Cheriaa pointed out the danger of this choice, as the government's erosion tactics would inevitably meet "dogged resistance" on the part of Western distributors; should the government give in once, it would lose the war (Cheriaa 1978, 99). In the confrontation with the Hollywood majors, the Tunisian government recurrently gave in, accepting a compromise over the 1960 legislation,[67] annulling the 1964 decree[68] and proving unable to have the SATPEC become sole distributor until 1979 (Shafik 2007, 21).

The third policy, favored by Cheriaa, was the "socialist way," in which cinema was considered as a "national heritage" to be placed wholly in the hands of the state, excluding any private players (Cheriaa 1978, 107, 105). He cited the Algerian nationalization of the exhibition sector in 1964 as an example (Shafik 2007, 21; Megherbi 1985, 45). Although in 1967, distribution was still shared between the Office national pour le commerce et l'industrie cinématographique (ONCIC) and private companies, two years later, the Algerian state decided to grant the ONCIC full monopoly over film distribution, thus signaling the end of private distribution in the country (Cheriaa 1978, 117; Shafik 2007, 21).

In the 1960s, the three North African states were thus trying to regain control of the distribution sector through moroccanization and nationalization; they were also restricting the flow of revenues remitted to the Hollywood majors' headquarters. Starting in 1960, Tunisia voted to levy tax on the entry of foreign films to fund the SATPEC and the building of movie theaters in rural areas.[69] It also blocked the transfer of funds, hoping to persuade the majors to use the frozen money in the country by investing in local production.[70] In the same way, after 1962, a percentage of foreign distributor's earnings had to remain in the country and accrue a special motion picture fund for film production in Morocco.[71] All means necessary were used in order to reach film independence.

Resisting Change

In the second half of the 1960s, the Hollywood distributors felt that their established film distribution structure was under constant attack in North Africa. Their reaction was dogged opposition to any measure that threatened their usual business practices. The confrontation was, in a sense, ideological. It played as a test of strength between national sovereignty and free market principles. During the conflict over the 1960 legislation instituting new taxes, Tunisian information secretary Masmoudi called

Tunisia the "leader of African cinema policies" and warned, "African eyes are on us awaiting the outcome of our disagreement with the MPEAA."[72] But the Hollywood majors were strong opponents that refused to create a precedent and warned "other countries contemplating cinema legislation similar to Tunisia's that the MPEA will withdraw from market entirely rather than submit."[73] The fact that the majors were facing increased difficulties in the Middle Eastern markets at the time must have played a part in the inflexible attitude toward the new legislations.

In order to stand their ground, the Hollywood majors resorted to three strategies. First, they refused point-blank to obey sovereign leg-islations, a fact that quite unsettled US embassy officers.[74] After 1964, the US majors refused to apply the moroccanization, buying time by leading negotiations.[75] In fact, they truly handed over distribution to independent Moroccan companies only in the early 1970s (Carter 2009, 115), after a 1973 Dahir, a royal executive order, moroccanized a large number of sectors (El Aoufi and Hollard 2011, 65). Warner Bros. gave a distribution permit to Abdelkader Benkirane, owner of the Rif cinema in Casablanca, and founder of Maghreb Uni Films. Columbia and MGM turned to another exhibitor: Mr. Bouamrani, owner of the Liberté and Lutetia. Fox made a deal with Mohamed Belghiti and Egyptian dis-tributor Kamal Barakat (Benkiran interview of 2017). In Tunisia, some majors simply refused to hand over distribution to the SATPEC in 1969, forcing the government to turn a blind eye to their continued activities for ten years (Shafik 2007, 21).[76] Confident in their strong position in the North African audience's heart, hubristically believing in their right to defend laissez-faire, the MPEA members chose to disregard the law.

When negotiations became increasingly tense, the US majors resorted to boycotts, which were, at the time, the weapon most commonly used by the MPEA in international negotiations (Mingant 2010, 117–20). If Morocco experienced only a brief one-month boycott in late 1963, Tunisia felt the full brunt of the majors' ire: the market was boycotted between November 1960 and April 1961 over the new tax, between June 1964 to July 1965 over the screen quota for Tunisian shorts, and again in 1969 (Bachy 1978, 40). As for Algeria, it experienced brief boycotts in 1965 and 1967 over remittances,[77] but a long boycott between 1969 and 1974 over the distribution monopolization by the ONCIC. Indeed, although the majors, who were taken by surprise by the 1969 decision,[78] decided not to oppose it,[79] they were very anxious to work out a satisfac-tory arrangement, especially percentage deals. Boycotts were not surefire weapons, however, and the disruption of their activities in Algeria were, indeed, wearing out the US distributors. After five years of boycott, the MPEAA finally had to lower its demands and accept the principle of individual arrangement between each major company and the ONCIC.[80]

The third strategy, on which negotiations and boycotts rested, was the alliance with other Western distributors. The commonality of interests between US and French distributors appeared as a given for the MPEAA. As the association executive Frederick Gronich negotiated the transfer of remittances in Morocco in 1961–1962, he "talked as much for the interest of the French industry as the American," since

> it has become apparent [. . .] in many parts of the worlds the two industries need each other to maintain a sound local situation for the film industry as a whole as neither the United States nor France alone produces a sufficient adequate number of films each year to maintain a healthy local market.[81]

The US and French negotiators kept each other informed,[82] made sure their positions were in unison,[83] and each breakthrough for one group of distributors set a precedent for the other.[84] This solidarity had, in fact, been sealed by 1951, when the MPAA joined the French-based International Federation of Film Producers (FIAPF) (Moine 2013, 96). When the MPEAA decided to boycott a country, it could consequently count on the solidarity of other Western distributors. Pressure on the Tunisian government grew when French and Italian companies joined the MPEAA boycott in December 1960,[85] while the Federation of UK Film Producers also recommended to stop sending films.[86] A similar logic prevailed during the boycotts of Algeria in 1965 and 1967.[87] Ironically, this type of alliance could not but exacerbate the determination of newly independent countries whose very aim was to fight Western domination.

By the late 1970s, the Hollywood majors' efforts to prevent the erosion of their position in the new North African nations had proved pointless. The MPEAA had to give in to the demands of the ONCIC in Algeria, the SATPEC in Tunisia and to moroccanization. The solid distribution structure established during the colonial era was dismantled. The new political context had, in effect, deeply altered the profitability in these markets. As the French population massively moved back to the motherland, the majors lost a significant part of their audience. This was a particular blow, as the colonial elite patronized the best movie theaters and paid higher ticket prices. Profitability had also rested on economies of scale, as prints circulated in staggered releases from the Algerian center to Tunisia and Morocco, and all the theaters of the region were linked "into a single continuous booking pattern."[88] As early as 1960, the MPEA noted that the impossibility to run a unified system meant it has "become uneconomic to continue servicing" the North African market.[89]

The end of the colonial era provides food for though both on the relation between state and cinema, and on the business strategies adopted by US film companies. The changed film policies subsequent to many countries' accession to independence foreground the centrality of the state in creating specific film business environments. For the observer of film policies, the new environment was both traditional and original. By gaining independence and taking control of their own film policies, the countries were reverting to a more traditional film policy situation in which legislations are conceived and implemented within national borders. The new criteria for censorship similarly followed traditional lines: defense of the national language, respect for national authorities and their domestic and foreign policy visions. The originality, on the other hand, lies in the means chosen to do away with the foreign domination of the film sector. A first step was to put the sector in the hands of nationals, as was done in Morocco and Syria. But many newly independent countries went one step further, and, inspired by leftist ideologies, nationalized the film sector, not only production, but also often distribution and exhibition, as in Algeria. The North Africa and Middle East region in the 1960s thus provides an interesting case study in this film policy choice that resonates with other areas in the world at the time such as the USSR and the Soviet bloc. The end of the colonial era was a sea change in North Africa and the Middle East as the newly independent states changed the rules.

This called for new adaptation strategies on the part of US film companies. At first, they did adapt, changing their distribution structure, moving their headquarters from Egypt to Lebanon, and creating separate offices, as in Israel, when required. However, a close study of the companies' decisions over the region from the 1950s to the late 1970s shows a mosaic of strategies, from compliance to resistance, from negotiation to outright violation of national legislations. It also shows that, in most cases, the situation reached a breaking point, leading to the US companies' departure from the markets. This raises a central issue: Why were companies that usually prided themselves upon their adaptability not able to operate in the new contexts? The argument used by the US companies—that the markets were not profitable anymore—holds, but one needs to look further, into cultural reasons. One can surmise that Hollywood companies could not adapt to the new business environments because they were indeed deeply entrenched in Western ideology. They had thrived during the colonial era, making Eurocentric films mostly targeted at the Western and westernized local elites patronizing picture palaces. They had monopolized the film activity as distributors, but also exhibitors. To some extent, they had also adopted the language and viewpoint of the colonizers on native spectators; hence the "natural" solidarity with the French during the North African film negotiations. As part of the "free world," the US film distribution executives were educated into capitalism and Eurocentrism. Adaptation, in this case, would means taking a big leap and learning to operate in a non-Western film environment; and this is what the US companies failed at. Hence the constant double movement of exclusion analyzed in this chapter: newly independent countries first excluded US companies—and sometimes their films—but, when the new government were ready for negotiations, the US distributors often ended up by excluding themselves from these markets. The US companies were not ready to face the postcolonial world.

The end of the colonial era was thus a political and economic but also cultural sea change. One can surmise—and more research would be needed there—that the rarefaction of US films opened up more space for films from other countries, either from the Arab world or the communist bloc. It also, however, led to the decline of the film sector in a number of countries and to the development of informal distribution patterns, as chapters 6 and 7 will show. In the meantime, one now needs to bring the history of the presence of US distributors in North Africa and the Middle East to its close. While political upheavals had already stricken a strong blow in the 1960s and 1970s, the sharp decline of the exhibition sector in the few remaining markets in the 1980s sealed the completed withdrawal of the Hollywood majors from direct distribution in North Africa and the Middle East.

Losing Interest

The Move to Indirect Distribution
(1970s–1990s)

I N THE NORTH AFRICAN AND THE Middle Eastern market of the early
1980s, the US distributors operated in a strictly circumscribed area.
They were subjected to nationalized distribution systems in Algeria,
Tunisia, Syria, Iraq, Iran, and Libya, and although they all had direct
distribution offices in Egypt, the market had become strictly regulated.
Two markets were still fully open: Lebanon and Israel. While the US
distributors were still dealing with reorganization after the political
upheavals of the 1960s and 1970s, the arrival of new media was already
eroding the commercial interest of theatrical distribution. The 1980s
marked the progressive deliquescence of the region as a profitable film
market and the consequent withdrawal of US distributors.

Challenges to the Exhibition Sector

In North Africa and the Middle East as in the rest of the world, two
new media revolutionized film viewing: television and the VCR. Kraidy
and Khalil noted that, "as Arab countries began gaining independence
from colonial powers, setting up broadcasting systems was an important
symbol of independence and a crucial instrument of nation-building"

(Kraidy and Khalil 2009, 13). The first state-owned television station was opened in Iraq in 1956 (Kamalipour and Mowlana 1994, 101). Algeria, Kuwait, and Lebanon followed in the late 1950s (19, 151, 166), Egypt and Syria in 1960 (67, 267), Tunisia in 1965, Libya and Jordan in 1968, and Bahrain, Oman, and Qatar in the 1970s (277, 181, 134, 35, 192, 237). In some countries, the adoption of television was delayed due to political resistance—notably Ben Gourion's vision of the medium as a source of corruption in Israel—and religious objections to the presentation of images of living beings by religious leaders in Saudi Arabia. Television stations did, however, open in Saudi Arabia in 1965 and in Israel in 1968 (248, 115). In 1970s Bahrain and Saudi Arabia, the VCR immediately followed on television's footsteps (37, 249). The new technology spread over the whole region in the 1980s; by 1986, about 75% of households in Oman, for instance, were equipped in VCRs (193). Political and social conditions proved to be fertile ground for the development of home viewing practices, which were soon to prove a challenge to the traditional film exhibition sector.

Safety First: The Adoption of Home Viewing

One reason behind the adoption of home viewing, which is not specific to North Africa and the Middle East, was financial: watching TV cost less than buying a ticket to a show. In the 1990s, Amin emphasized, most "urban Egyptians live[d] at a subsistence level and [could not] afford the cost of entrance tickets, child care, and transportation" to go to the cinema (Amin 1998, 320). However, specific conditions also led to the particular popularity of home viewing in the area. In the Gulf countries, this new practice solved the issue of female spectatorship, which had been a reason behind the ban of movie theaters in Saudi Arabia. It thus comes as no surprise that Saudi Arabia was one of the earliest adopters of VCR technology in the 1970s. Kamalipour and Mowlana also note that "Bahraini women, faced with traditional restrictions on their social activities, especially welcomed television and video technology" (1994, 39). By the early 1990s, "the Gulf area [had] the highest VCR ownership rate in the world, with a penetration rate far exceeding that of the United States and Western Europe" (154). With television and the VCR, women could have access to entertainment programs, while remaining within the confines of the socially acceptable private sphere.

Safety was additionally at the heart of the adoption of home viewing, as cinema-going became a potentially dangerous social activity.

Safety issues appeared in Israel as early as 1968. After bombs planted by terrorists were discovered in and outside movie theaters, filmgoers had to develop new habits, such as not carrying large bags or leaving in the middle of a show, to avoid the hassle of being searched and interrogated by reservists standing guard. Exhibitors also started to have the rooms systematically searched between performances.[1] This threat unambiguously brought to light the danger of public entertainment. This was clear also in Palestinian territories, as theaters in the West Bank and Gaza started closing in the late 1970s due to "the deterioration in the state of security" (Gertz and Khleifi 2011, 190). After the December 1987 uprising, the imposed curfews led to people staying home, further sealing the fate of traditional movie exhibition (Kamalipour and Mowlana 1994, 224).

In Lebanon, security issues also prevented people from seeking outside leisure activities as civil war broke out in 1975. By 1988, the *Hollywood Reporter* noted that movie-going in Beirut was "hazardous if not fatal," as several bombs had exploded in movie theaters, which were also targeted by shelling; as a consequence, "most Lebanese [. . .] opted to the safe environment of their home to watch videos,"[2] all the more so as acquiring VCRs had been rendered easy by the development of "illegal ports along the Lebanese shore" (Kamalipour and Mowlana 1994, 169). Exhibitors did try to adapt. Aware that the streets in West Beirut were deserted by 5:00 p.m., theaters in Hamra Street started proposing matinees.[3] However, by the mid-1980s, distributors estimated that 50% of the population had lost any cinema-going habit.[4]

Similarly, the civil war that raged between 1991 and 2002 in Algeria led people to abandon the theaters. With the rise of religious fundamentalism, at least one instance of a bomb exploding in a cinema was recorded, in 1996.[5] For many in North Africa and the Middle East, home viewing had thus become the only safe way to access films. As people turned their back on traditional cinema-going practice, illegal circulation of films became rampant.

The Spreading of Piracy

US film distributors had from the start been wary of the possible illicit use of VCRs in their home market (Decherney 2012, 155–200). In North Africa and the Middle East, as the cinema-going culture was starting to wane, piracy developed on a dramatic scale. MPAA executive William Nix noted in 1986 that "every video tape sold in those two parts of the world [Far East and Middle East], with the exception of Japan and

Israel, is a bootleg tape" (quoted in Segrave 2003, 167). A new type of distribution outlet started to appear all over the region: the video club. In 1989 Egypt, there were 1,000 registered and an estimated 2,000 unregistered such premises.[6] By the mid-1990s, about 65% of the tapes they rented were Hollywood hits, such as *Scarface* (1983), *Lethal Weapon* (1987), *Bloodsport* (1988), *Pretty Woman* (1990), *The Bodyguard* (1992), and *Forrest Gump* (1994) (Amin 1994, 324). In mid-1980s Lebanese video clubs, all available titles were, in fact, pirate copies.[7] Similar outlets bloomed in North Africa. In late 1980s Algeria, 60% of the VHS proposed by the registered video clubs were pirated products (Labandji 2011, 129). In Tunisia, although importing VCRs was officially illegal until 1992, the number of registered video clubs doubled from 400 in 1987 to 800 in 1992, with an additional 25% being unregistered (Ferjani 2011, 79). Even recent markets at the time, such as Abu Dhabi, saw piracy develop from the mid-1970s onwards.[8]

VCR recording and tape circulation also led to the development of illegal television stations. In 1985 Israel, 160 unregulated cable television operations showed US films, such as *Rambo: First Blood Part 2* (1985), shortly after they opened in movie theaters.[9] In 1989 Lebanon, there were five pirate TV stations, some of them operated by the militia in West Beirut. As fighting raged outside, homebound Lebanese were offered recent Hollywood films such as *Rain Man* (1988).[10]

Three factors encouraged piracy. First, spectators tended to be dissatisfied with state television, whose programs were largely censored in Egypt and deemed unattractive in Israel and Tunisia (Amin 1994, 324; Kamalipour and Mowlana 1994, 116; Ferjani 2011, 79). Secondly, since there was no fully legal videocassette distribution in many markets, piracy turned out to be the only option.[11] Finally, in the 1980s, piracy remained unchecked by government legislations, either because war situations led to the absence of stable governmental authority, such as in Lebanon,[12] or because no copyright legislation existed, such as in Israel or Bahrain (Kamalipour and Mowlana 1994, 39).[13] In Morocco, not only was there no legislation, but "state piracy" also developed as the state let video clubs rent illegal copies as long as a visa number was applied for and a tax paid (Benchenna 2011, 106). In a similar vein, Tunisian video clubs were sometimes in fact operated by civil servants (Benamor 2017).

Pirated film streams found their source in the US and Europe (Kamalipour and Mowlana 1994, 154). Copies of Hollywood films for the Middle East, including Israel, came from London.[14] Copies for North Africa came from France. In Algeria, the trend started with Algerian immigrants and tourists circulating in Europe (Labandji 2011, 129). In Morocco, video club owners simply bought videocassettes in French supermarkets (Benchenna 2011, 106). The Spanish enclaves of Sebta and Melilia also played an important part as a hub for the illegal import of VCRs and television sets (107). In 1984, Lebanese distributor Mario Haddad drew a dire picture of the pervasiveness of piracy. While some of the tapes came from Europe, some were pirated within the country: the prints of US films legally distributed in the country were copied "either from the censorship department, or from the subtitling laboratories and theatre projection room," and sometimes even "enroute to these locations."[15] Prints also crossed regional borders: Egyptians bought VHS in Saudi Arabia, which they visited on pilgrimage, and Dubai became an important piracy hub (Mattelart 2011, 33).[16] Sophisticated pirates even took into account linguistic accessibility in the Middle East: copies pirated within Lebanon were preferred, since they were subtitled,[17] and, in Israeli video-clubs, "if required for a particular film, Hebrew subtitles could be provided."[18]

Impacts on the Exhibition Sector

These factors, which appeared to various degrees in each country, strongly impacted the exhibition sector. The three major markets left for the Hollywood distributors by the late 1970s were hit by a strong decline—and for some a complete collapse—of the number of movie theaters. In Israel, the development of home viewing and the threat of terrorism, combined with a high ticket price[19] led to a slump in attendance: "While 62.9 percent of the population attended a movie theater at least once a month in 1969, only 41.5 percent did so during 1986–1987" (Kamalipour and Mowlana 1994, 118). An additional issue for exhibitors was the existence of high taxes, which made it difficult to gather enough funds to renovate the theaters.[20] The number of movie theaters steadily decreased from 223 in 1974 to 146 in 1984.[21] In the early 1980s, Egypt also had a "drastically insufficient total of 160 cinemas," including only 30 first and second run theaters, in which ticket prices would be higher. Hollywood distributors bemoaned the closing down of a number of theaters and the absence of new theater building. Nationalist legislations also made it more difficult for US distributors to find screen time. In 1982, Cairo had 15 first-run cinemas, but only four actually showed foreign films. Hollywood distributors heavily relied on theaters owned by US companies, such as Metro's theater in Alexandria. Twentieth-Century Fox, United Artists, and Disney actually only released their films at the Fox theaters in Cairo and Alexandria.[22] In Lebanon, although some cinemas stayed open, especially in the East Beirut area resort town of Jounieh (Khatib 2006, 41), most were destroyed, closed down, or used as bomb shelters during the war (Thoraval 2003, 42–43). Some also converted into supermarkets and shopping centers (Dönmez-Colin 2007, 7).[23] The number of theaters in Lebanon decreased by 85%, from 180 in 1975 to 27 in 1990 (Khatib 2006, 41).

The exhibition sector was also hard hit in North Africa. In Tunisia, piracy led to a decrease in the number of movie theaters in the late 1980s (Benamor 2017) with 102 theaters in 1966, 90 in 1985, and 88 in 1990 (Sadoul 1966, 139; Brahimi 2009, 202).[24] In Algeria and Morocco, piracy was only one factor of the exhibition sector decline, alongside the slow material deterioration of theaters. In Morocco, high ticket prices in comparison to the cost of living aggravated audience desertion. Faced with low profitability and high taxes, exhibitors were unable to invest in maintaining the premises. The slow dilapidation of theaters further pushed the audience away (Carter 2009, 115; Benchenna 2016, 218). The number of movie theaters slowly decreased from 251 in the early 1980s to 225 in 1990 (Dwyer 2011, 327; Benchenna 2016, 216). In Algeria, the lack of theater maintenance was also an acute issue. In the mid-1960s, a law had nationalized the approximately 300 movie theaters present in the country (Mingant 2016b, 203). Operated by civil servants with little knowledge of and interest in film exhibition, theaters were mismanaged and neglected (Mingant 2016b, 203; Shafik 2007, 262). Attendance declined from 20 million admissions in 1980 to around 16 million in 1989.[25] By 1992, the official number of theaters was 200, although only 130 were actually active (Kamalipour and Mowlana 1004, 22). In the 1990s, the civil war struck the coup de grace to the neglected exhibition sector.

The dereliction of the exhibition sector was accompanied by a deep change in the nature of the movie-going audience. Not only did women desert movie theaters, but families tended to stay home (Kamalipour and Mowlana 1994, 269).[26] Amin notes that "group VCR watching" involving "friends and extended family members" had become the rule in Egypt by the early 1990s (Amin 1994, 323). Deplorable theatrical conditions were also responsible for the desertion of upper-class audiences at the dawn of the 1990s, as noted by exhibitors in Morocco and Iraq.[27] Over the 1980s, cinema audiences thus became younger and male. In his 1995 study of cinema-going in 14 Casablanca theaters, Jaidi notes that 83.5% of respondents were aged between 15 and 34, and 73% were men (1995, 32–33); he underlines that theaters were "perceived as places of relaxation and moral perversion, unsavory to 'respectable people' " (33). In Egypt, as early as the 1980s, exhibitors noted the appearance of a "new audience," made of "exuberant" young people, "many with film buff roots," as well as "artisan and working class population."[28] The new predominance of young men was noticeable from Algeria to Israel, Bahrain and Qatar (Kamalipour and Mowlana 1994, 118, 39, 240).[29] This changed audience seems to have influenced the type of film that was successful at the box office, with young men attracted to "action, mild eroticism and war and police stories,"[30] to Rambo and Bud Spencer films.[31] In Lebanon, the success of action films can also be linked to the war context, as the *Hollywood Reporter* noted in 1988:

> Stars Arnold Schwarzenegger, Sylvester Stallone, Chuck Norris, Charles Bronson and Clint Eastwood are idolized among Lebanese youth for their macho posturing and heroic acts on the screen. And it is not surprising in a country whose youth grew up during a chilling civil war, dating back to 1975. This is a segment of the audience that is closely familiar with almost every type of weaponry the film heroes arm themselves with. Another genre of movies that has been attracting local audiences is slapstick comedies like the Police Academy series and its cheap imitators.[32]

The 1980s were marked by the contraction of a commercial exhibition market, which came to be characterized by the limited availability of screens, but also by the decrease in audience diversity and consequently taste.

Toward an Indirect Distribution Structure

By the late 1980s, the North Africa/Middle East market had been transformed to the point that the US majors started seriously questioning its profitability. This decline was actually occurring at a point in the history of Hollywood when international concerns were put on the back burner. While the international market, which had been of major importance since the end of World War II, started shrinking, especially due to declining attendance in Europe, the domestic market boomed with the revival of the exhibition sector and the development of ancillary markets, notably cable television and video (Mingant 2010, 22–23). The refocusing on the domestic market also finds its roots in the 1969–1971 crisis in the US film industry, which led major companies to restructure. Finding they could not maintain a vast international distribution structure anymore, the US distributors started to look for streamlining options. While some majors merged their distribution outfit in specific markets, signing ad hoc agreements aiming at achieving economies of scale, Universal and Paramount took the drastic decision to create a common international distribution company in 1970, Cinema International Corporation (CIC) (Mingant 2010, 58–59). Three years later, they were joined by MGM. In 1981, MGM brought in United Artists' distribution structure and the CIC was renamed United International Pictures (UIP). The alternative to such inter-major alliances was to partner with local companies. The combination of the necessity to streamline their international distribution structure and the decline in profitability of the Middle Eastern market led the Hollywood companies to move from a direct to an indirect distribution model in the three countries where they still had branded offices: Israel, Egypt, and Lebanon.

The Withdrawal Two-Step

In Israel, the crisis in the exploitation sector, which led to a general decrease in the number of distributed films, was accompanied by strong inflation issues starting in the late 1970s (Kamalipour and Mowlana 118).[33] Israel was thus the first Middle Eastern market affected by Hollywood's new streamlining policy, with the merging of the Paramount and Universal offices into CIC (Tav-Nof 1974). Soon, however, the US majors decided to turn distribution over to local companies. As early as 1970, MGM signed a deal with Itzfilm (*Film Daily Year Book* 1970). Seven years later, Fox, which had for some years been distributed through a joint venture with Warner Bros., signed with Albert D. Matalon.[34] By early 1980, only CIC and United Artists still owned direct distribution offices in the country.[35] However, given the context, later that year, UA signed a deal with Matalon, which was distributing not only Fox but also Columbia and independent US companies.[36] UIP was the last American company to hand its distribution over to a local partner, signing a deal with Cannon International in 1983.[37] By the mid-1980s, the distribution of US films was in the hands of three Israeli companies: Cannon (UIP), Gil'ad (Warner Bros., independent companies), and Matalon (Fox, Columbia, UA, independent companies).[38] Little room was left for smaller companies, such as Seven Stars, distributor of Orion and PSO.[39] The US majors could all the more trust these companies as their managers and leading personnel had previously been working in their own offices. S. Itzhaki (Itzfilm) had been manager of the MGM Israeli office in 1967 (*Film Daily Year Book* 1967), and Gil'ad manager for the Warner Bros office in 1970 (*International Motion Picture Almanac* 1970); the Columbia office had been headed by Albert D. Matalon in 1963 and Charlotte Matalon in 1970 (*Film Daily Year Book* 1963, 1970). Other leading distribution personnel in Israel had also begun their careers in the offices of Hollywood distributors: David Mallah had worked as a manager for Universal in 1963 before creating his own company (*Film Daily Year Book* 1963, 1970); Rachel Surkis had been the head manager of the United Artist office in 1980[40] and of UIP in 1983[41] before moving on to Cannon.[42] This relation of trust may explain why the US majors accepted the plea from the Organization of Israeli Film Distributors for a reduction of royalties when devaluation threatened their operations in 1983.[43] In a few years, the streamlining trend initiated by the majors led to a consolidation of the film sector, with Israeli distributors moving into exhibition to guarantee screen time to their products.[44] In 1989, Cannon, renamed Globus Group, snatched the distribution of Warner Bros. from Gil'ad. The smaller company could not compete with the strong exhibition presence of the Globus Group.[45] Alliances shifted among a small number of companies, in a locked market characterized by an ongoing "distribution war."[46] By the early 1990s, the most important distributors of US films were: Globus Group (UIP, Cannon, Warner Bros., Touchstone/Disney, Pathé), Matalon (Fox, Columbia, Tri-Star, Orion), Seven Stars (Vestron, Lorimar, Miramax), and Forum Film (Samuel Goldwyn Co., Castle Rock).[47] Far from being detrimental to the majors, putting the distribution of their films in the hands of strong and trusted local companies acted as a guarantee that their best interests would be preserved (Mingant 2010, 61).

In the 1980s, the nearby Egyptian market was also losing its attraction for US film distributors. Not only was the exhibition market declining, but the nationalist legislations and the bureaucracy represented constant hassles for distributors. Censorship was a particularly sensitive issue under Mubarak's regime. In 1982–1983, MGM saw five of its films banned: *Victor/Victoria* (1982), *An Officer and a Gentleman* (1982), *Cat People* (1982), *The Thing* (1982), *The Best Little Whorehouse in Texas* (1982).[48] Columbia's troubles in Egypt were of a more worrying nature. The broadcasting of a Columbia-produced mini-series entitled *Sadat* (1983) on US television triggered the ire of the Egyptian government.[49] From 1984 to 1987, the company was officially blacklisted and all of its films prohibited.[50]

Additionally faced with mounting subtitling and advertising costs, US distributors were also becoming more selective, circulating only films that were sure to bring profits and rejecting weaker productions.[51] In 1982, a Hollywood executive soberly admitted, "Egypt is a losing proposition. We are here only to keep the flag flying and to feed the family."[52] By the mid-1980s, Egypt was bringing "scarcely $1,000,000 a year."[53] The decreasing profitability and the increased operational difficulties made the decision to streamline quite logical for the US distributors, which started merging their offices in the late 1970s. Fox took over distribution for UA in 1976, Columbia in 1980, and Warner Bros. in 1983.[54] By 1984, two Hollywood distributors were servicing the others: MGM of Egypt (Universal, Paramount, UA, CIC) and Fox (Columbia, Warner, Disney).[55] In the late 1980s, however, the majors moved to the next stage in the two-step withdrawal process and signed subdistribution agreements with local companies. In 1988, Fox handed over its films to the Egyptian company United Motion Pictures (UMP).[56] As in Israel, this meant passing on the responsibility to trusted hands: Antoine Zeind, the head of UMP, had been working for Hollywood majors since 1960. Starting as an assistant accountant at United Artists, he had moved on to become head of the Fox Cairo office in 1980 (Zeind interview of 2013). In 1992, UMP also signed a deal with Warner Bros (Zeind interview of 2013). In 1987, Columbia moved its distribution to another trusted name in Egypt: Anis Ebeid and Sons.[57] By 1990, only MGM retained an office in Egypt (*International Motion Picture Almanac* 1990).

The same two-step process took place in Lebanon. In line with the international MGM-Fox alliance, the Beirut offices were merged in 1972 (Mingant 2010, 169). The situation was more disturbing than in Israel and Egypt, however, as war broke out in the country only ten years after the US distributors had moved their central headquarters there. The first reaction was to consider moving back to Egypt,[58] but as the war intensified and profits waned, the majors opted for subdistribution contracts (Haddad interview). By 1984, it seems that only a merged Warner Bros./Fox office, under the management of Joseph Chacra, was still open. Hikmat Antypas's Four Star Films distributed UIP (Universal, Paramount, MGM/UA); Empire Circuit represented Columbia and Disney; Joseph Vincenti's Italia Films managed Orion and PSO.[59] Although initially a default option, the move towards indirect distribution turned out to be a profitable choice. As Mario Haddad, Sr., notes, "Instead of disappearing, [the majors] handed over [distribution] to Lebanese, with long-term contracts. They realized that the deal was not bad; that they earned more money than if they actually were there" (Haddad interview, 2014). Distribution was left in the hands of men who had solid film experience. Mario Haddad, Sr., was born into cinema: his father had opened the first movie theater in 1919 Beirut, as well as the distribution company Cattan and Haddad. Mario Haddad, Sr., himself created Les Fils de Georges Haddad and Co. in 1956, and his Empire Circuit distributed UA films from 1958 to 1974. The company became entrenched as a distributor of American films, especially after the deals with Columbia in 1964, Columbia Tri Star Home Entertainment in 1986, and Twentieth Century Fox in 1988.[60] In 1984, the *Los Angeles Times* attributed the strong efficiency of "middlemen" such as Antypas, Haddad, and Vincenti to their epitomizing "the quintessential Lebanese, who, with one foot in each culture, has long served as the perfect bridge between Western business interests and Arab consumers. Polyglots all, they slip effortlessly from Lebanese Arabic into French, English, and sometimes Italian."[61] During the war, these highly competent managers also proved their strong determination and inventiveness in maintaining film distribution. Due to frequent shelling in Ashrafieh, East Beirut, Joseph Vincenti had established his offices in a bomb shelter. In a context where "electricity [was] rationed, mail arrive[d] two or three months late (if at all) and each new outbreak of violence [put] more phone lines out of order,"[62] he relied on a portable generator to be in constant telex communications and had his mails and films "sent to the neighboring island of Cyprus," where they were "collected by an agent who [forwarded] them to Lebanon by boat."[63] Films were subtitled in French and Arabic in Beirut. While one copy remained in Lebanon, the others were "returned to Cyprus and dispatched from the country's minuscule international airport to clients throughout the Arab world."[64] In 1984, Vincenti proudly declared, "I've never stopped importing films into Lebanon, and I've never failed to supply my clients in the Gulf, Jordan, Iraq, Libya and Syria."[65] In an attitude reminiscent of the above-mentioned executive who kept the flag flying in Egypt, the Lebanese distributors were not making any profit, but keeping the market open, betting on the future.[66] Hamra Street exhibitor Khalid Itani seemed to summarize the dominant spirit in 1984: "We can't close now just because business is bad. [. . .] No, we must be patient and wait. *Inshallah* ["God willing"], things will be better."[67]

A Last Local Effort: The MPEA Fight against Piracy

As the move to deal with competent local companies shows, the US distributors were not completely abandoning the market. In the late 1980s, the MPEA was in fact active in the area, as it launched into a battle against piracy from its offices in Tel Aviv and Cairo. Since its creation, the majors' association had mostly fought trade restrictions, but the development of new technologies in the 1970s and 1980s led it to shift its attention to piracy issues, and that became its number one priority in the mid-1990s (Mingant 2010, 105). The MPEA partnered with the US federal government as it gave increased attention to its copyright-based industries (Bullich 2011, 58). By signing the Berne convention in 1989, the US signaled that it intended to become a major player in the field of international copyright regulations (59). The first focus of the MPEA's attention in the late 1980s was Europe, "a major area of pirate activity," and the point of origin of the pirate programs circulated in North Africa and the Middle East (Segrave 2003, 147): Britain, notably, had "the justified reputation of being the major world exporter of pirated cassettes" (152). Pirate routes were, indeed, numerous between European countries and their former colonies (148). For the US distributors, the fight against piracy was also a matter of principle and had to be led in all markets, regardless of their level of profitability. In the early 1990s, Warner director of European sales Gary Hodes said about Eastern Europe, "We're not abandoning [any territory] because if we did, we would never recover it from the pirates" (quoted in Segrave 2003, 161). The same spirit prevailed regarding the market in North Africa and the Middle East.

As in other regions of the world, the MPEA had a two-pronged approach. First, it established working relations with local companies, which shared the same economic concerns. In Israel, exhibitors, who often had both film and video distribution arms, contributed 2.5% of their income from ticket sales to antipiracy operations led by the MPEA.[68] When the association held an awareness-raising conference, entitled the Pan-Arab Antipiracy Forum, during the 1988 Cairo Film Festival, it invited US companies' regional managers, independent distributors, and film and television executives from Egypt, Lebanon, Jordan, Saudi Arabia, Morocco, Iraq, and Kuwait.[69] This business-to-business approach was complemented by state-to-state relations.

With the US government now putting its full weight in the fight against copyright infringement, the MPEA gained a new weapon in the late 1980s: trade sanctions. The 1983–1984 trade laws made it possible for American companies to lodge an unfair trade complaint at the office of the United States Trade Representative (USTR) against countries in which copyright was not respected. This was reinforced by section 301 of the 1988 Omnibus Trade and Competitiveness Act, which established a Watchlist and a Priority Watchlist of copyright-infringing countries (Mingant 2010, 111). Since 1988, the MPEA has participated to the elaboration of these lists. At the 1988 Pan-Arab Antipiracy Forum, the association was thus able to wield that weapon, threatening that the US was "prepared to impose economic sanctions on all Arab countries unable or unwilling to stamp out film/cassette piracy."[70] Two Middle Eastern countries appeared on the lists at the end of the 1980s: Egypt and Saudi Arabia.[71] Pressured internationally by the US government[72] and lobbied locally by MPEA's antipiracy director for the Middle East, Walid Nasser, and Cairo lawyer Samir Hamza, whose firm Baker and McKenzie represented the MPEA's interest, the Egyptian government pushed for the adoption of a bill that would close copyright loopholes. The law, which updated the previous 1954 copyright, was voted in 1992, after a six-year examination and amendment process.[73] The MPEA was, however, not satisfied with the watered-down version passed, and in 1992 and 1993, Egypt remained on the Special 301 Priority Watchlist.[74]

By signing subdistribution agreements with former employees and trusted local companies, the US majors were able to streamline their international distribution structure while maintaining efficient local distribution. The withdrawal from direct distribution was, however, an indication that the market had become further removed from the Hollywood preoccupations and worldview. The US distributors' involvement was then limited to action through their common association, the MPEA, as part of the worldwide effort against piracy. In markets where subdistribution contracts were signed, the US companies maintained a degree of visibility. In some markets, however, US distributors had completely lost control over the circulation of their films: as distribution choices came to be made by politically motivated civil servants, US films lived a life of their own.

US Films sans US Distributors

In a number of markets in the 1970s and 1980s, the circulation of American films was the responsibility of nationalized distribution arms such as the Tunisian SATPEC, the National Company of Kuwaiti Cinema, and the Qatar Cinema and Film Distribution Company (Kamalipour and Mowlana 1994, 155, 240). State control did not necessarily bring in the expected results on the circulation of American films or for local film industries, as the cases of Iran and Algeria show.

Although the 1979 revolution had spelled the end of US distributors' presence in Iran, their films continued to trickle into the country. In

1983, the government gave distribution monopoly to the Farabi Cinema Foundation (Thoraval 2000, 66). In spite of anti-American rhetoric, some US films were admitted on Iranian screens as domestic production was not large enough yet. Naficy notes the strong political filtering that was operated: "Officials permitted a film regardless of its origin as long as it could be made to fit Islamic values" (2012a, 167). In 1983–1984, Iran admitted war films and comedies by US independents (*War Hunt*, 1962; *Law and Disorder*, 1974; *A Bridge Too Far*, 1977), films showing the dark side of the US (*The Chase*, 1966), and escapist films (*Star Wars*, 1977). Interestingly, it also admitted films that would prove problematic for the Arab countries: Bible epic *Ten Commandments* (1956), Spielberg's New Age science-fiction movie *Close Encounters of the Third Kind* (1977), and Palestinian terrorism story *Black Sunday* (1977). Quantity was also guaranteed by allowing the reentry of western movies, although only after manipulating the dubbing and editing to "give them an anti-American edge" (Naficy 2012a, 167). American programs were also sometimes broadcast on Iranian television, such as prison drama *Brubaker* (1980).[75] Besides being subjected to many cuts, films such as *High Noon* (1952) and *3:10 to Yuma* (1957) were "released through official channels without permission."[76] In a context of strict state censorship and lenient copyright considerations, a strong pirate market developed in Iran. In the mid-1980s, VCR owners could rent films such as *E.T.* (1982), *Never Say Never Again* (1983), *Octopussy* (1983), *48 HRS.* (1982), and *The Day After* (1983) from video clubs. The original tapes were obtained from England, copied, and then "moved into Iran by an Indian ring."[77] Authorities turned a blind eye to illegal distribution circuits and pirate tapes viewers.[78] Paradoxically, such rampant piracy could be viewed with less than disapproval in the US. On the one hand, it meant that the Iranian public was not losing the habit of viewing American films, a familiarity that might prove profitable in case of political changes. On the other, such underground penetration was clearly considered as a strong propaganda asset by the US government (Lobato 2012, 47).

Algeria is another example of public policy ending in unexpected results. About ten years after the Hollywood majors agreed to hand over distribution to the national agency ONCIC, Megherbi painted a striking picture of the film situation on Algerian screens. He contends that, in spite of the nationalization of distribution, there was no great visible change in the type and nationality of films present in the country (Megherbi 1985, 44, 51). The number of American programs circulating in Algeria did fall from 48.19% of screened films in the second quarter of 1968 to

13.9% of the total number of films imported by ONCIC in 1972 (33, 46). They were dethroned by French films and Italian westerns. But what Megherbi really laments is the continued domination of Western cinema, which constituted 87.27% of screened films in the second quarter of 1968, and 70.8% of imported films in 1972 (33, 46). He is particularly critical of ONCIC's negotiations with the MPEA, deriding the fact that the Algerian agencies were sold "worn-out and overexploited" film prints in 1969 (35), and denouncing the deal finally signed in 1974 as being "all about the big bucks" (44). The fact that ONCIC was more preoccupied by keeping Algerian screens filled than by ideological consideration was particularly visible in the lax censorship applied to US imports (96–98). Closed down in 1984,[79] ONCIC was replaced in 1987 by the Centre algérien pour l'art et l'industrie cinématographique (CAAIC) (Armes 2006, 45). The agency continued to rely on American films, importing French-dubbed prints from Paris for which it paid an average of $6,400 per film for five years.[80] The CAAIC practices were far removed from the nationalist consideration that had led to nationalize distribution in 1969 to the point that about 90% of the films shown in movie theaters were in fact US (Ali-Yahia interview). By the late 1990s, Shafik noted that the nationalized agencies had not really altered the US dominance (1998, 21). The lack of foreign exchange preventing importation in the 1980s (262), the consequent drastic reduction in the number of films imported, from 262 in 1987 to 4 in 1992 (Kamalipour and Mowlana 1994, 21), and the dereliction of nationalized exhibition in fact led to the destructuring of a film sector in which, by the 1990s, even exhibitors relied on pirated film copies (Mingant 2016b, 205).

Despite the sidelining of Hollywood distributors, US films thus continued to circulate in the strictly controlled markets of the area, from the *Rambo* franchise that was popular at the Iraqi Atlas movie theater in the 1990s,[81] to the SATPEC-distributed *Fort Apache, the Bronx* (1981) in by-then Western-friendly Tunisia.[82] For the Hollywood majors, however, commercial distribution in these markets had become anecdotal. In 1981, three years after the majors finally accepted a deal with the SATPEC, the agency monopoly was abolished and private companies took over the sector (Armes 2006, 52). The majors, however, did not reopen their offices and by 1990, the local distributors were struggling to keep the sector alive.[83] Tunisia had in effect been written off by the Hollywood majors. The map of the distribution of Hollywood films in North Africa and the Middle East in the 1980s (figure 5.1) thus offers a strong contrast to the map of the vast network of direct distribution offices established during

Map : Overview of the distribution of US Films in the MENA market in the 1980s

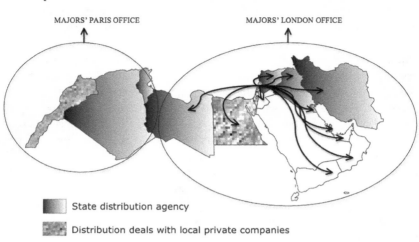

MAJORS' PARIS OFFICE   MAJORS' LONDON OFFICE

State distribution agency

Distribution deals with local private companies

Distribution zone of Beirut sub-distributors

Figure 5.1. US major companies' distribution network in North Africa and the Middle East in the 1980s

the colonial era (figure 1.1). By the 1980s, eight markets were closed to direct distribution by state decisions; and the dire economic or security conditions had led the majors to withdraw from the remaining markets.

The study of film distribution and consumption in the 1970s–1990s North Africa and the Middle East tells us about the history of Hollywood and the history of entertainment technologies, and opens reflections on the concept of film culture. The distribution strategies adopted by the US distributors in Egypt, Lebanon, and Israel at the time need to be interpreted in the larger context of Hollywood's relation to its international market. US companies' choice to hand over distribution to local companies is part of more general process: US distributors had been withdrawing from direct distribution in many markets all over the world, radically streamlining their distribution networks. The international market, as a whole, began to take a secondary importance in Hollywood, as companies focused on their dynamic domestic market, producing films that would please their domestic audiences. As the MPEA's fight against piracy shows, the international market was not fully abandoned. It only remained on the back burner until the end of the 1990s.

This case study also provides original insight into the adoption of a new entertainment technology, the VCR, by bringing to light situations with a marked difference from the US and European markets. New technologies are adopted because they respond to audiences' needs and enable them new access to content. The Middle East/North Africa region offers the picture of very specific needs: the social need of segregated viewing in the Gulf; the security need in case of war or conflict, as in Lebanon and Israel. The chapter thus proposes to join current reflection on the adoption of a variety of technologies, including the Internet, by factoring in social and security issues. The case of this region also joins efforts such as Lobato's to theorize piracy as creator of transnational film circulation. While the link to the international film world had hitherto been largely mediated by Western companies, the withdrawal of these companies did not condemn the region to cinematic insulation. The existence of legal distribution but also the development of piracy maintained the area firmly within the international film world, though often through alternative and less visible transnational patterns.

The extent to which the VCR was adopted in North Africa and the Middle East, finally, provides useful insights for observers of film cultures. As the cinema-going habit came largely to be replaced by the home viewing habit, a new culture of consumption was born. Cinema-going culture and film culture came to be divorced. This changed the nature of audiences that were still going to the cinema, mostly young males; in some countries, such as Iraq, the cinema-going culture came to be associated with a film culture focused on action films and disreputable viewing atmospheres. On the other hand, home viewing meant a diverse film culture. The new gatekeepers of this film culture were not the official distributors anymore by the agents of the pirate circuits and the video club owners. Although US companies withdrew from the markets, their films remained very strongly present, but the official distribution routes, managed by local distribution companies, now ran in parallel to numerous informal circulation paths. Today Hollywood films are still largely present in a region that offers a mosaic of film cultures.

Part III

US Films Galore in the Digital Era (2000s–2010s)

In the late 1990s, North Africa and the Middle East were hit by a "global cinematic phenomenon" that carried away most spectators around the world: James Cameron's 1997 *Titanic* (Klinger 2010, 109). As Egyptians flocked to movie theaters, film critic Khaled Farahat noted, "There is something that takes them away from what they see on the street [. . .] back to the romance of the old Arabic movies."[1] A graduate student at the American University in Cairo confided to *The New York Times*, "It's not an American movie [. . .]. It is a human movie." In Israel, Emil Knebel, head of Tel Aviv University's film department, noted the "special magic from America which appeals to Israeli youth and adult alike," and Mr. Barak, distributor for Twenty-Century Fox in the country, added, "Israeli's movie tastes are exactly the same as an American or European. We have become part of the small village called the universe."[2] Putting aside foreign policy considerations, viewers in North Africa and the Middle East responded enthusiastically to the production value and star quality of Hollywood entertainment;[3] in fact, "*Titanic*'s extensive success in international markets allowed it to attain the status of a common experience among communities within different world populations" (Klinger 2010, 112). In her 2010 article on the popularity of *Titanic* in Afghanistan, Klinger provided substantial warning about the laudatory accounts of

127

the film's global success in the English-language press, in which Western media tend to be unquestioningly presented as forces of modernity and liberation (120–22). Indeed, there is more to *Titanic* than a unilateral story of Hollywood know-how and international desire. In the context of our study, the *Titanic* success opens up specific avenues of reflection. It does foreground the commonality between the existing film culture in North Africa and the Middle East, and the rest of the world, with Hollywood films serving as a common denominator. Spectators in North Africa and the Middle East envision themselves as citizens of the film world, sharing a global culture. This communion, however, does not preclude diverse reappropriations in specific local contexts. Far from being evidence of cultural standardization, the worldwide reception to *Titanic* invites one to consider the multiple ways in which spectators interact with Hollywood films, in a tension—and complementarity—between local, regional, and transnational contexts. While all communed in the global *Titanic* enthusiasm, some experienced the pathetic love story in modern theaters and others turned to pirated DVDs. Internationally, *Titanic* became a milestone in world film history both as "the first film in history to gross more than $1 billion in legitimate worldwide distribution and as a remarkably hot property in the piracy market" (Klinger 2010, 109). In the region, veteran distributors in Israel, Egypt, Lebanon, and Morocco remember *Titanic* as their biggest success (Awad interview; Benkiran interview of 2013; Haddad interview; Zeind interview of 2013).[4] To this day, the historical distribution company Empire features the poster of *Titanic* on some of its advertisements.[5] *Titanic* has also been one of the most asked for films at Najeh Slouma's video club, an informal DVD distribution outlet in Tunisia (Caillé and Slouma 2016, 251). Additionally, the *Titanic* success brought to light the potential of new markets worldwide, and notably in the Gulf. Before *Titanic*, Empire sold its films outright to the entire Gulf area, that is, for a flat fee. After *Titanic*, Empire decided to open a full-fledged office in the Gulf and became the first distributor in Dubai (Haddad interview). Twenty years later, the Gulf has become the most profitable market in the region.

More than a hundred years after the first US film entered the region, Hollywood cinema is still very much part of the cultural landscape in North Africa and the Middle East. It is, however, experienced in myriad ways. In many markets, audiences enjoy a fully operating exhibition sector, as in Israel, Egypt, and Lebanon. In some, movie theaters exist, albeit with difficulties, as in Tunisia and Morocco. In other countries, piracy is virtually the only means of access to films either because movie theaters are banned, as in Saudi Arabia, or derelict, as in Algeria. In Egypt and Iran, films allowed in movie theaters are faced with strong ideological constraints that directly impact US productions. In cases where political regimes limit the presence of American films, or films in general, Hollywood programs become what Klinger calls "contraband" products and represent "both an act of civil disobedience and contact with a different world." (2010, 116, 118). In others, informal circulation and consumption have more to do with economic consideration, fall into Lobato's definition of "piracy as access" (2012, 82), and have become an unquestioned routine activity. Moreover, in the early twenty-first century, movie theaters and pirated tapes are not the only means of access to films and TV series, as new platforms have developed, from the Internet to satellite television channels. The chapters in part 3 will offer the reader a dual aim and tonality. Following encyclopedic efforts such as Sadoul's 1962 *Histoire du cinéma* and 1966 *Les cinémas des pays arabes*, part 3 will first draw a series of portraits of the different film markets in the late 2010s North Africa and Middle East, detailing the number and types of movie theaters, the other legal and illegal means of watching films, and the local audiences' film genre preferences. In the course of each chapter, these data, compiled for the use of current and future observers of the North African and Middle East film sectors will serve as a basis for a reflection on the variety of modes of access to and consumption of films, and open up a discussion on film cultures.

6

The Porous Nature of
Closed Markets

NOWHERE IS THE DISCREPANCY between the official story of the distribution of US cinema and its actual reality more striking than in markets where these films are not commercially distributed. At the dawn of the twenty-first century, five countries remained officially closed to the theatrical distribution of Hollywood films due to geopolitical and ideological reasons. The legacy of the anti-US policies of the late 1960s and 1970s played differently, however, in Syria, Libya, Iraq, and Iran, while in the Gulf, Saudi Arabia devised a way to combine the century-old rejection of the theater experience with the popular desire for entertainment.

Cinema-Going in War and Strife

Syria and Libya: Dereliction and War

The diplomatic tensions of the late 1960s and 1970s, which had spelled the end of the commercial distribution of American films in Syria and Libya (chapter 4) had lasting—and damaging—effects on the film exhibition sector. In Syria, the nationalized exhibition sector faced a slowly decline. In 2003, there were about 90 theaters in the country, 20 of them situated in Damascus (Thoraval 2003). By 2008, the estimated number was 38 cinemas, mostly in Damascus and Alep (Layadi 2013, 3). In larger cinemas, tickets cost about $5, in smaller cinemas, about $1.50 (3). Lebanese film distributors interviewed in the 2010s mentioned only two cinemas in Damascus, one of which comprised two screens (El-Azar interview; Saliby interview; Chakra interview). Many theaters were in a state of dereliction, which led to audience desertion. In the first decade of the twenty-first century, 90% of the audience was comprised of men, who attended cinemas to watch Indian films, violent karate films from Hong Kong, and films from the US (Thoraval 2003, 87). Although, officially, the state managed film import, no distributor actually sold any films to the Syrian authorities in the 2010s (El-Azar interview; Saliby interview; Chakra interview). The civil war that has engulfed the country since 2011 marked the demise of the theatrical experience. A similar ruin of the nationalized exhibition sector occurred in Libya. After the nationalization decision of 1975, the government proved unable to import foreign films; this led to the decline of the exhibition sector (Ramadan Salim, quoted in Layadi 2013, 3). Although Libya is still part of the territories for which Lebanese distributors hold rights in their contracts with American studios, no film seems to have been sold there in the past fifteen years (El-Azar interview; Saliby interview). Since the 2011 revolution that put an end to Al-Qaddafi's regime, civil strife has seized the country. Not only is cinema-going impossible, but no information is accessible on whether the populations use other means of access to films.

Two lessons can be drawn from the film situation in Syria and Libya. First, the presence of a strongly popular cinema appears as a core ingredient to the health of the exhibition sector. In many countries, Hollywood films have acted as a key attraction; popular cinemas from Egypt and India have played a similar role in a number of markets. This is also visible, to some extent, in the area of television: the development of Syrian television series was a factor of attraction to the small screen in the country, but also in Middle Eastern markets where they were exported. The second lesson is that cinema can only thrive in the context of a stable industry structured on three pillars: production, distribution, and exhibition; and a stable political context is paramount to maintain the balance. In 1960s and 1970s Syria and Libya, theatrical exhibition became a pawn in a political game focused on independence from Western influences. The advent of war in the 2010s marked the final destructuring of the commercial film market, at a time when survival has become the main issue for the population.

Palestinian Territories and Iraq: Cinemas against all Odds

Wars and conflicts, however, do not necessarily entail the disappearance of film culture, as the repeated attempts to revive film-going in the Palestinian territories show. In the 1980s, inhabitants of Nablus would regularly attend shows at the city's four cinemas. Recent Egyptian comedies, Hollywood blockbusters, and Bollywood romances were the habitual fare. During the weekend, both families and young people frequented cinemas that could welcome as many as 870 spectators. But in 1987, the First Intifada, the Palestinian uprising against Israeli occupation of the West Bank and Gaza, marked a breaking point; many commercial venues, including theaters, closed subsequently. Some cinemas were destroyed by Israeli shells; others were turned into parking lots.[6] In 1993, at a time when the Oslo Accords seemed to offer hope for a return to normalcy, cinemas reopened. They closed again with the start of the Second Intifada in 2000 (Gugler 2011, 191). In the early 2000s, the Al Kasaba Theatre and Cinémathèque in Ramallah was the only functional screening facility in the entire Palestinian Authority. Financed by an unnamed French benefactress, the theater, which had opened just before the uprising, was a state-of-the-art venue with 700 seats. By 2002, it was facing challenging conditions: roadblocks and curfews made it impossible for potential spectators to reach the cinema; the closed borders made it impossible to obtain prints except from diplomatic sources or through smuggling; the cinema made no profit and was dependent on ever-dwindling funding.[7] Hopes for a more peaceful situation came in 2005 with the Sharm el-Sheikh summit and the end of the Second Intifada. With peace came the reopening of theaters. By 2011, an estimated number of five screens were servicing the 3.7 million inhabitants of the Palestinian Authority (Layadi 2013, 2). Given the dire economic situation in the territories, however, most of the screening facilities are internationally supported culture-oriented initiatives, such as Ramallah's Al Kasaba Theatre and Cinémathèque, which presents Egyptian cinema, as well as film weeks organized through diplomatic channels (Caillé and Arasoughly 2016, 274).[8] In East Jerusalem, the Al Quds Cinema, originally an 800-seat cinema founded in 1950 and closed in 1987, was renovated in 2007, becoming the Yabous Cultural Centre, an NGO functioning with international support.[9] In the 81-seat hall dedicated to cinema, which opened in 2012, audiences can watch recent US films, quality Arab films and Palestinian films (Caillé and Arasoughly 2016, 274). Even internationally supported cultural initiatives have found it hard to survive. Closed since 1987, the Jenin Cinema in Jenine reopened in 2010, with support from the German government. After failing to find an audience, it was closed and was razed in 2016.[10]

Alongside these cultural initiatives, two commercial cinemas were operating in the 2010s. In Nablus, the Cinema City was opened in 2009 by two businessmen: Marwan Masri and Bashir Sheka. Sheka's family had opened a cinema in the city in 1921 but had to close it in 1987.[11] Cinema City is situated in a new shopping mall in the commercial city center, just outside of the Old City.[12] The programming includes commercial American and Egyptian films (Caillé and Arasoughly 2016, 274). In 2009, a reporter noted that the entrance to the theater was framed by a still from Charlie Chaplin's *The Kid* (1921):

> Sheka explained the symbolism of the choice, saying the people's sense of humor in Nablus is that of the underdog. He quoted the title screen from The Kid, which reads "A comedy with a smile, and perhaps a tear," echoing the same attitude of many Nablus families during the years since the cinemas closed down.[13]

The second commercial theater is the Clack, a six-screen multiplex in Ramallah opened in 2014 and renamed Palestine Tower Cinemas (Caillé and Arasoughly 2016, 274).[14] Situated at the center of the Ramallah financial district, the Palestine Trade Tower is also home to a radio, a luxury hotel and restaurant, a spa, a fitness club, and a "sky gate terrace and bar."[15] Advertising itself as "the first movie multiplex in Palestine," the Palestine Tower Cinemas offers a modern cinema experience with six screens, high quality surround sound, 2D and 3D films released day-and-date with the US, concession stands and friendly employees.[16] Its program for the week of October 18, 2018, available through the cinema's Facebook page, included one Egyptian action film and seven Hollywood films of various genres: children's movies (*Smallfoot*, 2018; *Goosebumps 2: Haunted Halloween*, 2018), a biopic (*First Man*, 2018), an African-American comedy (*Night School*, 2018), a superhero movie (*Venom*, 2018), a horror movie (*The Nun*, 2018), and a melodrama (*A Star is Born*, 2018).

The same desire to revive cinema-going against all odds has been visible in Iraq. In the 1990s, the exhibition sector declined, due to a context of insecurity and strict state control. Although foreign films were purchased for a flat fee, censorship drastically controlled the type of programs imported (Saliby interview).[17] In the wake of the Iraqi invasion of

Kuwait in 1990 and the 1991 Gulf War, international sanctions by the United Nations further isolated the country economically and culturally (Thoraval 2003, 19). One consequence was the continued decline of the exhibition sector during the following decade.[18] By the end of the 1990s, 40 cinemas still existed in Baghdad.[19] The US invasion of the country in 2003 and the ensuing war situation sounded the death knell for the exhibition sector. In 2009, Saad Hashim, manager of the Atlas cinema in Baghdad, sadly noted that only 8 cinemas were still operating. As a film-lover, with nostalgic memories of Kirk Douglas' *Spartacus* (1960) and Costa-Gavras' *Z* (1969), he was distressed by the new type of audience attending his cinema: "riffraff and lowlifes" eager for films with "the 'racy' scenes and 'sexy' shots not readily available under Hussein's tight censorship."[20] Exhibitors were discouraged by this uneducated audience, as well as by security concerns, irregular electricity supplies and mounting pressure from Islamists demanding they "black out the sensitive body parts" in the films shown.[21] Most theaters closed in 2003; some had burnt down during the guerilla fights.[22] In a 2010 article, a fifty-two year-old Iraqi explained that he "ha[d] not taken his family to a movie theatre since the mid-1980s."[23] Cinema-going culture seemed to have been lost.

Political instability plagued the country with the development of an insurgency against the US occupation from 2003 to 2011, but in the safest zones, a few entrepreneurs were striving to revive cinema-going by introducing state-of-the-art multiplex theaters. As US troops started leaving in 2011, entrepreneur Zaid Fadhel was busy opening Iraqi Cinemas, a two-screen mini-cinema in Baghdad's Hunting Club. With a hosting capacity of 75 seats per screen, the first Iraqi Cinema had "luxurious red seats imported from Spain, sophisticated sound and light systems and projectors from Italy and Germany."[24] Fadhel's aim was "to bring back the culture of cinema to Iraqis" by reconnecting them with the global film culture.[25] The following year, Fadhel opened an Iraqi Cinemas theater in the Royal Mall in Erbil, the capital of Kurdistan (Mekary interview).

While the rest of Iraq was sinking into a bloody civil war, the autonomous region of Kurdistan indeed remained a safe area (Mahajan 2012, 67). Attracting viewers was an uphill battle, and the exhibitor's first challenge was to change the bad reputation cinema had acquired in the 1990s (Mekary interview). The potential for growth in the relatively safe region soon proved equally attractive to Empire, a historical player in the field of distribution in the Middle East and exhibition in Lebanon. Looking for expansion opportunities abroad, Empire opened a movie theater in Erbil in June 2013.[26] Erbil seemed full of promises due both to its stable political situation and the lack of alternative entertainment opportunities. As Financial director Gino Haddad emphasized, "When it comes to cinema and entertainment, Iraqi Kurdistan is a virgin territory."[27] Future phases of expansion were planned to include the creation of cinemas in two other cities of the region, Sulaymaniyah and Dohuk, as well as Basra, Iraq's third biggest city. Locations were chosen based on their political stability: in 2014, Mario Haddad, Sr., explained Basra, a Shiite city, was chosen due to the absence of any community tensions.[28] In line with the types of cinema built around the region—and the world— Empire opened a fourteen-screen multiplex in a commercial building, the Family Mall.[29] The cinema is equipped with 3D digital projectors and DTS digital surround sound system, and has a comfortable hall with confectionary stand. The programming is composed of Hollywood blockbusters, released day-and-date with the US, as well as commercial Arabic and Indian films.[30] On October 19, 2018, for example, spectators could pick between American mainstream entertainment (*A Star Is Born*, *First Man*, *Goosebumps 2: Haunted Halloween*, *Night School*, *The Nun*, *Venom*) and genre fare (*Bad Times at the El Royale*, 2018; *Mayhem*, 2017), as well as two Egyptian films (crime drama *Diamond Dust* and comedy *El Badla*), one Russian animation film (*The Princess and the Dragon*, 2018) and an international coproduction (*Johnny English Strikes Again*, 2018). Modern cinema-going culture however has to be built from scratch. At a one-off British film festival organized in 2011, Kurdish government representative Bayan Sami Abdul Rahman noted that, "for most, eating popcorn and watching a movie on the big screen was an entirely new experience."[31] Developing the market thus also meant developing film culture. The Empire cinema has, for example, been part of an educational project, organizing weekly film sessions for neighboring school (Haddad interview). Another obstacle to developing cinema-going is language. In view of the fact that people in Kurdistan do not speak Arabic but Kurdish, Empire tried showing a film with Kurdish subtitles . . . only to realize that many people could not read. Faced with the prohibitive cost that dubbing in Kurdish would entail, the cinema now only shows films in English with French and Arabic subtitles (Haddad interview), a fact that seems to breed discontent in the audience, as can be seen in the Facebook page comments.[32]

The competition from the Lebanese giant proved too much for the Erbil Iraqi Cinemas theaters, which closed around 2013 (Mekary interview), but Fadhel consolidated his pioneering position in Baghdad with the opening of multiplexes in Mansour Mall in 2013, Nakheel Mall in

2015, Zayouna Mall in 2017, and Baghdad Mall in 2018. Iraqi Cinemas also opened a multiplex in Dohuk in 2015 and in Hilla in 2017 (Mekary interview). Iraqi Cinemas offers the same state-of-the-art experience as other multiplexes. As explains Pierre Mekary, Iraqi Cinema operations manager in Baghdad, the theater mostly shows Americans films, but also includes Egyptian, Lebanese, and Iraqi films when available (Mekary interview). The most popular movies are American horror films (*The Nun*, c. 2018; *The Meg*, 2018) and Egyptian films with stars (*El Diesel*, 2018; *El Badla*, M2018). *Mission Impossible: Fallout* (2018) was also a box-office success in 2018 (Mekary interview). In Baghdad as in Erbil, attracting an audience that has been alienated from the cinema experience is the central focus. The usual audience is a diverse mix of families, university students, and groups of young men or women. Every Monday, Iraqi Cinemas proposes a "buy one, get one free" ticket offer in order to enable people from all classes to experience films in cinemas (Mekary interview).

At the time of writing, there were eight operating cinemas in Iraq: the six Iraqi Cinemas in Baghdad (Mansour Mall, Nakheel Mall, Zayouna Mall, Baghdad Mall), Hilla (BDC), and Dohuk, the Empire Cinema in Erbil, and one smaller cinema in Basra (Mekary interview). Empire and Iraqi Cinemas have not only been faced with the difficult task of attracting spectators back into cinemas, they have had to do so under unstable political circumstances. With the end of US occupation, the country fell under the domination of the Islamic State of Iraq and the Levant from 2014 to 2017. This directly impacted Empire in Erbil: the expats from the US, Europe, and Arab countries who had been the core of movie-goers left Kurdistan. The cinema did not shut down but its potential audience has been drastically reduced (Mekary interview). In Baghdad, the audience was mostly local and the cinemas continued to operate through the commitment of the local employees who worked in spite of the dangerous conditions (Mekary interview). Today film exhibition remains a risky business and all cinema owners and managers can do is invest, work, and hope for the best. As Iraqi Cinemas' Pierre Mekary explains, the aim of Fadhel's theater chain is less to develop a business than to turn a new leaf after years of war, to develop a new and lively culture (Mekary interview).

As the situations in the Palestinian territories and in Iraq show, the reopening of cinemas is part of a return to the "normalcy" of peacetime. Some initiatives are culturally motivated, often led by NGOs and artists, such as the Jenin Cinema. Others are led by entrepreneurs aiming at creating a viable commercial sector through a two-pronged strategy:

creating a link with the audience, by offering state-of-the-art movie theaters, and with the region's distributors by convincing them that they could be stable business partners.[33] These entrepreneurs often have a cinephile history of their own. Cinema exhibition and distribution has often been a family history, as in the case of Bashir Sheka in Nablus or the Haddads from Lebanon. Sheka's choice of *The Kid* for his cinema's façade epitomizes a taste for, and knowledge of, world cinema and its history. Fadhel is also viewing his commitment as culturally motivated. These commercial initiatives thus have deep roots in the entrepreneurs' own vision of culture and cinema. The movie-going culture described here is, however, partial on two accounts. The nature of multiplex film culture is to favor mainstream cinema, so that viewers can fully enjoy the quality screen and sound system. This culture, in which Hollywood cinema is very present, is thus different from the more art-house fare offered in cultural initiatives. The selection also operates in terms of audiences. Many are excluded from this experience due to language issues, as in Erbil. The high cost of ticket prices and the geographical distance are also factors of exclusion. Just as cultural initiatives primarily reach the educated elite, these multiplexes can cater only for a small portion of the Palestinian and Iraqi population. Most people, in fact, continue to favor other modes of access to films, notably through the small screen.

Turning on the Small Screen: US Films on Satellite Television

The importance of television as a means of access to cinema is particularly visible in Saudi Arabia. While cinemas remained banned until the late 2010s, films have been largely available on the small screen. The absence of movie theaters actually increased the demand for films on television (Sakr 2007, 130). In fact, in the late 1990s, Saudi Arabian businessmen became the driving force behind the development of satellite television in the region. Investment into the nascent satellite television market was, at first, politically motivated. CNN coverage of the 1990–1991 Kuwait crisis brought to light the political and commercial power of high-standard television, but Arab entrepreneurs, many of whom had studied in the US, winced at the channel's Western bias and decided to create quality satellite channels that would reflect an Arab point of view (Rugh 2004, 211). In 1991, the first pan-Arab station was created by Shaikh Salih Kamel and Shaikh Walid Ibrahim, who both had strong ties to the Saudi royal family. Based in London, Middle East Broadcasting Center (MBC) was assumed to be politically and financially supported by the Saudi authorities (Rugh 2004, 212). While MBC was a free-to-air channel, the Saudi business group al-Mawarid founded the pay-TV channel Orbit in 1994 in Italy (213). Al-Mawarid was also controlled by a businessman close to the royal family, Prince Khalid bin Abdullah. The first pan-Arab channels were thus "offshore Arab television stations" based in Great-Britain and Italy, where they found skilled human resources and quality logistic services, while remaining geographically close to the Arab world. For Saudi authorities, supporting offshore television was also a way to encourage the development of friendly media, while placating the antagonism of the religious clergy, which had been opposed to television since the 1960s (Kraidy and Khalil 2009, 19–20). Competition boomed in the 1990s, and while MBC, Orbit, and Arab Radio and Television Network (ART) were linked to Saudi Arabia, other pioneering channels were created by Lebanese (LBCI, Future Television) and Kuwaiti interests (Showtime), all based in Europe (Rugh 2004, 213; Kraidy and Khalil 2009, 22). In order to provide state-of-the art services, these offshore channels routinely employed British executives (Sakr 2007, 169) or were created in partnership with Western media, such as the—short-lived—collaboration between Orbit and BBC in 1994 (Rugh 2004, 213) or the cooperation with US Viacom Inc. in the Kuwaiti-American joint venture Showtime (Kraidy and Khalil 2009, 22). By the early 2000s, the channels left Europe due to "the clashes between Saudi political practices and British journalistic norms" and "the high cost of operating in London and Rome" (23). In order to be closer to their Arab audience and gain in cultural authenticity, the companies settled in the newly developed media free zones in the Gulf area. In 2002, MBC relocated to Dubai Media City, ART to Jordan Media City. Showtime relocated to Dubai Media City in 2004, and Orbit to Bahrain in 2005 (23). The sector was also marked by consolidation. In 2009, Orbit and Showtime merged to become the largest pay-TV channel, OSN. By 2015, the leader of the free-to-air broadcasters in North Africa and the Middle East was MBC; its competitors were Saudi Prince Al-Walid's Rotana, as well as state media organizations from Qatar (Al-Jazeera Network), Abu Dhabi (ADM), and Dubai (DMI) (Dubai Press Club 2012, 45).

Originally focused on news, the satellite channels also broadcast entertainment. Created to counterbalance Western programs, ART, for example, started by broadcasting Egyptian films (Rugh 2004, 213). As it reorganized in 2001, ART also added non-Arab movie channels: Turner

Classic Movies (TCM), which showed MGM, Warner Bros., RKO Pictures, and United Artists films of Hollywood's Golden Age, the Film Channel, and the Hindi channel B4U (Sakr 2007, 130). In the early 2000s, viewers who wanted to watch foreign films with Arabic subtitles could turn to pay-TV offer from ART, Orbit, and Showtime (130).

The turning point for access to US films on television came in 2002–2003 when the free-to-air channel MBC developed a new strategy centered on Hollywood cinema. MBC's owner, Sheikh Walid al-Ibrahim presented this new orientation as politically motivated by his avowed desire to "get rid of [. . .] the Taliban mentality" in the Arab world (quoted in Sakr 2007, 112). Showing American films and sitcoms (*Seinfeld*, 1990–1998; *Frasier*, 1993–2004; *Friends*, 1994–2004) as well as localized versions of US programs such as *Big Brother*, MBC's Channel 2 aimed to bring about a cultural change for young people (Sakr 2007, 170). Created two years later, MBC4 was also to "expose the modern Arab woman to the best of what the West has to offer," according to MBC's director of public relations Mohammed al-Mulhem (172). One cannot help but notice that MBC's marketing proposes to equate Hollywood with modernity, developing the very discourse that Klinger questions in her research on *Titanic* (Klinger 2010). In commercial terms, investing into attractive American programs meant reaping large advertising revenues (Sakr 2007, 171). The turn to such programs was engineered by British network director Tim Riordan. Until the early 2000s, American programs were sold to television stations through agents. Relying on his experience and network, Riordan offered a new modus operandi in the form of a stable and reliable relationship.[34] By the end of 2005, Riordan had obtained exclusive long-term deals with Paramount, Fox, and other studios for MBC2 (Sakr 2007, 130). By 2011, he noted, "We have contracts with all Hollywood studios, some on a more exclusive basis than others."[35] When Riordan retired from the company in 2011, he could boast that "MBC [had] created a whole new way of doing business."[36] By that time, the Middle Eastern television sector had turned into an attractive market for the Hollywood majors. Companies traditionally not selling their films and programs to free-to-air, such as Warner Bros., signed deals with MBC on the faith of this new relationship.[37] The attractiveness of the Middle Eastern television market for the majors became increasingly visible in 2010 when Australian-American News Corp bought a 9.09% stake in Rotana Group. For Rotana, this meant access to News Corp media experience and to Fox films; for News Corp chairman James Murdoch, the deal meant expanding News Corp's presence in a region with "a young and growing population where GDP [gross domestic product] growth is set to outstrip that of more developed economies in the years ahead."[38] The Saudi group was all the more attractive as by 2007, it had taken control of the Lebanese channel LBC (Gonzalez-Quijano 2012).[39] Alongside its free-to-air channels dedicated to Arab cinema (Rotana Masriya, Rotana Cinema, Rotana Classic, Rotana Aflam), Rotana also broadcasts Fox TV, FX, and Fox Movies. In 2009, Rotana and Fox signed a deal with Disney to broadcast Disney and ABC programs on Fox channels.[40] By 2012, News Corp had increased its participation to 18.97%.[41]

The second half of the 2010s was marked by the entry of an aggressive player in the field of pay-TV: the Qatari news network Al Jazeera, which branched into sports locally in 2003, and internationally in 2012 with the creation of beIN Sports. In January 2012, Al Jazeera ceased its involvement when the beIN Media Group was created and established in London.[42] In November 2015, beIN MENA started expanding into movies and entertainment, first by signing deals with Italia Films and Front Row, two historical distributors of US major and independent productions in the Middle East.[43] In March 2016, beIN Media signaled its determination to enter the world of cinema by acquiring Miramax.[44] The same year, beIN signed a deal with Turner Broadcasting System, a division of Time Warner, to have exclusive distribution rights to channels such as Cartoon Network and TCM in the Middle East and North Africa.[45] TCM thus left the ART network, which had by that time refocused its strategy on Arab content. In 2016, a deal was also signed with the television network AMC.[46] The following year, beIN added the Fox channels to its roster (Fox Action Movies HD, Fox Family Movies HD, Fox HD).[47] As of 2019, beIN also had a long-term multiyear deal with Warner Bros., with exclusive rights for first-run programming, series and first pay-window feature films.[48] By the late 2010s, the concentration of power in the hands of a few companies and their aggressive expansion policies were opening a new television market for US films, series, and TV show formats.

The development of satellite television in the Middle East, and especially in Saudi Arabia, has thus provided a new space in which Hollywood films can circulate, and the satellite television universe is vital to understand the twenty-first century regional filmscape. American films are part of a satellite television world comprising other types of entertainment options, mostly sports, TV series, reality TV, and talk shows. A study of pay-TV subscriptions by content type showed that film packages come second after sport packages. In the early 2010s, 82% of channels subscribed to in Saudi Arabia were sports channels, while 40% were dedicated to films (Dubai Press Club 2012, 50). When it comes to film-dedicated channels, US productions are clearly dominant. Out of the 10 MBC channels, 7 are wholly or partially dedicated to these programs. Out of the 17 OSN channels, 10 are wholly dedicated to US films. All films are shown in their original English-language version, with Arabic subtitles, an option favored by the audience (Gamal 2008). Films are not necessarily shown in their original versions in terms of editing, however, as free-to-air channels routinely practice self-censorship. In 2008, the information ministers from the Arab League countries issued a charter to respond to the rapid development of satellite channels and their increased accessibility to the Arab world population. The charter prohibits obscenity, pornography, and scenes that glorify smoking; it also calls for the respect of Arab leaders, pan-Arab solidarity, and respect for religious symbols.[49] Satellite TV executives themselves feel protecting families, moralities, and Arab values is part of their mission. MBC, for example, has clear guidelines for what it calls "editorial control."[50] The channel's objective is to provide "safe content" for the whole family.[51] Although free-to-air channels cover the whole region, censorship criteria are mostly based on the Gulf countries' traditions.[52] The censorship guidelines for Dubai One TV, a free-to-air entertainment channel in English, are directly derived from government policies; language, nudity, and political references are big no-nos.[53] Rotana executives are similarly cautious about religion, politics, and sex scenes, adopting the standards of their target audience: Saudi Arabia.[54] Though Hollywood films seem to require a higher dose of censorship, all cinemas are scrutinized. The MBC website notes that films and series on MBC Bollywood "have all been cherry-picked for originality, significance and relevance to our Arab audiences."[55] On the other hand, pay-TV channels, which target a more restricted audience, show films uncensored and without commercial breaks, the lack of censorship being actually a major factor of attraction.[56] Hollywood films thus circulate in different versions, which respond alternatively to a need to localize and a desire of access to the "real thing."

Television is the dominant medium not only in Saudi Arabia, but also in the Arab world as a whole. Free-to-air and pay-TV channels offering US films are largely accessible all over the region through ArabSat and NileSat.[57] In 2011, more than 60% of TV households in the Arab region were watching free satellite channels, and about 5% were watching pay-satellite (Dubai Press Club 2012, 43). Consumption varied depending on the country, as shown by a study of the top ten

TV channels in several Arab markets in 2012 (45). Egyptians preferred local content, and eight to the top ten channels were Egyptian (Al Hayat, Al Mehwar). The only two non-Egyptian pan-Arab channels in the top ten were Rotana Cinema and MBC2 (Dubai Press Club 2012, 142). In Morocco, the most watched TV channel was the local 2M TV, but Gulf channels ranked high, with six channels (Al Jazeera, MBC 4, MBC 2, MBC 1, Rotana Cinema, MBC Action) in the top ten (150). MBC channels also clearly dominated the UAE market, with MBC 2 and MBC Action as the top two channels (45). Saudi channels were also strongly successful in their home country, with 6 MBC channels as well as Rotana Cinema in the top ten (45). A closer look at audience tastes in Saudi Arabia showed another characteristic in the varied TV market: high segmentation. In the mid-2010s, the "most preferred (Top 3) TV genres in Saudi Arabia [were] movies, news (driven by males and by the region's unrest) and drama series (driven by females especially with Turkish series continuing to capture a strong following in the region)" (159). The strongly target-oriented nature of satellite television leads to the existence of a variety of potential media landscapes according to gender and age. Women watching MBC 4 live in a world of localized shows, imported American talk shows, and series such as *Friends*, as well as Turkish series. Young men targeted by MBC Action are offered American series (*CSI*, 2000–2015; *Supernatural*, 2005–) and talk shows (*Car Matchmaker*, 2014-), as well as local lifestyle shows (*Eish El Dour*). Segmentation is also operated in terms of cultural backgrounds, with distinct channels for programs from the US, but also Egypt (MBC+ Drama as well as the ART channels) and India (MBC Bollywood, Stargold, Zee Cinema). Language is part of the segmentation strategy with channels in English with Arabic subtitles (OSN), Hindi films dubbed in Syrian Arabic (MBC Bollywood), and channels in Arabic, but also channels targeting audiences speaking Hindi (Stargold), as well as Tamil (KTV) and Malayalam (Asianet Movies). Intended as a commercial means of maximizing the audience, segmentation also entails the creation of a number of parallel mediascapes that do not necessarily overlap. This variety of television cultures is also accentuated by the fact that pay-TV is not widely accessible. For spectators of American films, this means the difference between watching original or edited versions. Pay-TV penetration in 2011 varied between 9% in Egypt, 20% in Saudi Arabia, 25% in Morocco, and 45% in the UAE. Pay-TV appears as a costly option, while free-to-air channels are widely accessible (Dubai Press Club 2012, 142, 151, 161, 170). Access to Internet services such as MBC's Shahid, a free video-on-demand TV catch-up service, or MoBC, a mobile services application, also depends on broadband penetration, which varies in the region.

In Saudi Arabia, the ban on movie theaters has thus largely been compensated by wide access to powerful channels conceived with this local audience in mind. In the mid-2010s, Saudi Arabia had the highest satellite TV penetration in the Arab region at 97% (Dubai Press Club 2012, 159), which is quite a paradox since satellite dishes were still officially banned in the country (Kamalipour 1994, 251; Dubai Press Club 2012, 159). From the point of view of production and distribution, the history of satellite television revolves around executive strategies and commercial deals, marketing and audience segmentation. From the point of view of consumers, however, satellite television is also very much about illegal access to films and programs. The dominance of Saudi interest in satellite television is actually based on a consumption that is, for the most part, illegal. Satellite channels have, in fact, played a key role in the informal circulation of Hollywood films in all markets officially closed to American cinema.

Multifaceted Piracy

Although satellite dishes are illegal in Iran, where authorities have curtailed all potentially corrupting foreign influences, they have been largely present there, "hidden in makeshift gardens and shrubbery atop buildings."[58] After one of the regular police raids to confiscate dishes, Culture Minister Ali Jannari admitted "using satellite is strictly prohibited, but most people use it."[59] As Sohrabi and Dowran noted, "Iranians have integrated satellite television into their daily lives," accessing a number of Persian-language entertainment channels such as Manoto, Gem TV, and Farsi One (2016, 170). A tribute to the strong presence of the Iranian audience is the launch of MBC Persia, a channel with international programs, including Hollywood films, translated in Farsi, in October 2018.[60] The issue of piracy in the Middle East does not only include illegal access to legal satellite channels, but also the existence of pirate channels. In 2012, while about fourteen free-to-air channels legitimately operated in the Middle East, another dozen channels operated without licenses.[61] In the aftermath of the 2011 Egyptian revolution, for example, at least five channels started illegal operations on Nile Sat. The channel operators obtained movies from video stores, copied them, added subtitles, and put them on air.[62] A study of the programming of three pirate TV channels (Top Movies,

Claquette TV, Panorama Action) between January and February 2012 showed that 35% of the films aired were copied from MBC. Over 50% of the pirated films aired on the three channels came from major US production companies (Dubai Press Club 2012, 52). Illegal use of free-to-air and pay-TV satellite televisions and their programs have notably enabled the circulation of Hollywood films in commercially inaccessible markets, such as Syria or the Palestinian Authority territories (Thoraval 2003, 87; Caillé and Arasoughly 2016, 273; Saliby interview). Following new technological developments, television piracy moved from the illegal channels of the 1980s to satellite piracy in the 1990s and early 2000s. As satellite channels started using the commercial possibilities of the Internet in the 2010s, piracy followed, with online channels offering free streaming services.[63]

Physical piracy also evolved and DVDs replaced the VHS format in the late 1990s. In Iran, pirate DVDs have been sold on the black market. In a 2000 report, the *New York Times* followed one of the "tape men," who never gave their names to clients, and met them on a weekly basis, always avoiding the Komiteh or religious police. The salesman they interviewed provided banned American films such as *Big Momma's House* (2000) to "more than 40 families in uptown Tehran."[64] In his 2015 pseudo-documentary *Taxi*, Jafar Panahi's dedicates a long sequence to a discussion with such an illegal DVD salesman or "filmi." Carrying a heavy brown shoulder bag, Omid meets his clients every week outside their homes, offering a variety of titles from Hollywood blockbusters and TV series (*The Walking Dead* 2010–2022; *The Big Bang Theory*, 2007–2019) to American independents (*Midnight in Paris*, 2011), international art-house cinema by young auteurs (*Once upon a Time in Anatolia*, 2011), and revered masters (Kurosawa). Pirated films, however, have sometimes undergone a process of reinterpretation and reappropriation. The main characters of the series *Shrek* (2001) have, for instance, enjoyed particular popularity in Iran, less thanks to their endearing personalities than to the existence of several dubbed versions that have become the subject of debate among Iranian viewers. As Brian Edwards noted,

> In some versions (since withdrawn from official circulation), various regional and ethnic accents are paired with the diverse characters of *Shrek*, the stereotypes associated with each accent adding an additional layer of humor for Iranians. In the more risqué bootlegs, obscene or off-topic conversations are trans-posed over *Shrek's* fairy-tale shenanigans.[65]

Four to five cinemas in Iran do legally show a few action and animation films by independent US film companies or films with anti-American undertones such as *Fahrenheit 9/11* (2004) (Saliby interview; Chakra interview), but the films sold illegally are the big-budget films the general population asks for. As an Iranian "filmi" expressed in 2008, "I will have my long list of customers as long as these films are not shown in cinemas."[66] In Iran as in Saudi Arabia, there are no sanctions for holding or selling pirated DVDs.[67]

The presence of pirated DVDs is also widespread in war zones and areas where political and economic instability do not make copyright issues a priority. Inhabitants of the Palestinian territories thus routinely access Hollywood in this way (Caillé and Arasoughly 2016, 273). Similarly, a French journalist visiting the Sabra and Chatila Palestinian refugee camps in Beirut around 2010 described pirate DVD shops that, behind a unassuming parlor proposing Egyptian and Syrian films, hid large and modern underground rooms with millions of recent CD, DVDs, and software. DVDs comprised the recent Hollywood films, but also Hollywood "classics" such as *Spiderman* (2002) (Martel 2010, 336–37). Pirate DVDs have also been present in the streets of Baghdad, where in the 2000s a nonlocal audience was also craving for access to Hollywood films: the US military. US soldiers had so much taken to buying pirate DVDs from Baghdadi stores that the MPAA sent an official request to the US military authorities to forbid this practice. The army, however, refused to intervene. Additionally, US soldiers were strong users of TorrentFreak in order to illegally download films and music.[68] Piracy in the markets closed to commercial theatrical circulation of Hollywood films is thus multifaceted and rampant. It is, for many, virtually the only means to access such films. In countries where copyright laws are inexistent or not implemented, pirate consumption of films has become an unquestioned practice, as is epitomized by the bad experience of a Syrian refugee in a German shelter who was issued a $900 fine for downloading films through file sharing to while away the hours.[69]

When drawing a map of the theatrical distribution of Hollywood film in the Middle East, Syria, Libya, Iraq, Iran, and Saudi Arabia would at first glance stand as blacked out no-go zones (Mingant 2016a, 130). This would be misleading as the borders between "closed" and "open" markets for Hollywood films are, in fact, quite porous. The variety of modes of access devised by entrepreneurs and consumers in those markets can serve as a blueprint for practices visible in the other markets of the area, from attempts to revive the exhibition sector to the importance of access through television, as well as the issue of rampant piracy. Similar issues are indeed at play in the three areas in which Hollywood films can legally circulate today but which face specific challenges: the dysfunctional film markets of North Africa (chapter 7), the mature markets of the Middle East (chapter 8), and the booming markets in the Gulf countries (chapter 9).

7

North Africa

Cinema and Informal Economy

O N PAPER, ALGERIA, MOROCCO, and Tunisia are part of the markets open to the legal distribution of US films. While political
obstacles are indeed absent on those markets, commercial film
distribution encounters difficulties due to the fragile structure of the film
industries. As a consequence, informal film distribution and consumption
thrive in the Maghreb.

Fragile Film Markets

One can in fact argue that the term "film industry" is questionably appli-
cable today to the North African film sector as it suffers from serious
difficulties. The ties between the traditional three pillars of any film
sector—exhibition, distribution and production[1]—have been broken. This
is particularly visible in Algeria, where the exhibition sector is virtually at
a standstill (Ali 2014, 96). The number of theaters in Algeria fell drastically from 424 in 1962 to 21 in 2008 (EuroMed Audiovisuel II 2008a).
By the 2010s, only 2 to 4 commercial theaters, all situated in Algiers,
were actually operational, alongside a number of state cinematheques
(Mingant 2016a, 138, 203). One of the reasons behind the dereliction
of the exhibition sector has been the lack of interest by managers and
employees since nationalization intervened in 1964. As civil servants with

no training or taste for cinema, exhibitors are not keen on investing to improve the comfort and technical qualities of the theaters. Anecdotes circulate such as the story of a film projectionist who canceled a 6:00 p.m. screening in spite of the presence of spectators in order to go home early. The exhibition sector is impacted not only by the lack of commercial impetus, but also by the outdated state of the material. Even theaters that underwent renovation at the beginning of the twenty-first century, turned out to be nonoperational or outdated. In Oran, the Maghreb Cinéma, formerly the Regent, was fully renovated . . . but without a projection booth. The Essaasa cinema, formerly the Colisée, was also renovated in 2008, but the new digital sound system was dismantled a year later (Ali 2014, 97). At a time when digital distribution has become the international norm, Algerian distributors are faced with an unsolvable conundrum. Films rented by distributors are now all on DCP (Digital Cinema Package) and thus cannot be circulated in any of the operating theaters, which are all equipped with a 35 mm projector (Ali-Yahia interview). Besides, digital renovation would hardly be useful given the lack of skilled projectionists. The technological dead-end is aggravated by state legislations. Distributors are required to provide the films to be evaluated by the film commission delivering the visas. However, although distributors can easily obtain DVDs for smaller European and auteur films, none can be obtained for big-budget Hollywood productions such as the *Harry Potter* franchise. Trying to follow the legal procedure would mean distributing the film eight months after its original release in the US. By that time, Algerian audiences would have found other means to watch the film and lost interest (Hachemi interview). Rather than renovate cinemas and collaborate with distributors, state exhibitors routinely use pirated DVDs, a practice which spelled the final break with distributors (Ali-Yahia interview; Hachemi interview). In effect, in Algeria, film distribution has become an impossible activity. In 2013, although there were officially 50 distribution companies registered at the Ministry of Culture, only two were still active (S. Ali 2014, 98). MD Ciné and Cirta Films, the representative for Warner Bros., distributed about two films each a year in 2013 (Al-Yahia interview). Being a film distributor in the three North African countries today is in fact a more than challenging occupation.

While Morocco's movie theaters are in better conditions, they illustrate a second problem: unequal access to cinemas over a given national territory. As in Algeria, the number of theaters has drastically fallen in the past decades. There were 251 theaters in the early 1980s, 43 in 2011, 35 in 2013, and 27 in 2018 (Mingant 2016a, 139).[2] In 2013, there was one screen for 470,000 inhabitants (Layadi 2013, 5). Out of the 68 screens in the country, 23 actually belonged to two multiplexes situated in Casablanca and Marrakech, while 45 one-screen theaters were spread over the territory. In 2013, only the two Mégarama multiplexes, the IMAX theater in Casablanca, and two theaters in Marrakech had been digitized (Layadi 2013, 4), but even digitized cinemas could not halt audience defection (Marrakchi interview). The big issue thus appears to be the geographical concentration of movie theaters in a few large or attractive cities such as Casablanca, Marrakech, Rabat, Tangier, Meknes, Tetouan, Fes, Oujda, Agadir, Settat, and Assilah (Ali 2012b, 112). In their 2019 study on film audiences in Morocco, Aït Belhoucine and Forest, provide a detailed inventory of movie theaters in the country. They note that only nine cities had one or several theaters: Casablanca (9 theaters), Rabat (4), Marrakech (4), Fès (1), Tangier (5), Tetouan (2), Meknes (3), Oujda (1), and Agadir (1) (Aït Belhoucine and Forest 2019, 136–47). Outside the four Megarama multiplexes and the IMAX cinema in Casablanca, the majority appears to be monoscreen theaters, and about six had been digitalized (Aït Belhoucine and Forest 2019, 136–47). In smaller cities on the coast from Agadir to Casablanca, cinemas have disappeared (Marrakchi interview). In fact, the Mégarama theaters in Casablanca, Fes, Marrakech, and Tangier attracted 65% of the Moroccan box office, 50% of the tickets sold, and 72% of the film distributed in 2013 (Layadi 2013, 4). While the upper-middle class of the larger urban centers can watch recent Hollywood films in the Mégarama theaters (Benchenna 2016, 221), the cinema-going habit has been fast disappearing for most of the population. By 2012, a report noted that "going to the cinema is not part of the leisure habits of Moroccans:" "60 % of Moroccans are absolute non movie goers, which means that they go less than once a year to the movies or never go at all" (S. Ali 2012b, 116). The report recorded the fall: "The attendance coefficient in movie theaters in 1982 (ratio of admissions/population in the country) was similar to that of a developed country; it is presently near zero" (114). As former president of the Moroccan Chamber of Movie Theatres, Hamid Marrakchi, lamented: "People have forgotten cinema" (Marrakchi interview).

The small Tunisian market presents similar dysfunctions. There were 17 theaters in 2008, 13 in 2013, and 15 in 2015 (EuroMed Audiovisuel II 2008b; Mingant 2016a, 139; Layadi 2013, 4; Caillé and Guiga 2019, 41)[3]. In the mid-2010s, the state of decay of existing theaters and their atmosphere of incivility routinely put off the audience (Caillé 2016; Caillé and Guiga 2019, 42). Out of the 13 existing theaters in 2013, 8 were concentrated in the same area in Tunis, and only 3 were digitized, leaving the rest of the country largely underscreened (Layadi 2013, 4). In their

2015 fieldwork, Caillé and Guiga listed 12 theaters in and around Tunis, and six cities with 1 theater each (Hammamet, Sousse, Monastrir, Bizerte, Menzel Bourguiba, Menzel Temime) (Caillé and Guiga 2019, 43). Additionally, Pathé opened a multiplex in Sousse in December 2019. Statistics are not available on the number of films circulating in these theaters, as no data collection exists (Caillé and Guiga 2019, 46). The last available figures dating from 2008 indicated that 4 Tunisian films were screened per year, about 8 European films, and about 8 American films, as well as 14 films from other countries (EuroMed Audiovisuel II 2008b, 64). In 2013, there were still four registered distributors (Layadi 2013, 4). Caillé and Guiga, however, identified only two companies still active: Société Ciné7ème Art, headed by Lassaad Goubantini, and auteur-film-orentied HAKKA Distribution founded by Kais Zaied and Amal Saadalah in 2013. Both groups are distributors and exhibitors (Caillé and Guiga 2019, 45). In an interview in the mid-2010s, a French executive for a Hollywood major indicated he actually no longer sold films to Tunisian distributors, as they usually offered fees deemed too low. Tunisia did not have the critical size to be considered an actual film market.

The dissensions between film professionals and the lost relationship with the audience convey the extent to which the film markets have become destructured. US distribution companies have been put off from providing films not only by the lack of profitability, but mostly by the disorganization of the sector, which translated into an absence of solid and stable interlocutors, and a lack of visibility over revenues. The surest sign that the markets are deemed unreliable is the fact that when US films are provided to local distributors, they are sold for a flat fee and not on a percentage deal. The collapse of the commercial film sector does not, however, spell the end of the popularity of American films. To discover the filmscape in which Algerians, Moroccans, and Tunisians live, one needs to look outside the movie theaters.

Far from the Movie Screen: The World of Informal Circulation

Points of Access

In the mid-2010s, the main point of access to films in North Africa was the world of street vendors and video-clubs selling pirated DVDs. The arrival of digital technology in the 1990s led to a consolidation in the illegal film distribution sector, and film duplication changed from cottage industry to an organized network of small businesses (Benchenna 2011, 107). In Algeria, during the VHS era, video club owners had managed the importation and duplication activities. With the digital turn, large distribution companies such as SOLI took over the business, supplying film to the video clubs. As these companies were legal, they were registered with the National Copyright Organization (ONDA) and paid for a fiscal stamp visible on the DVD covers (Labandji 2011, 130). The pirate sector has thus evolved with each new technology. In Tunisia, a typical video club offered VHS until 2004, VCD (Video Compact Disk) between 2004 and 2006, and DVDs between 2006 and 2008, stocking films on hard drive and providing them on DVX or USB sticks in the 2010s (Caillé and Slouma 2016, 249). Video club owners also provide viewers with boxes featuring programs from Netflix (Mounim interview). The proliferation of different formats actually made consuming films easier (Caillé and Slouma 2016, 249–50). In Morocco, blank DVDs can legally be imported from China, and then burnt locally. The films themselves come from pirated versions either obtained in local cinemas or sent from Canada via the Internet (Ali 2012b, 155–56; Marrakchi interview). In Algeria, the pirated films have traditionally come from Canada (Ali-Ya-hia interview; Hachemi interview). Pirate companies can then burn up to 10,000 DVDs an hour (Marrakchi interview). Pirate DVDs from flea markets such as Derb Ghallef in Casablanca are then circulated into other large urban centers on small town markets (Benchenna 2011, 109; Marrakchi interview). Video clubs in North Africa are an integral part of the "informal film distribution" networks described by Lobato in *Shadow Economies of Cinema* (2012).

For the consumer, pirated DVDs means an easy access to films that are widely available on market stalls or through vendors "around each street corner" for a low price (Marrakchi interview). While movie tickets can range from $3 to $6, a pirated DVD in Morocco would cost about 5 dirhams, that is 50 American cents (Marrakchi interview). It also means the possibility of watching the film simultaneously with the rest of the world. In Morocco, American films are often available on the streets before they have obtained a legal distribution visa. In 2005, Oliver Stone's *Alexander* was available to Moroccan viewers before French spectators had seen it in movie theaters (Benchenna 2011, 107). In 2013, *Oblivion*, a Joseph Kosinski film starring Tom Cruise, was available on Moroccan streets six hours after its US release in movie theaters (Marrakchi interview). The downside for the consumer is the lack of quality of the film viewed on pirated DVDs. In Algeria, big-budget Hollywood films that are illegally circulated a few hours or days after their US release are called "previews" and are renowned for their bad quality, as they are obtained through camcorder piracy (Labandji 2011, 131). They nevertheless satisfy novelty-hungry teenagers (135). Bad image quality, green hues, synchronization issues can affect pirated films. In the early 2000s, films arriving from Canada would also have the additional surprise of being dubbed in Canadian French (Ali-Yahia interview).[4] Consumers have, in fact, little alternative, given that there is no operational legal DVD distribution. When the French retail store chain FNAC entered the Moroccan market in 2011, it decided to offer DVDs with similar pricing as in its French outlet, at about $20, a price much above the purchasing power of most Moroccans (Benchenna 2011, 111). In Tunisia, the DVDs sold by large retail stores such as Carrefour, Géant, and Monoprix are, in fact, provided by illegal local distributors (Ferjani 2011, 82). While the illegal distributor and video-owners now routinely use downloading, this option was not necessarily available to the average consumer in theearly 2010s due to the lack of access to high-speed Internet, especially in Algeria and Tunisia (Ferjani 2011, 82; Labandji 2011, 134).

The main competition for video clubs, and the other point of access to films for North African spectators in the mid-2010s, has been pirated television. In Tunisia, the practice of intercepting the protected signals of foreign televisions dates from the late 1980s, when viewers turned their back on state television. On the coast and in the center of the country, people used boxes imported from Libya to intercept Italian channels. In the early 1990s, when French pay-TV channel Canal Plus tried to enter the market, 95% of the decoder's accessing the signal were in fact pirate. When Canal Horizons Tunisia changed decoders, inhabitants of working-class neighborhoods started to buy one subscription to service a dozen homes. Property management companies took up the idea to provide illegal access to their residents. The Canal Horizons Tunisia experiment ended in 2001 (Ferjani 2011, 79–80). Illegal access continued with the development of satellite television in the 1990s. Piracy technology simply evolved to follow that of satellite television providers. Viaccess receivers, patch receivers, and Dreamboxes imported from South Korea and China have enabled Tunisian viewers to follow the pay-TV programs from the French Canal Plus, but also Dubai-based OSN (Orbit Showtime Network) (Ferjani 2011, 80–81; Mingant 2015b, 78). In 2009, Canal Plus tried to develop a legal channel package in Algeria and Morocco; two years later, it withdrew due to excessive piracy (S. Ali 2012b, 35).

The mid-2010s seem to have marked another turning point in the history of pirate access. A 2019 study of film audiences in four African countries records the signs of a transition. In Tunisia and Morocco, DVDs and the more recent USB sticks are losing the audiences' favors and are being replaced by the multiplication of television offerings and digital platforms (Caillé and Guiga 2019, 51; Aït Blehoucine and Forest 2019, 122). Aït Belhoucine and Forest observed a collapse of the legal and illegal DVD sector from the early 2010s in Morocco, and, in fact, predict the disappearance of the physical video market in the near future, and its full replacement by downloading and streaming platforms that offer similar, and even better, factors of attraction: "home consumption, increased ease of access and transfer, absence of marginal cost, dematerialization," as well as a large access to recent international—mostly US—films (Aït Belhoucine and Forest 2019, 161).

Ineffective Antipiracy Initiatives

The informal economy film distribution sector, which appears as inventive, reactive, and well-organized, does not seem to suffer from North African authorities' antipiracy actions. In fact, film professionals recurrently point out that, beyond the few much publicized raids on pirate DVD warehouses, little is done to counter the phenomenon (Mingant 2015b, 79). Although copyright laws exist, they are rarely enforced. The main reasons behind state passivity might be an unwillingness to put an end to a very profitable sector of the economy. The informal economy is a large job creator, and it could be against the state's best interest to suppress it (Carroll 2001, 591–92). It is a means to avoid social unrest, by providing jobs for many young people (Benchenna 2011, 117). Another reason for the lack of efficiency of antipiracy efforts might be their inadequacy. As Euromed legal expert Gyory noted, piracy has been addressed through repressive legislations that were conceived in Western countries for markets where legal consumption is the norm and piracy is perpetrated by organized networks. The Southern Mediterranean countries, however, are characterized by a "widespread piracy" perpetrated by isolated individuals. In countries where illegal access to films is the norm for consumers, the enforcement of repressive legislations "is often difficult and has no real impact on markets, even when the effort is important" (Gyory 2007, 24–25).

The Motion Picture Association (MPA) itself discontinued its active antipiracy presence in North Africa and the Middle East in the early

2000s. The shift from physical piracy (DVDs) to digital piracy led the Hollywood majors' association to reconsider piracy as a global phenomenon to be dealt with on a supranational level. The MPA's approach is now two-pronged. Should a local issue arise, the Brussels office hires a local lawyer and works with local producers and distributors who are equally affected by piracy (Marcich interview). Although local distributors would have welcomed MPA support, it appears that, since the early 2000s, the MPA has actually not been directly involved in North Africa on piracy issues (Mingant 2015b, 80). The initiative is very much left in the hands of local film professionals. On a more global level, the MPA acts from its Washington office, through organizations such as the International Intellectual Property Alliance (IIPA), by lobbying for the inclusion of stringent copyright legislations in all free trade agreements signed with the US. Benchenna noted that the Moroccan legislation on copyright and related rights was modified in 2000 in order to comply with the conditions demanded by the US for the signing of a free-trade agreement between the two countries four years later. Under the pressure of the US—and the MPA—the sanctions were also strengthened in 2006 (Benchenna 2011, 109, 118). Through the IIPA, the MPA also participates in the compilation of the lists of countries infringing copyright rules for the Special 301 report of the United States Trade Representative (USTR). Algeria appeared on the watch list in 2008 and has appeared on the priority watch list since 2009. In this context, films are subsumed in the larger intellectual property context. In Algeria, the challenges underlined in the report are mostly linked to infringement of pharmaceutical products and patents, as well as the use of unlicensed software (USTR 2018, 52). Thus, the pressure applied through the USTR lists is not about the occasional solving of a piracy case, but more generally about raising "awareness of and building capacity on IP issues" (USTR 2018, 52). This is a long-term strategy and, for the moment, the more stringent state legislations have not been followed by actual enforcement (Marcich interview) or any substantial change in the culture of piracy.

Film Culture in a World of Informal Film Circulation

The widespread circulation of illegal film copies in North Africa corresponds to Lobato's definition of "piracy as access":

> For billions of people around the world, piracy is an access route to media that is not otherwise available. This kind of

piracy is not usually a self-consciously political act but an everyday activity practiced in a context where legal alternatives do not exist. (Lobato 2012, 82)

In North Africa, consumers tend to view piracy as fully acceptable. In fact, illegal access has become so rampant that it is not considered so. Ferjani noted that interviewees in Algeria did not understand her when she asked, "But aren't you bothered by the fact this it's illegal?" The respondent would usually protest that they had bought the products (Labandji 2011, 133; Gyory 2007). Consumers thus fully participate in this informal economic system, accepting it as the norm. As anthropologist Keith Hart suggested, an informal economy can also be considered as "a market-based response of the people to the overweening attempts of bureaucracy to control economic life from above" (1992, 223). The consumers' agency in the alternative film paths in North Africa is epitomized by the resourcefulness developed locally to access TV signals (Labandji 2011, 126). Another testimony to this strong desire for cinema is the creation of a dubbing studio by Algerian Samir Ait Belkacem, a former biologist and self-taught dubbing translator, in Ain-El-Hammam. Studio Tamughli, later renamed Studio Double Voice, screened American children's movies dubbed in Kabyle for viewers in the region of Tizi-Ouzou. By 2012, the studio had adapted *Shrek* (2001), *Cats and Dogs* (2001), *Ice Age 2* (2006), *Alvin and the Chipmunks* (2007), *The Tale of Despereaux* (2008), and *The Smurfs* (2011).[5] Retitled *Pucci 2* and enriched with Idir music, *Ice Age 2* became a top sale in video clubs in the Kabyle area of Algeria, to the point that children playfully called each other Zenhof, Micha, Pucci, Mascara, Zmimouche, and Zinouche.[6] For Northern African viewers, films are, in effect, "windows open on the outside world" (Labandji 2011, 127).

The rare field studies in the world of informal film circulation in the area all point to the overwhelming presence of US films. In Morocco, "recent Hollywood blockbusters dominate the counterfeited DVD market" (Benchenna 2011, 115). Virtually all US blockbusters are made available to Moroccan consumers. A video club owner in Tunisia confirmed that his business was mostly based on the sale of Hollywood action films. His top sales were *Titanic* (1997), *Avatar* (2009), *Troy* (2004), *Gladiator* (2000) and *The Patriot* (2000) (Caillé and Slouma 2016, 251–52). Similarly, young Algerians keep an eye out for the release of the latest installments in the *Star Wars* and *Pirates of the Caribbean* franchises (Labandji 2011, 135). The same type of films is also present on television channels Canal

Plus and OSN—as well as on the legally accessible MBC channels.[7] As Caillé and Guiga noted,

> films watched in movie theaters, even though they mark an event and contribute to the fame of the national cinematography much beyond the spectators who actually see them, constitute a small minority in the whole of the films in Tunisia, which are entertainment films, mostly from the USA, watched in private spaces, on TV or on the computer screen. (Caillé and Guiga 2019, 96)

Beside the general predominance of big-budget Hollywood films, the specific film mix can vary according to each consumer's gender and social class. In Slouma's video club, men favor action movies with famous actors, but women buy romances and horror films, as well as Arabic films (Caillé and Slouma 2016, 252). In Marrakech, blockbusters predominate on stalls located in the touristic areas, while they stand alongside documentaries produced by Arte and Planète in the student neighborhood. In working-class areas, a mix of American B movies, and Egyptian and Indian movies are on offer (Benchenna 2011, 114–15). While local films were originally not present in video clubs, the revival of Moroccan cinema since the 1990s has led to its increased illegal presence (114). Thorough field studies on audiences and their film tastes are now needed to fully gather the variety of filmscapes in the region. In their path-breaking study, Caillé and Guiga foreground the existence of varied "film cultures" in Tunisia, depending notably on class and gender (2019, 88). Beside the predominance of US films, they show the attachement to Tunisian cinema as well as a taste for other cinematographies. Scutinizing the list of favorite films given by the interviewees, they note the presence of US, French, Tunisian, and Egyptian films, "with a marginal presence of Indian and Asian films, except in working-class neighbourhoods where Egyptian films is appreciated by 72% and Indian films by 50% of women of all generations" (84). The predominance of Hollywood cinema should thus not hide the varied film cultures experienced by spectators.

When it comes to Hollywood cinema, consumers can also be more or less demanding in terms of quality. Penniless young Algerians eagerly buy "previews" in spite of the lack of quality, while middle-class clients insist on the availability of language choices and 5.1 sound (Labandji 2011, 135). Upper-middle-class consumers can also decide to buy a low-quality pirated DVD to watch the film at the time of its international release, then buy a legal DVD version from France to enjoy their favorite movies in full quality (136). The same impetus seems to move most consumers: the possibility to be tuned to a global culture symbolized by Hollywood blockbusters. As former head of the Béjaïa Film Event, Abdenour Hochiche remarks,

> Algerians have not severed all ties with cinema, have not severed the ties that bound them to films. [. . .] When you see the number of films that are illegally downloaded, when you see the number of films sold by street vendors or in shops, when you discuss with young people under 40 and they tell you about the recent films they've seen. . . . What the young people their age watch in France, in Switzerland, in Belgium or in American, they also watch it. (quoted in Bouzar and Zénine 2015)

Reviving the Theatrical Film Market?

This vivacious film-watching habit suggests the existence of an audience base that would make a revival of North African markets possible. Because they are very much favored by the young and the middle class, US films are at the heart of existing efforts to rebuild the market. A first series of initiatives originated from France. In 2002, the French cinema chain Mégarama opened a multiplex with fourteen screens in Casablanca. By 2018, Mégarama also operated multiplexes in Marrakech, Fes, and Tangiers, and was planning construction in Agadir and Rabat.[8] Mégarama also owns 18 cinemas in France and 3 in Spain. The French company entered the market at a time when the exhibition sector was at its lowest. Jean-Pierre Lemoine, who had been strategically moving his company away from traditional theaters toward multiplexing since the mid-1990s, viewed investing in Morocco as a business opportunity. Not only were real estate and operating overhead costs lower, but the Moroccan state was also striving to attract foreign investment through tax incentives (Benchenna 2016, 219–20). The ground to build the Marrakech multiplex was, for example, offered by the *wilaya* (or prefecture) as a way to develop a new area (220). For Moroccan film authorities, Mégarama was bringing long-needed innovation that would revive the exhibition sector as a whole. Mégarama was viewed as a potential "national champion" investing to develop multiplexes in the country (222, 229). Jean-Pierre

Lemoine did bring a number of innovations. First, he offered the same programming in his French and Moroccan multiplexes. Rather than screen the big American and French films two or three months after their world release, Lemoine offered them day-and-date, thus fulfilling the audience's desire to be up to date. Mégarama also offered a state-of-the art film experience comparable to multiplexes worldwide, with wide screens, vast halls, easy parking space, and confection stands. By focusing its programming on Hollywood blockbusters, the multiplexes followed the global trend and responded to the demands of upper-middle-class youths, its core target. In 2011, out of the 101 films screened at the Mégarama, 74 were American, 24 were European, 2 Moroccan, and 1 Egyptian (Benchenna 2016, 223–24).

The presence of Mégarama did not, however, lead to the hoped-for revival of the exhibition sector, but actually complicated the situation for local entrepreneurs. At the turn of the twenty-first century, a number of historical Moroccan distribution companies had informal partnerships with the Hollywood distribution companies, buying films from the majors' French offices for a flat fee. When Mégarama entered the market, those companies were slowly disappearing, and Mégarama took over distribution. Jean-Pierre Lemoine bought up and closed Specima and Maghreb International, and established direct contact with the majors' Paris offices. By the mid-2010s, the films shown at the Mégarama multiplexes were bought for a flat fee by Mégarama France, which then sold them to Moroccan companies (Benchenna 2016, 227). Not only has the strong presence of Mégarama accelerated the disappearance of the fragile historical companies, but it seems also to be endangering the current distribution sector. Moroccan distributors have complained that Mégarama has, in effect, a monopoly, and routinely refuses to sell Hollywood films to other companies. In 2011, Mégarama distributed 74 of the 87 US films circulated in the country, and all of the European films (Layadi 2013, 4). In 2017, Mégarama Maroc held about 47% of the distribution market shares and about 74% of the exhibition market (Centre cinématographique marocain 2017, 41, 56). The state attempt at exhibition revival by bringing in foreign investment in fact backfired. Far from striving for the development of the film market as a whole, Mégarama has followed its own logic—that of foreign investment and strategic international expansion—favoring its company's interest by guaranteeing its privileged access to attractive products and weakening potential competition. In a similar way, the presence of an IMAX theater in the Morocco Mall in Casablanca since 2011 is by no means contributing to the rejuvenation of exhibition. Included in a mall cofinanced by Moroccan group Akwa and Saudi group Al Jedaie, the theater is managed by the Société Al Amine d'investissement immobilier, which held about 12% of the distribution market in 2017 (Centre cinématographique marocain 2017, 41, 56). The theater, which shows big-budget Hollywood productions, is part of a plan for mall development for the Moroccan and Saudi companies, and a strategy of international expansion for IMAX.[9] In the late 2010s, more French investors were poised to enter the exhibition market in North Africa. Pierre-François Bernet, the head of Chrysalis Films, a company behind the opening of the first multiplex in Rabat, the Ciné Atlas Rabat Colisée, in August 2018, enthusiastically described the growth potential of the Moroccan film market and its position as a beachhead to conquer Africa as a whole. Multiplexes equipped with 3D, 4K, and Dolby 7.1 are at the center of this strategy.[10] The announcement of the creation of an eight-screen multiplex by the French Cinémas Gaumont Pathé chain in the Tunis City Mall for 2018[11] belongs to this trend—a combination of local economic development objectives and French companies' international expansion strategies, but not a long-term project to revive the film market. The apparent lack of profitability of the Mégarama circuit in Morocco should also be a warning to foreign investors. In the mid-2010s, the attendance rate was estimated at 10% and by 2018, rumor had it that eighty-year-old Jean-Pierre Lemoine was soon to sell the circuit.

Considering the limitations of large investment initiatives, the rejuvenation of the film markets might come from local film professionals with few funds but strong personal involvement. A first initiative is the creation of nonprofit association Save Cinemas in Morocco by French-Moroccan former actor and entrepreneur Tarik Mounim in 2007. The association was first created to document the existing cinemas and strive toward their revival. Its core activity has been the launching of awareness campaigns.[12] By 2014, the association has obtained the support of the minister of communications for the preservation of twenty cinemas as historical monuments. Faced with lack of funding and support, however, it has been less successful in its attempts to revive cinema-going culture. Defending a vision of cinemas as vital spaces of cultural exchange, Mounim warns that state support for the creation of multiplexes that are financially inaccessible to the average Moroccan will not be a long-term solution.[13] The state initiatives he calls for would favor diverse programming of Moroccan, Arab, and European films.[14] Ten years after the creation of his association, faced with the continued downfall of the exhibition sector, Mounim now calls for a new model based on a vast education programs (Mounim interview). Created in 2018 and supported by the Moroccan Chamber of Movie Theaters, the Cinemadrasa Maroc project, based on the word *madrassa* meaning "school," is a collaboration between twenty-one cinemas and a number of Moroccan state schools aiming at "democratizing cinematic art" by making it accessible to more than 80,000 pupils and their teachers.[15]

While Mounim's initiative has focused on the long-term recapture of the Moroccan audience by rekindling interest of state authorities, two entrepreneurs have put their efforts in reactivating the partnership with Hollywood. In Algeria, Malek Ali-Yahia found himself reviving the spirit of movie pioneers with his company MD Cinéma, founded in 1997. Faced with the impossibility of importing films for the state exhibition sectors, Ali-Yahia decided to import a projector and to turn event planner, organizing showings in various venues, such as a screening of *Skyfall* (S. Mendes, 2012) at a Sofitel for a Heineken event (Ali-Yahia interview). Fully aware that, in the eyes of US distributors, Algeria is not a market, Ali-Yahia has decided to "invent the market" (Ali-Yahia interview). His strategy has been to start with a clean slate. Doing away with the old distribution structure, he established a direct contact with the majors' London offices. In terms of exhibition, he has also called for a break with the past by actively promoting the use of digital technology to screen recent films in theaters such as the Cosmos in Algiers, as well as nontheatrical venues such as the 5-juillet sports complex in Algiers.[16] He has also striven to develop commercial multiplexes with affordable ticket pricing.[17] In his estimates, the Algerian market could ultimately reach an attendance of 100 million. The film market Ali-Yahia has in mind would both enable young Algerians to be attuned to the global film consumption and create a dynamic film sector beneficial to Algerian film production.[18] By 2018, MD Cinéma had distributed *Mad Max: Fury Road* (2015), *Mission Impossible: Rogue Nation* (2015), *Fantastic Four* (2015), *Inside Out* (2015), *Star Wars: The Force Awakens* (2015), and *Avengers: Infinity Wars* (2018). In the rejuvenated Cosmos theater in Algiers, screenings have attracted young people, but also couples and families. Although tickets are more expensive, the theater has attracted both middle-class people in their thirties and forties, and young people.[19] It remains to be seen whether Ali-Yahia's strong determination will reveal a game-changer for the Algerian film market.

In Morocco, historical film distributor and exhibitor Mohammed Layadi (Marrakech Spectacles) has actively pursued the development of regional as well as international alliances to revive the film market.

On the one hand, he has been part of the 2012 creation of MEDIS, the Mediterranean Distribution Network gathering distributors from the whole North Africa and Middle East region under the aegis of the EuroMed Audiovisuel program.[20] MEDIS has developed both awareness and educational programs. On the other hand, Marrakech Spectacles has reactivated its contracts with Twentieth Century Fox in 2014 (Layadi interview). Both Ali-Yahia and Layadi are proposing a new vision of the North African market. By acting as reliable partners, by foregrounding their knowledge of local markets and their determination to make them profitable, the two entrepreneurs are trying to put North Africa back on the film map. Today, Hollywood films are deeply engrained in the film texture of North Africa. Their strong power of attraction makes them a favorite choice on the informal economy market, but also a key asset to revive the film exhibition and distribution sector. Although the seeds of revival have been sowed by hopeful and determined local entrepreneurs, the day when North African film markets become viable still lies in the distant future.

8

Historical Markets

The Age of Maturity

THREE MARKETS HAVE HISTORICALLY been the core of film circulation and consumption in the Middle East. Egypt has been the biggest film market in terms of exhibition, with the most important attendance rate per screen in the region (table 8.1). Israel has dominated in terms of box-office revenues, with a total receipt of nearly $100 million in 2011 and a high ticket price comparable to some profitable European markets. Lebanon has been the home of the most important distribution and exhibition companies of the region and can boast its modern theatrical sector (Layadi 2013, 6–7). For these three

Table 8.1. The three mature Middle Eastern film markets in 2013

	Egypt	Israel	Lebanon
Box office in million USD (2011)	74.7	99	18.4
Tickets sold, in millions (2011)	31	10	4
Ticket price in USD (2011)	2.40	9.90	5.11
Attendance rate (2013)	0.4	1.3	0.9
Number of inhabitants per screen	207,853	19,241	33,613

Source: Layadi 2013, 6.

markets, the early twenty-first century has also been the age of maturity: theatrical sectors are fully operational and the market structure is well established, but there seems to be little room for additional growth.

Israel: An Oligopolistic Market with Western Tastes

The Israeli exhibition sector, which had faced a crisis in the early 1990s, went through a process of renovation that led to its revival a decade later. The first multiplex was opened by the Greidinger family, a historical player in film exhibition in Israel: Moshe Greidinger had opened its first movie theater in Haifa in 1931, and the family had moved into film distribution by buying Forum Films in 1967. In 1982, their company, the Chen movie theater chain, opened the first Israeli multiplex in Tel Aviv's Dizengoff Center, with five screens, modern sound systems, elegant design, comfortable seats, and computerized box offices.[1] By 2005, the market could be described a "buoyant,"[2] and in 2011, cinema-going reached a peak of admission at 11 million tickets sold. In the 2010s, the multiplexing wave continued and was considered by Israeli exhibitors as the key to continued market development (Mingant and Lifshitz 2016, 188–89). Exhibition company Globus Max, for example, opened a Yes Planet multiplex in Rishon LeZion in July 2014, including the most modern equipment and services: twenty-four screens, IMAX and 4DX technologies, VIP seats, and a large range of restaurant and food options.[3] The following year, it opened another state-of-the-art nineteen-screen Yes Planet theater in the Sherover complex in Abu Tor, Jerusalem.[4] In 2015, there were 7 megaplexes and 18 multiplexes in Israel (Mingant and Lifshitz 2016, 187). Between 2011 and 2017, screen density per million inhabitants increased from 34 to 52, box office admission from 12 to 18.2 million, and box office from about $98 million to $158 million.[5]

Though piracy has been present, it has not been a major obstacle to the film distribution business. The presence of the country on the Watchlist and Priority Watchlist of the United States Trade Representative Special 301 report from 1997 to 2013 was mostly linked to pharmaceutical rights infringement. Film piracy, viewed by some as inevitable in the Internet era, has not reached a high level in Israel. Accordingly, the MPA has not been overly involved in the market, and Hollywood distributors have mostly adapted by extending day-and-date release to Israel (Marcich interview; Sigaro interview 2013). According to Globus Max marketing director Efi Lifshitz, although the Internet does represent competition for theaters, it is also a way for audiences to develop a taste for cinema: "The more audiences watch films, whatever the media, the more likely they are to go to the cinema" (quoted in Mingant and Lifshitz 2016, 188). The major challenge for exhibitors in Israel seems to be the political context. Film attendance indeed must be considered in light of the tensions between Israel and the Palestinian territories. In November 2000, two months after the beginning of the Second Intifada, cinema registered a 30% attendance decrease and distributors had to postpone releases for their new films. The fear of a terrorist attack in malls, where the multiplexes are situated, led spectators to stay home and turn to other options, especially television (Mingant 2016a, 141). In 2004, security issues were so important that guards patrolled twenty-four hours a day in some multiplexes, and spectators routinely submitted to bag search on entering cinemas. In July 2014, during a new surge in political tensions, a bomb alert disrupted the Jerusalem International Film Festival (Mingant 2016a, 141–42). Providing a safe environment, by investing in the presence of security personnel, is thus a necessary requirement for film exhibitors.[6]

The stability of the Israeli film market is visible in the lack of major obstacles to film distribution, but also in its oligopolistic structure. The market is currently controlled by a few companies involved both in exhibition and distribution. Three companies hold 90% of the exhibition sector: Israeli Theatres (Yes Planet, Rav-Chen), New Lineo Cinema (Cinema City), and Globus Max. The remaining 10% mostly correspond to art-house circuit Lev. Film distribution is mostly in the hand of three companies: Forum Film, which is a branch of Israeli Theatres and represents Disney, Fox, Sony, and independent companies; Globus Max, which represents Warner Bros., Universal, Paramount, and independent US companies; and United King, a company in which New Lineo Cinemas has shares, and that distributes Israeli and US independent films. The level of competition on the Israeli market is thus quite low. While theaters reserve the best screens and screen time to their own distributors, companies maintain win-win relationships (Mingant and Lifshitz 2016, 187–88). Viewed from Hollywood, and especially from the London offices with which Israeli distributors have exclusivity contracts on percentage deals, Israel is a market that runs smoothly and, though small, is not negligible (Mingant 2016a, 142–43).

American movies are a favorite among this film-loving audience (Layadi 2013, 6–7). In 2017, Israeli films enjoyed a record 9.1% of the box office due to the success of *Maktub* (2017) (Union Internationale des Cinémas [UNIC] 2018), but Efi Lifshitz estimates that the usual share for

Israeli films is about 5%. European films, which have a niche audience, can represent up to 10% in case of a surprise hit. The rest of the box office consists in American films (Mingant and Lifshitz 2016, 188). The most successful genre is family films dubbed in Hebrew, which represent about 40% of tickets sold. Hebrew-subtitled action films targeted at young people come second (188). Comedies are very successful, too, particularly films starring Jewish-American comedians Adam Sandler and Ben Stiller, and one of the reasons behind the popularity of *Borat* (2006) might be that under cover of speaking "kazakh," Sacha Baron Cohen was actually speaking Hebrew.[7] The specificity of the Israeli market is that it is very European-minded when it comes to movie preferences. A US distributor interviewed noted that the Israeli audience is very close to the German audience in its taste for comedies and family films, as well as to the Polish audience when it comes to disliking superhero films (Mingant 2016a, 141). The European ancestry of much of the population thus creates film preferences that mark a sharp contrast with the rest of the Middle East, with horror, science fiction, and superhero films faring less well at the box office. In 2016, the top five films at the box office were four animation films (*The Secret Life of Pets*, *Ice Age: Collision Course*, *Zootopia*, *The Angry Bird Movie*) and a European coproduction about the life of a Latvian journalist in Stalin's Siberian work camps in the early 1940s (*Melanijas hronika*) (UNIC 2017). In 2017, the top five pictures at the box-office were the local hit *Maktub*, two animations (*Despicable Me 3*, *Boss Baby*), and one action film (*The Fate of the Furious*). That year the top spot was exceptionally occupied by a superhero film, *Wonder Woman*, starring . . . Israeli actress Gal Gadot (UNIC 2018).

In terms of film sector, Israel stands as a case study on fixed monopolistic structuration. In terms of film tastes, it points to the eminently transnational nature of film culture, with bridges linking Israel both to Europe, through the ancestry of its inhabitants, and to the US, with the special attraction of Jewish-American and Israeli talent active in Hollywood.

Egypt: Protecting National Cinema

The Egyptian market is characterized by a tight control exercised not only by private companies but by the state as well. The film sector is managed by a few vertically integrated companies. Founded in 2000, the Al Arabia Cinema production and distribution company is also the most important exhibitor in the country, through its chain Renaissance

(S. Ali 2012b, 57).[8] It currently manages twelve multiscreen theaters in Cairo, Alexandria, and Suez.[9] The other major player is the trio Oscar/ Al Massa/Al Nasr (Shawky 2016, 174). The companies distributing US films are similarly part of vertically integrated groups. Misr International, the production company founded by Youssef Chahine in 1972 and now led by the Khoury family, also operates two multiplexes (American Plaza, Point 90 Cinema) and one art-house cinema (Zawya) in Cairo.[10] It also distributes art-house films through Zawya Distribution, and commercial Egyptian and foreign blockbusters through MIF Distribution. Since the early 2000s, it has had a partnership with Allied Films Distribution, the Egyptian subsidiary of Lebanese distribution company Italia Film, distributor of Walt Disney, Columbia, and US independent films in the Middle East (Saliby interview).[11] United Motion Pictures (UMP), sole distributor for Warner Bros. and Twentieth Century-Fox in Egypt, also has shares in circuits in Cairo and Alexandria through its subsidiary Silver Screen.[12] UMP, for example, manages the Amir Cinema in Alexandria, a cinema formerly owned by Twentieth-Century Fox (Zeind interview of 2013). While the film sector presents an oligopolistic structure, it is also tightly controlled by the state.

The protectionist measures devised in the late 1940s (chapter 4) have been maintained in the twenty-first century. The presence of foreign films has been discouraged through various means. The number of copies allowed to circulate, which was limited to 2 in the 1960s, rose to 3 in the 1980s, and 4 in the 1990s.[13] By 2008, the number had increased to 8.[14] Cinema owners have to pay a 20% tax on foreign films, as opposed to 5% for national films (Layadi 2013, 6). There are import duties as well (Layadi 2013, 6). Screening seasons are also limited; foreign films are not to be released during the most profitable periods (the summer, the religious celebration of the Eid and the Ramadan).[15] This strongly protectionist system has enabled Egypt to be one of the rare countries in the world where national films hold the box office. In the early twenty-first century, Egyptian films routinely represented 80% of the box office, with Hollywood films holding the remaining share (Layadi 2013, 6). Egyptian authorities have not only limited the physical presence of US films, but also their content through very strict censorship procedures.

Egypt has a rating system based on two categories: General Audiences and Adult. Scrutiny of the films released in the General Audiences is very strict. Religion is a particularly touchy issue that has led the censorship committee to refuse release permits to a number of US films, such as DreamWorks' *Prince of Egypt* (1998) that contravened Islamic prohibition to visually represent God and the prophets (Mingant 2012; Mansour 2012, 11). *Da Vinci Code* (2006) was banned a few years later for fear that its plot, which called into question the Holy Scriptures, would upset the Christian communities in the country and create sectarian strife (Mingant 2012). *The Matrix Reloaded* (2003) was also banned on religious grounds. Madkour Thabet, head of Egypt's Department of Monitoring Artistic Products, explained that a committee comprised of academics, psychologists, sociologists, and writers had found that,

> despite high artistic and technical levels, the film deals explicitly with issues of creation and existence related to the three monotheistic religions we all respect and believe. This includes discussions of the issue of the Creator and the created, the origins of creation, free will and predestination and other theological issues that have caused controversies and tension.[16]

Beside the religious argument, there were "scenes of excessive violence [that] could cause harm to social peace and affirm the concept of the culture of violence."[17] Politics is another bone of contention. *Exodus: Gods and King* (2014) was thus banned for historical inaccuracies on the apparent claim that "Moses and the Jews built the pyramids."[18] Egyptian culture minister Gaber Asfour explained, "It is a Zionist film. [. . .] It gives a Zionist view of history."[19] *You Don't Mess with the Zohan* (2008) epitomizes all the elements that are likely to block distribution. The film tells the story of a former Mossad agent, played by Jewish-American comedian Adam Sandler, who flees to New York and finds a job as a hairdresser in the city's Palestinian neighborhood. Its satirically irreverent tone, political subject, and hero's obsession with sex were more than enough to have the film banned in Egypt.[20] Though spectacular, bans are only the visible tip of the censorship iceberg. Film distributors interviewed for this book list other means to prevent film distribution, from making the bureaucratic procedure last for six months, as happened to *Meet Joe Black* (1998) and *The Matrix* (1999), to refusing to subtitle offensive portions of the film, as happened with the final speech in *The Devil's Advocate* (1997) (Mansour 2012, 10). Another routine procedure is to cut scenes involving nudity (10). This operation is carried out by distributors of US movies before submitting them to the committee.

As in other markets, such strong censorship has led to a thriving informal sector. After the announcement that *The Matrix Reloaded* was to be banned, pirate DVDs were sold "for three times the regular rate on the black market."[21] Piracy of satellite pay-TV is also important.[22] Egypt has, in fact, featured in every Special 301 report of the USTR since 1989, and is currently on the watch list (USTR 2018). The US Trade Representative reports have regularly pointed out the high level of piracy, both in video and on satellite television. They have also signalled the lack of enforcement, of strong customs control, of deterrent sanctions, and of training of Intellectual Property Rights enforcement officials and especially judges. Invariably, the Report has noted that, from the US point of view, "challenges and concerns remain" (USTR 2018). The film distributors interviewed, however, all resignedly pointed to the fact that authorities have other priorities given the tense political context.

Over the past two decades, two events of a different nature have modified the context for Hollywood films in Egypt. The late 1990s was marked by the revival of the Egyptian film market. The surprise hit *Ismailia Rayeh Gay* (1997) led to the increased production of commercial comedies drawing large audiences (Mansour 2012, 5). At the same time, the exhibition sector underwent a process of renovation, with the turn to multiplex theaters. As early as 1998, the Renaissance circuit planned the opening of 100 screens.[23] In 2002, six new multiplexes opened in Cairo and Alexandria.[24] The trend towards multiplexing triggered a change in terms of audience, as noted a journalist in 2005: "For decades, dilapidated cinemas alienated the middle and upper classes, who didn't want to walk down an aisle littered with pumpkin seeds to sit in a seat with broken springs."[25] The luxury multiplexes built in suburban malls offered a new experience, drawing in family audiences that had hitherto fled theaters (Awad interview). The revival of the film market also meant changes for distributors of US films. In the early 1990s, Italia Film used to sell its films for a flat fee to Egyptian distributors. As the market started booming again, it founded a local branch, AFD, and allied with the established local company Misr International (Saliby interview). The multiplication of the number of available screens led distributors to ask for an increase in the quota of American films. For the release of *Titanic* (1997), for instance, UMP CEO Antoine Zeind obtained five prints in 1998. The film set a box-office record in Egypt, grossing more than $2 million.[26] In 2005, the distributors' argument that more screens meant the need for more prints was heeded by the state and the quota for foreign films was raised to eight.[27] The national cinema still remained strongly favored, since there was no limitation on its number of prints. By that time, Egypt was described by *Variety* as a "fairly vibrant market."[28] The trend toward state-of-the art movie theaters has continued in the 2000s and 2010s. Misr International Films spearheaded the turn toward new technologies, opening an IMAX theater in Cairo in 2012 and two MX4D screens in 2016.[29] The dynamic exhibition sector has also attracted foreign investors, such as the UAE shopping mall company Majid Al Futtaim, which operates twenty-eight screens in Egypt through its chain VOX Cinemas.[30] Reports on the number of screens vary from 382, estimated by Layadi (2013, 6) in 2011 to 221, estimated by the UNESCO in 2015 (UIS 2021). As in other countries, however, the new multiplex experience has been only accessible to the middle-class urban audiences. In the Nile Delta, Upper Egypt, and in the urban peripheries, one-screen cinemas still exist. While the ticket price is cheap, the theaters are uncomfortable, still using 35 mm prints. Those second-category cinemas cater to an audience belonging to lower classes living far away from the IMAX and 4DX movie experiences (Shawky 2016, 171).

The second event that shifted the place of Hollywood films is the 2011 revolution. The immediate consequence of the revolution was a drastic decrease in movie attendance, notably due to the curfew (Fahim interview). Distributors postponed releases of their Egyptian films (*Tahrir 2011*, 2011) and US films (*Yogi Bear*, 2010).[31] Total box-office revenues fell from $66 million in 2010 to $37 million in 2011.[32] The revolution also had an unintended impact on national film production, which decreased (Awad interview) and continued to face harsh censorship, first under the Islamic rule of Mohamed Morsi (2012–2013), and then under the strong hand of Abdel Fattah al-Sissi.[33] During the unrest, many cinema owners did not respect the limitations on foreign films, preferring to offer noncommittal escapist films over national products.[34] In the immediate aftermath of the revolution, American films thus filled the void. In 2011, US films caught an unprecedented 50% of the total box-office receipts, with *Harry Potter and the Deathly Hallows: Part 2* (2011) obtaining $1.3 million, the highest revenue for a foreign film in Egypt.[35] After the revolution, the quota for US films was also increased to ten prints, with one additional print for IMAX films (Zeind interview of 2013). Quotas remain, however, very much in favor of the national cinema. An American blockbuster such as *Interstellar* (2014) was released with about eight prints, while up to forty prints of a local blockbuster like *El Gezira 2* (2014) were allowed to circulate, thus earning ten times more (Shawky 2016, 173). By 2018, the quotas had continued to evolve, with a marked favor toward the development of state-of-the art multiplex experience: distributors of American films were allowed ten prints in 2D and 3D, one print in IMAX, four prints in DBox immersive format, as well as two prints in 4DX. American films managed to keep on benefitting from this more favorable environment, holding 55% of the box office, while the share of Egyptian films has fallen to 45% (Zeind interview of 2018).

National cinema still remains at the heart of the Egyptian film experience, however. The two biggest Egyptian hits in 2017 were action films *El Khaleya* and *Horob Edterary*, each reaching a total revenue of about $3 million (elcinema.com). The other top films of the year were a drama (*Tsbah ala Kher*, $1,5 million), a historical drama (*EL Kenz*, $1 million), an action film (*Jawah Ieteqal*, $900,000), and a comedy *Khair W Baraka* ($560,000). When it comes to Hollywood films, blockbusters— whether action, superhero, or comedies—are the audience's favorites. *Gravity* (2013) was a big hit in 2013 with a revenue of $124,000 over five weeks (elcinema.com). Not only was the space action film impressive, but it also starred two dark-haired, brown-eyed stars, George Clooney and Sandra Bullock, close to the local beauty standards (Awad interview). American dramas and art-house fare are, however, generally spurned by Egyptian audiences. *Lincoln* (2013), for example, stayed only three weeks in cinemas, obtaining $12,000. Successful American films in 2017, with revenues ranging from $400,000 to $500,000 were action films (*The Mummy*, 2017), superhero films (*Spider-man: Homecoming, Thor: Ragnarok, Logan, Justice League*), and a horror film (*It*) (elcinema.com). The three top US films in 2017 were *Beauty and the Beast*, a children's live-action film that stayed for ten weeks in cinemas and grossed $597,000; *Anabelle: Creation*, a horror film that stayed nineteen weeks and grossed $798,000; and the record-breaking comedy action film *Jumanji: Welcome to the Jungle* that stayed twenty weeks in cinemas and grossed $1.4 million (elcinema. com). All the films were shown with Arabic subtitles. While a few studios apparently attempted to dub their animated films in the late 1990s, such as *Toy Story* (1995) and *The Lion King* (1994), all films are now shown with subtitles (Awad interview; Fahim interview). With the digital turn, subtitles formerly created in the Middle East in Egyptian Arabic, are now made in the US or in Great Britain in literary Arabic (Zeind interview of 2013). With the strong presence of national and American cinemas, there is little room for films from other countries. Hardly any European film is distributed in mainstream theaters (Fahim interview). As for Bollywood cinema, which was very successful in the 1970s and 1980s, it faced so many obstacles from Egyptian authorities that distribution altogether stopped in the 1990s. Zeind's attempts to revive the popularity of Indian cinema by distributing *Krrish 3* (2012), *Dhoom 3* (2013), and *Chennai Express* (2013) largely failed. Only the US-Indian production *My Name is Khan*

(2010) met any success, probably more due to its topic: a Muslim hero trying to pass on a message to the US president, "My name is Khan, and I am not a terrorist." Fans of Bollywood prefer to turn to satellite television and watch MBC Bollywood and Zee Aflam (Srour and Zeind 2016, 155, 158). The Egyptian film market stands as a revealing case study on several accounts. Decades-long nationalistic policies created one of the rare markets in which national films dominate the box office, thus creating a unique filmscape. State intervention, however, had strongly limited expression of local and foreign cinema and can be compared to other tighly controlled nations. Students of film industries will notice the film sector's tendency toward oligopolistic structure observed in many other countries around the world, as well as the strong link between the global multiplexing phenomenon and the development of big-budget 3D Hollywood action films.

Lebanon: Doors Wide Open to US Cinema

As a country that has been largely open to foreign cultural influences from the Western world, Lebanon offers a contrast to Egypt. In the 1990s, the challenge in Lebanon was to rebuild the market after the end of the civil war in 1990. Although the exhibition sector had badly suffered during the war, film distributors had continued their operations, managing distribution over other territories in the Middle East (chapter 5). Historical players thus quickly set out to reconstruct the market, choosing to join the global multiplexing trend. Film distribution veteran Hikmat Antypas invested in "American-style" multiplexes as early as 1994. Two years later, his company, the Circuit Planete theater chain, was managing 23 screens, including 21 in Beirut and 2 in Tripoli. Through his distribution company Four Star Films, Antypas had a guaranteed access to attractive US films from UIP (Universal, Paramount). The second largest exhibitor at the time was also a distribution company. The Haddad family's Empire company, which handled Fox and Columbia films, was managing 15 screens.[36] In 2007, UAE-based Lebanese film entrepreneur Selim Ramia joined the sector, opening Grand Cinemas theaters in Lebanon.[37] By 2012, there were 94 screens in Lebanon, spread over fifteen multiplexes. Exhibition was mostly in the hand of three companies, all with ties to distribution. Empire had 34 screens, Grand Cinemas 30, and Circuit Planète 15 (S. Ali 2013a, 85–86). By 2018, Majid Al Futtaim's UAE shopping mall company had 15 screens in Lebanon.[38] By the 2010s, the market was fully digital

(Ali 2013a, 85), and a Lebanese spectator visiting cinema platform CineK-lik was given a choice not only between different theaters, but between different cinema "experiences" as well: standard, Dolby Atmos sound, VIP and Gold services, 3D, 4D, and 4DX, IMAX, and theater in laser.[39]

In 1996, the success of Antypas's new multiplex theater in the Abraj area of central Beirut was especially put down to the opening film: *Mission: Impossible* (1996).[40] As in other countries, multiplexing has been accompanied by the strong presence of Hollywood films. In a country where no film policy exists to support the national industry, and where distributors have historically handled American films for the whole Middle East, the strong presence of Hollywood films at the box-office is unsurprising. American films have thus regularly held 90% of the market share (Saliby interview; Ali 2013a, 91; Layadi 2013, 7). The only local films that seem to have met success have been those of Nadine Labaki (Caillé and Sfeir 2016, 181). In 2011, *Where Do We Go Now?* was the top film at the box office, grossing $2.2 million, twice as much as the second film, *The Smurfs* (Layadi 2013, 7). *Where Do We Go Now?* was the third film in terms of grosses in the history of Lebanon, after *Titanic* and *Avatar* (Mingant and Chakra 2016, 193). The most successful Hollywood genres are animation for family audiences and action blockbusters, which are particularly appreciated by teenage audiences (Caillé and Sfeir 2016, 182; Saliby interview). In a country with a vibrant film festival culture, dramas can also find an audience (Saliby interview). Little room is left, however, for films beyond those from the US. French and European films do find a niche audience among the educated elite attending the Metropolis, while Egyptian cinema is favored by the working-class audiences (Caillé and Sfeir 2016, 181–82).

The Lebanese market presents a number of traits in common with other Middle Eastern markets. First, it has been plagued by piracy. Lebanon has appeared on the Special 301 report of the USTR lists since 1999, the year when the country implemented copyright legislation (Ali 2013a, 102). Illegal circulation of Hollywood films in Lebanon takes the usual forms of physical DVDs sold in the streets and pirate access to television channels (Ali 2013a, 102; Saliby interview; Chakra interview; USTR 2001). Cable piracy was a sensitive issue from 2001 to 2009. In 2001, the USTR report stated there were "over 1,000 cable operators in the country, many of whom retransmit[ed] domestic and foreign programming without authorization from right-holders," and by 2005, "well over 80 percent of Lebanon's cable subscribers view pirated content, one of the highest rates in the world" (USTR 2001, 2005). In spite of the existence of copyright legislation, enforcement has remained weak. The reports, however, took due note that the tense political context, such as the 2006 Israeli-Hezbollah war and the parliamentary paralysis between 2009 and 2018, makes IPR defense far from a priority (USTR 2007, 2018).[41]

In Lebanon, as in other Middle Eastern countries, the lack of political stability has impacted the film industry. During the 2006 war between Lebanon-based Hezbollah and Israel, the Empire circuit had to close all theaters but one. Audiences could not attend cinemas due to the destruction of roads and bridges, and distributors could not import film prints because of the blockade. Releases that were supposed to be day-and-date with the US had to be postponed. Empire theatrical director Bassam Eid noted that "usually we have 40,000 people a week coming to our theaters but for the past month we've only had 200."[42] As soon as a cease-fire was signed, theaters had to woo audiences back, offering cut-price tickets and donating part of their grosses to the Lebanese Red Cross.[43] The political stability necessary for the smooth running of the film business cannot be taken for granted. The tense political context that plagues the region is also sporadically visible through highly debated censorship cases. Censorship of foreign films, dealt with within the Directorate for General Security, is reputed to be quite lenient in Lebanon (Mingant 2012; Ali 2013a, 105). Sex, nudity, and even drug usage will routinely pass; politics, however, remains a sensitive issue (El-Azar interview; Mingant and Chakra 2016, 197). A reminder of the existence of the Israel boycott list (chapter 4) came with the banning of Steven Spielberg's *The Post* (2017). The director had been put on the blacklist after the release of *Schindler's List*, a 1993 World War II drama with scenes shot in Jerusalem.[44] In 2017, political motives had also been behind the banning of *Wonder Woman* (2017) due not only to the Israeli citizenship of main actress Gal Gadot, but also to her time in the Israeli Defense Force and her pro-Israel remarks.[45] The strict implementation of the Israel boycott seems variable, however, as the release of Spielberg's *Bridge of Spies* (2015) and *The BFG* (2016) suggests, as well as the first—and more minor—appearance of Gadot as Wonder Woman in *Batman vs. Superman: Dawn of Justice* (2016).[46] More recently, the banning of horror film *The Nun* (2018) on religious grounds illustrates that politics remains a very complicated issue even in one of the reputedly more liberal-minded countries in the area.[47]

In the early twenty-first century, a number of countries in the Middle East are closed to commercial distribution of Hollywood films for geopolitical reasons. In North Africa, the markets officially exist but the exhibition sector is struggling to varying degrees. Israel, Egypt, and

Lebanon are, in effect, the only territories commercially functioning and open to Hollywood films. The three historical markets present a number of similarities: a stable—even locked in—film structure around a small number of players, a thriving exhibition sector that does not suffer exceedingly from existing piracy and that underwent renovation through multiplexing, and a vulnerability to geopolitical crises. Each, however, retains a strongly individual identity, directly linked to its past. The trace of European immigration is felt in the genres and stories favored in Israel; the legacy of Nasser's nationalistic vision—and policies—is reflected in the strong success of Egyptian films; and the history of Lebanon as a cultural crossroads shows in its making room both for Hollywood blockbusters and European, as well as a few North African and Middle Eastern, auteur films. The strength of each market is also visible in the fact that each has its own local distributors. For US distributions companies, the three markets are actually to be separated into two categories. While the US companies work with all three territories from their London offices, different executives are in charge of Israel and of the two Middle Eastern markets, a legacy of the regional film distribution structure break after the creation of Israel (chapter 4). In the 1950s, nationalistic policies in Egypt had moved the heart of the Hollywood film distribution system to Lebanon, a country with an established film-going habit and openness to other cultures. During the civil war, the country had maintained its importance through the activity of its local film distributors. As the home base to key regional distributors, Lebanon is today valued less for its size—it is a small market—than for its symbolic importance. The influence of Lebanese distributors was long visible in the presence of both Arabic and French subtitles on prints circulated throughout the Middle East, even in territories that had not been colonized by France (El-Azar interview). By the early twenty-first century, Lebanese film distributors continued as key players, as the heart of Hollywood film circulation shifted East once more, to the Gulf region.

9

Film Boom in the Gulf

NOTHING PREDESTINED THE Gulf region to become a dynamic film market in the twenty-first century. For decades, Hollywood films had trickled to the area, originally distributed in movie halls within the Western compounds of petroleum companies such as Shell Oil in Qatar, Aramco in Saudi Arabia, and BAPCO in Bahrain and strictly restricted to Europeans (Kamalipour 1994, 239, 253; Oruc 2020, 20). British colonial personnel in fact resisted to the establishment of movie theaters open to the local population in Bahrain. Stringently rejecting requests by South-Asian and Iranian entrepreneurs to establish commercial cinemas for a decade, Charles Belgrave, British advisor to the government of Bahrain, finally had to reconcile himself to allowing the opening of the first commercial public cinema in 1937 (Oruc 2020, 24–27). Situated in Manama, the Bahrain Cinema, operated by Hussein Yateem, opened with Umm Kulthum's *Wedad* (1936) (Oruc 2020, 27). A second theater was opened only after World War II, by an "entrepreneur from India, S.M.G. Badshah (apparently encouraged by the physical dilapidation and permit expiration of the Bahrain Cinema)" (27). In the late 1940s, the Bahraini theaters were showing mostly Egyptian and Indian films (31). In the 1950s, Bahrain had 5 commercial cinemas. In Kuwait, the 1954-created Kuwait Cinema Company opened 3 theaters in the decade (Oruc 2020, 31). Though a few countries in the Gulf had had operational movie theaters since the 1950s, these had declined after the arrival of VHS technology in the 1980s. In the early 1990s, there were 3 movie theaters in Bahrain and 5 in Qatar, showing mostly Indian films for Asian expatriate workers (Kamalipour and Mowlana 1994, 39–40, 240). The few theaters in Oman, Muscat, and Salalah were generally attended by US, British, and Indian expatriates (193). Kuwait's 14 movie theaters were destroyed in the 1991 Gulf War, and only 7 were subsequently rebuilt by the National Company of Kuwaiti Cinema, which has a monopoly on exhibition and distribution (155). Jordan counted 45 cinemas, half of them in Amman, but they had a low attendance rate (136–37). As for the United Arab Emirates (UAE), the federation of seven emirates (Abu Dhabi, Ajman, Dubai, Fujairah, Ras al-Khaimah, Sharjah, Umm al-Quwain), which was to be the center of the film boom in the early twenty-first century, it was still a young nation, born in 1971, and lay largely outside the paths of film circulation. This area with few movie theaters, no film industry, and no film culture was turned into a dynamic film market in two decades partly through the efforts of two pioneers: Ahmed Golchin and Salim Ramia.

A Film Market is Born

Ahmed Golchin migrated from Iran to Dubai in the 1960s (Srour 2018, 369). Forced to stay in Dubai after his identity papers were stolen, the young Iranian publisher decided to launch into film distribution. He bought used prints of Indian, Arab, Iranian, British, and US films from Lebanese distributors and organized film showings in Dubai (370). In 1971, Golchin became a UAE citizen. As better-quality movie theaters were opened in Jumeirah, Dubai, Golchin tried to obtain films at the Cannes film market. No major film company, however, was interested in this unknown market. In the 1970s, Golchin became "the number one distributor of independent films in the Middle East, in Bahrain, Qatar, Kuwait, Dammam, Jordan and Egypt" (quoted in Srour 2018, 372). He was also developing partnerships with businessmen from India, Lebanon, Egypt, Australia, and South Africa in order to improve the exhibition and distribution market in Dubai (Srour 2018, 372). Selim Ramia was also active in film distribution in Dubai in the 1970s. Originally working in the record industry in his native Lebanon, Ramia made a first foray into film distribution in Dubai between 1975 and 1979. After forming a distribution company in Lebanon, he came back to Dubai in 1986, competing with Golchin.[1]

In 1989, the two men decided to partner, creating a company origi-nally called 2001 Films. Renamed Gulf Film two years later, the company distributed independent films, and became the agent for Paramount and Universal for the Gulf region (Srour 2018, 372). Ramia himself insists on the pioneering nature of their company, as "in the Gulf in particular, cinemas were a foreign concept, and so was the idea of a centralized distribution network for international titles."[2] Starting the film business, meant not only rationalizing distribution, but also developing exhibition, and in 1992, Golchin and Ramia leased a cinema in the Al Nasr Club in Dubai, calling it the Al Nasr Cinema, refurbished it, and opened it in September with Eastwood's *Unforgiven* (1992). The movie was a flop, and the cinema was saved only by the release of *The Bodyguard* (1992) three months later.[3] Attracting audiences was an uphill task at the time, as cinema-going was reputed to be an activity for the laboring classes patronizing Bollywood films, but Golchin and Ramia's renovated theater introduced a new vision of cinema, and middle-class viewers started attending during the weekends (Salem interview).[4] While the second half of the 1990s was marked by the opening of new cinemas in Dubai, Abu Dhabi, and Sharjah, film exhibition became a "big business" only in 2000, with the creation of Golchin and Ramia's exhibition company Grand Cinemas, and the opening of two multiplexes: a 9-screen cinema in Al Mariah Mall, Abu Dhabi, and the 12-screen Grand Cineplex in Dubai (Srour 2018, 373).[5] Between 1995 and 2003, under the influence of Golchin, Ramia, and other entrepreneurs, the number of screens in the UAE quadrupled to 142, leading to an admission rise of more than 160%.[6] Grand Cinemas soon became the leading exhibition chain in the Gulf region, absorbing rival companies Al Massa Cinemas in 2003 and Century Cinemas in 2006 (373). By 2011, the number of screens in the UAE had reached 250.[7] In 2014, Grand Cinemas was rebranded Novo Cinema. In 2018, it operated 4 theaters in Qatar, 1 in Bahrain, and 9 in the United Arab Emirates. The Grand Cinemas brand still exists. Based in Lebanon and owned by Selim Ramia and Co., it presents itself as "the leading cinema chain in Lebanon, Jordan and Kuwait," operating 1 theater in Bahrain, 2 in Jordan, two in Kuwait and 6 in Lebanon.[8]

Entrepreneurs from other sectors soon joined the exhibition boom. In Dubai, movie theaters have become part of the strategy of real estate companies branching out into leisure activities such as malls, aquariums, ice rinks, and safari parks. Emaar Entertainment Co. operates Reel Cinemas, and Meraas operates Roxy Cinemas. While Reel Cinemas and Roxy Cinemas are located within Dubai's urban projects, UAE shopping mall company Majid Al Futtaim has invested regionally through its VOX Cinemas company, operating 345 screens over 35 locations, in the UAE

(186 screens), Oman (47), Bahrain (30), Egypt (28), Qatar (18), Kuwait (17), and Lebanon (15).[9] In Oman, for example, Majid Al Futtaim allied with the Oman Arab Cinema Company and the Jawad Sultan family to open City Cinema, the country's largest exhibition chain with 9 theaters.[10] In Kuwait, the real estate group Tamdeen Holdings renovated the state Cinescape theaters in the 2000s (Mingant and Chakra 2016, 199). In Jordan, many cinemas in Amman, such as Taj Cinemas, were opened through a collaboration between Al Taher Cinemas, a branch of Omani construction, engineering, trading, and real estate company Al-Taher Group, historical exhibitor Selim Ramia and Co., and regional film distributor Eagle Films.[11] While the original impetus came from the development of the UAE market by two Iranian and Lebanese entrepreneurs, the exhibition boom expanded all over the Gulf region, sustained by a collaboration between real estate groups, on the one hand, and film exhibition and distribution companies, on the other.

The historical Lebanese distributors quickly identified the opportunities of the newly born market. Italia Films, which distributes Disney, DreamWorks, and US and European independent films, opened an office in Dubai in the late 1990s.[12] So did Empire, after the success of *Titanic*. In 2004, Lebanese company Joseph Chacra and Sons, distributor for Warner Bros., set up a sister company, Shooting Stars, in Dubai to cater to the new Gulf market.[13] Four Star Films, the distributor for Universal and Paramount, decided to partner with local giant Gulf Film for the Gulf area.[14] By the late 2010s, Lebanese distributors such as Empire International (Twentieth Century-Fox, Sony Pictures, DreamWorks Animation), Eagle Films (independent US films), and Jaguar Film International (independent US films) all had offices both in Beirut and Dubai. The UAE also attracted Lebanese-Italian Gianluca Chakra, son of film distributor Michael Chakra, as he established his company Front Row Entertainment in Dubai in 2003. Two years later, Front Row had signed a key strategic alliance with the state-owned Kuwait National Cinema Company, reinforcing its status as the leading distributor of independent US films.[15]

The rapid development of the UAE theatrical market, through the efforts of regional exhibitors and distributors, started to attract the attention of the Hollywood majors around 2007–2008 (Viane interview).[16] Between 2009 and 2010, admissions in the UAE grew by 94% to 11.8 million. That year, the growth in the Chinese market had been 64%.[17] The number of tickets sold between 2008 and 2012 has increased by 75% in the UEA and 112% in Oman.[18] The rise continued in 2012–2013 with an increase in attendance of 15% in the UAE, 30% in Kuwait, 45%

in Bahrain, and 60% in Oman (El-Azar interview). Between June and December 2015, there were 100 new screens in the UAE, 45 in Qatar, and 13 in Kuwait (Mingant and Chakra 2016, 191). As the region's power of attraction was growing, the perspectives seemed endless to film professionals (El-Azar interview; Mingant and Chakra 2016, 191). One could hope for long-lasting growth, as the market was based on sound foundations. The steady economic rise of the Gulf countries over the past thirty years had led to the development of a wealthy middle class. The Gulf region attracted both foreign companies and tourists (Mingant and Chakra 2016, 191).[19] The 2012 per capita GDP in the UAE and Qatar was actually comparable to developed economies (Mingant 2016a, 140). The population's disposable income has thus enabled exhibitors to fix high ticket prices (Cripps 2013; Chakra interview). Besides, cinema appeared as a welcome leisure opportunity in Gulf countries where alcohol consumption and night clubs are largely banned, and restaurants too expensive or inexistent (Saliby interview; Salem interview; Chakra interview). In Kuwait, where nightclubs and alcohol consumption are forbidden, people routinely go to the cinema two to three times a week (Chakra interview). A second element of stability is the managing of the film market by a small number of historical companies. The Hollywood distributors deal with companies that have distributed their films sometimes for decades. Based on such track records, these partners are considered as reliable and trustworthy. Distribution deals can be run all the more smoothly as the expected results are quite predicable. The Gulf region thus has all the elements of a fully operational film market: a solid audience base as well as a stable exhibition and distribution sector. Although the region has been plagued by piracy, and copyright enforcement has not been, from the point of view of American distributors, up to US standards, this has not been a major obstacle to the general growth rate (El-Azar interview; Saliby interview; Viane interview; Chakra interview).

By the 2010s, the Gulf region has become an extremely profitable market for Hollywood. Although the Middle East does not seem important in terms of box-office revenues compared to other markets for US films, it is highly so in terms of profitability. In the Gulf, very little money is spent on marketing, which mostly consists in US trailers and theater marketing material such as standees, posters, and banners. Once they deduct the low print and advertising (P&A) from the box-office revenue, US distributors find themselves with a profit margin that can reach about 90%, as opposed to 20%–30% in other markets (Mingant 2015b, 81). A former Hollywood major sales manager for the EMEA

(Europe, Middle East, and Africa) region noted that, in the late 2000s, the Middle East had the fourth most profitable margin for his company (81). Around 2010, Italia Films was named "Disney's most profitable and Biggest Contributor Sub-Distributor Market" for five years in a row (81). Within the Middle East, the UAE is the most important market in terms of revenues, followed by Kuwait, Qatar, Bahrain, Lebanon, Oman, Jordan, and Egypt. In terms of number of tickets sold, the list would be UAE, Kuwait, Lebanon, Bahrain, Egypt, Qatar, Oman, and Jordan (El-Azarint- erview). When one considers profitability, the Middle East as a block can be placed after Western countries such as Great Britain, France, Spain, and Italy, but before countries from Northern and Eastern Europe such as Denmark, the Netherlands, Poland, and Hungary (Haddad interview). By the 2010s, the Middle East could be estimated to belong to the top 15 markets for the Hollywood majors. The December 2017 announce- ment by Saudi Arabia's Ministry of Culture that movie theaters were to be allowed in the country as of 2018, as part of the Vision 2030 social and economic reform program, opened further vistas for growth in the area. In 2018, *Variety* noted that, "with a population of 32 million, 70% of whom are under the age of 30, and a relatively affluent citizenry, some analysts expect that Saudi Arabia could eventually produce $1 billion in revenues and be among the top 10 markets for theatrical revenues."[20] AMC chair Adam Aron summarized the huge hopes raised thus: "Where else are you going to find a movie market that does not exist today that could be a billion dollars three or five years from now?"[21]

The Gulf market has, indeed, not only caught the eye of Hollywood distributors, but also of North American exhibitors. IMAX, the Canadian large-format movie exhibition company, identified the region's potential as early as 2005, with a deal to open an IMAX screen at the Scientific Centre of Kuwait.[22] Through deals with local partners such as Gulf Film (now Novo Cinemas), Vox Cinemas, and Cinema City, IMAX had steadily expanded its presence in the Middle East. By 2018, there were 20 the- aters offering IMAX in Jordan, Kuwait, Qatar, Oman, Bahrain, and the UAE. In 2018, IMAX also opened its first screen in the newly opened Vox Cinemas theater at Riyadh Park Mall in Saudi Arabia.[23] The first license to operate movie theaters in Saudi Arabia was actually granted to US exhibition chain AMC, which opened its first theater there in April 2018.[24] Distributors of films and TV programs on other platforms also entered the new market. The Hollywood major companies' television branches turned their attention to the UAE market, especially with the development of satellite television (chapter 6). In the 2010s, NBC

Universal, Sony, Fox, and Disney opened direct television distribution offices in the UAE.[25] Distribution through VOD platforms also started developing. Front Row Entertainment established itself as a key player in this area in 2014, when it became the sole official iTunes Aggregator for the Middle East, providing the platform with independent, Bollywood, and Arabic content. Front Row Entertainment signed further aggregation deals with GooglePlay and YouTube as well as S-VOD platform Netflix in 2016.[26] The new audiences in the Gulf have thus enjoyed a wide and state-of-the-art access to films.

Film Culture between Modernity and Tradition

The beginning of the twenty-first century marked the birth of a film culture in a region that had hitherto been virtually a *"cinéphile* desert" (Weissberg, quoted in Yunis 2014, 280). This culture has, however, developed in a tug-of-war between modernity and tradition. As cinema-going has developed with the introduction of state-of-the art multiplexes, the budding film culture is linked to new technologies. Cinema chains have been competing to offer the newest innovations. In fact, cinema-going is first and foremost marketed as a technological experience. Visitors of the Novo Cinemas website in 2018 were invited to "search for a movie, location, experience or language."[27] The website advertised 3D technology, inviting the audience to "take a sensory thrill-ride." MX4D technology would allow the spectator to "take part in the action," while IMAX offered "larger than life entertainment."[28] In this context, the film itself takes second stage, becoming the vessel through which the technological innovations are to be enjoyed. Cinemas hold a similar function to that of a park ride and stand on par with other exciting experiences such as waterparks, laser mazes, and inflatable playgrounds.[29] Reel Cinemas' parent corporation, property developing company Emaar, unambiguously describes itself as "the provider of premium entertainment and leisure choices."[30]

In addition to the technological attraction, movie theaters have developed a variety of premium services. Novo Cinemas offers to let one "experience cinema in the lap of luxury," with "the opulent luxury of premium recliner seating," "gourmet dining menu [. . .] served by your very own butler," and "private entrance."[31] Roxy Cinema Box Park in Dubai offers the first "boutique cinema experience," with "hand-stitched Italian leather-trimmed seats," "gourmet menu," and Western-style "retro interiors and ambience."[32] These premium offers also target families. The

Roxy Mamas offer invites mother to attend the cinema with their small children. The Platinum Lounge is presented as the place to chat with friends before the film, and the session is made comfortable by the large Platinum Plus seats "big enough for you to kick back and cuddle with your baby."[33] Cinema thus becomes an experience to be understood in terms of the technology and services offered. These luxury services are only enjoyed, however, by the wealthiest (Mingant and Chakra 2016, 191).[34] The multiplex audience is comprised of the wealthy local elite and executive expatriates (Cripps 2013). In 2018, VIP tickets cost about $43, 4DX tickets $25, IMAX 2D tickets $17, and 3D tickets $14. Most people would thus go to the regular 2D ticket priced at about $10, including a voucher for food and beverage. Even for the majority who buy regular tickets only, the VIP experience, although often inaccessible, can be viewed as a new cinema norm.

While the experience around the films is marked by innovation and modernity, the films themselves have been shaped by the strength of traditions in the Gulf area through multifaceted censorship. In the UAE, there is an age classification system, whose aim is "preserving the values of the UAE society and its cultural heritage, and [. . .] protecting children from the negative influences from various media platforms including movies, videos, electronic games and video games, as well as comic books and printed and online books."[35] Films are examined by two committees: the first decides on a classification, the second on whether cuts should be made.[36] Hollywood films are routinely cut before they reach screens in the Gulf area in general. Kuwait, which banned 62 films in 2010 and 47 in 2011, is considered to be the strictest country, followed by Qatar and the UAE, while Jordan is reputed to be more liberal (Mingant 2012).[37] A film distributor interviewed for this volume notes that, for the same Hollywood film, 2 to 3 scenes would be cut for the UAE, 5 to 6 for Bahrain, and 20 to 25 for Kuwait. As in other areas of the world, the key issues are nudity, religion, and politics. Scenes involving nudity, sex, or simply kissing are routinely cut.[38] For instance, the romcom *Love and Other Drugs* (2010) was banned in the UAE for "excessive sexual content,"[39] and *Girl on the Train* (2016) in Qatar because it had sex scenes and focused on drinking problems.[40] Homosexuality is also a strong taboo in countries where it is considered a moral perversion and punishable by law (Hammond 2007, 43). *Black Swan* (2010), *Brüno* (2009), and *Brokeback Mountain* (2005) were all banned (Mingant 2012). Films touching upon political issue are also most likely to be targeted. *Syriana* (2005), which explores the shady relations between the Gulf countries and the US, was banned in Jordan.[41] In the UAE, two minutes were cut, especially a scene depicting migrant Asian workers roughly handled by the police in a Gulf country (Mingant 2012). Censorship strikes films that depict both Gulf authorities and their allies in a negative light. For instance, Kuwaiti authorities banned *Fahrenheit 9/11* (2004), as they considered the film insulted two key allies: the US and Saudi Arabia.[42] One particularly tense political issue remains the relationship with Israel. The Israel Boycott Office for example has a representative on the board of the UAE censorship committee.[43] While *Wonder Woman* was released in the UAE, Oman, and Bahrain, it was banned in Qatar and was nearly banned in Jordan.[44] Today not all Hollywood films are affected by censorship to the same degree. Small-budget comedies or politically committed films, originally created with a Western audience in mind, are more likely to encounter trouble. On the other hand, the majority of bigger-budget Hollywood films, which are from the start conceived for PG and PG-13 ratings, are well-adapted to international distribution, especially in countries with strict censorship systems (Mingant 2012).

Though mainstream Hollywood films are released on Gulf countries screens, censorship is a major obstacle for distributors. One difficulty is the lack of unity in censorship criteria, which forces them to try and meet the varying demands from different committees (Mingant 2012). The process is also time-consuming, from the red tape in each country, to sending the required cuts to the US producers for approval, to contacting the London office so the DCP can be digitally adapted. And in an era when films are released day-and-date to fight piracy, time is of the essence. The process of modifying the DCP is also costlier than was the cutting of the physical print. Although accepted by distributors as part of the business, censorship is thus a key determinant to film distribution in the area. It also directly impacts viewer's experience. One can consider that Gulf countries spectators do not have access to the film version intended by the director, but to a localized version, adapted to what authorities believe to be the desirable cultural and moral standard. The audience is fully aware that the films are cut. They have access to the same films through legal channels, such as pay-TV OSN, as well as through illegal channels. Yet in spite of censorship, people still go to the cinema. Pointing out that Kuwait both has the strictest censorship and the highest screen average in the Middle East, a local distributor offers two explanations: the audience is used to cuts, and, although the "films are unwatchable," "it's their only entertainment." The strict control over film content cannot but participate in the shifting of the emphasis from the film to the technological and service experience.

With their focus on state-of-the art production value and a PG-13 audience, Hollywood films combine the main ingredients guaranteeing access to and success in the Gulf markets. In the 2010s, US films held about 85% of the market share in the UAE.[45] In Jordan, the share of Hollywood films reached 90%.[46] In the Gulf countries in general, US films have held on average 50% (Saliby interview). American films are followed by Bollywood films, which hold about 20% to 30% of the GCC[47] market (Saliby interview) and are particularly aimed at the large Asian population in the region. Up to 60% of the Gulf population is of Asian origin (Mingant and Chakra 2016, 193). The other important cinema in the region is Egyptian films, which make up 10% to 15% of the box office (Saliby interview). The mix varies for each country. In Jordan, films favored at the box office come from the US (90%) and Egypt (10%).[48] In 2010, in the UAE, Bollywood films held about 10% of the market and Egyptian films 3%.[49] The decreasing Egyptian production in the 2010s might, however, very well be replaced by a new entrant on the film scene: UAE cinema. Abu Dhabi is a case in point of the new interest for media and film production in the country. In 2007–2008, the emirate launched a diversification strategy focused on knowledge-based economy, thus preparing for the post-oil era. In the space of two years, Abu Dhabi set up filming infrastructures, a film production support program, training opportunities, a film festival, and a state-supported film production company, Image Nation (Mingant 2018, 169–80; Mingant and Tirtaine 2018, 282–95). On November 28, 2018, Novo cinemas in the UAE offered 4 Arabic-language films: 1 from Egypt (*Gunshot*) and 3 from the UAE (*Hajwala 2, Shabab Sheyab, 11 Days*). Diversity also characterized films coming from India. In the top fifteen films at the UAE box office for November 15–18, 2018, 5 films were from India: 2 in Hindi (*Thugs of Hindostan, Badhaai Ho,*), 2 in Tamil (*Sarkar, Kaatrin Mozhi*), and 1 in Mayalayam (*Mangalyam Thanthunanena*).[50] The first films released in the new Saudi cinemas confirm a cultural landscape based on mainstream films from the US (*Black Panther, The Emoji Movie, Sicario*), India (*Kaala*), and Egypt (*El Badla*).[51] In terms of genre, action is the most popular in the area (Mingant and Chakra 2016, 192). Six of the UAE box-office top ten for 2010 were Hollywood action films, such as *Avatar, Prince of Persia: The Sands of Time*, and *Iron Man 2*.[52] While action attracts young people, families are drawn to animation and family films, such as *Despicable Me* (2010) and *The Smurfs* (2011) (El-Azar interview). In 2010, *Shrek Forever After* was the second film at the box office in the UAE.[53] A third genre is particularly popular in the Gulf: horror (El-Azar interview); films such as *Anabelle: Creation* (2017) and *Halloween* (2018) found enthusiastic audiences in the area.

This young cinema culture based on mainstream movies and luxury theaters relegates many films and spectators to the margins. European cinema, for example, benefits neither from the high production quality of Hollywood cinema nor from the cultural proximity of Egyptian, UAE, and Indian cinemas. In 2013, French cinema took 0.6% of the UAE market share (Mingant, Renouard, and Baubiat 2016, 162). Language seems to be a key issue. In a region with a diverse population including locals and Western and Asian expatriates, English, which is spoken by 90% of the population, has become the lingua franca (Chakra interview). The only French productions that have made a mark on the UAE market so far have been action films financed by French conglomerates but shot in English with Hollywood stars, for instance *The Family* (2013), *Lucy* (2014), and *Collision* (2013) (Mingant, Renouard, and Baubiat 2016, 164). In 2014, Gulf Film, Novo Cinemas, and the French Institute in the UAE launched the Ciné 13 initiative which aimed at releasing one English-dubbed French film a month (Mingant, Renouard, and Baubiat 2016, 165). British films fare better due to the country's historical link with the region (194). Many, however, are, in fact, coproductions with the US, such as *The King's Speech* (2010), *Les Misérables* (2012), and *Johnny English Strikes Again* (2018). While the preference for mainstream films marginalizes cinemas perceived as art-house, the luxury associated with cinema-going excludes spectators who cannot afford to pay $10 or more. Old theaters, with 1,000-seat halls, still exist. The cinema experience is thus clearly divided between top theaters offering a mix of mainstream American, Arabic, and Indian films to the wealthy elite, and second-class theaters offering Bollywood films to the laboring classes (Mingant and Chakra 2016, 193; Haddad interview). The tale of booming development of the exhibition and distribution sector in the past twenty years seems to draw the portrait of a capitalist success story, with a market being suddenly born, rapidly growing, and largely open to US film distributors through their collaboration with local companies. The dominance of the multiplex film culture, with its emphasis on technology and the spectacular, places the Gulf region within a strong global trend. This should not, however, cloud the very diversity of film cultures that also exist in this region, where the luxury cinema experience is offered only to the urban middle class, and where the very diversity of the population present points to a variety of tastes, in terms of genre and language, as well as a variety of access, from cinema to television screens.

Conclusion

THE HISTORY OF HOLLYWOOD films in North Africa and the Middle East is not simply a one-directional affair, but stands at the intersection of commercial, political, and cultural issues, involving a variety of players, from film companies to state authorities to audiences. In its exploration of film markets during the colonial era, part 1 showed that scrutinizing the circulation of Hollywood film in North Africa and the Middle East meant not simply studying each market separately, but rather uncovering regional dynamics, as well as transnational exchanges with Europe. The circulation of Hollywood film in North Africa and the Middle East today is similarly dipped in transnational issues and experiences. Commercial film distribution has often been a regional affair, which remains true to this day with the large number of territories covered by Lebanese distribution companies. Similarly, Saudi television channels were always meant to have a regional reach. Informal circulation paths—be it through DVDs, downloading, or pirated channels—also trace global networks that span from Canada to Europe and China. Film distribution is a transnational activity par excellence. Exhibition, on the other hand, tends to be imagined as local. This is contradicted by the findings of this volume, and especially by the data on the development of multiplexing over the past decades. The move towards multiplexing has in effect been operated through regional dynamics, along the expansion strategies of companies such as Lebanese Empire and the UAE Grand Cinemas. That the UAE market was born through the influence of an Iranian and a Lebanese is no coincidence. Multiplexing has additionally attracted new types of regional players: real-estate companies. Gulf companies have in particular extended their leisure strategy, reaching North Africa. The transnational nature of exhibition, in its multiplex format, is all the more

191

striking as North American and European companies also start to invest in the Middle East and North Africa. AMC's ground-breaking involvement in Saudi Arabia and IMAX's international expansion strategy would be two case studies worth scrutinizing for observers of transnational exhibition phenomena. The development of numerous legal and illegal platforms and the rejuvenation of the market through multiplexing have both reinforced the transnational nature of cinema.

Spectators have directly felt these evolutions as their access to films has greatly increased, perhaps to the point of being seemingly unlimited. Modes of access have proliferated beyond theaters, with the development of television and DVDs. Film consumption has become a routine gesture, trivialized by free access through regional satellite channels as well as piracy. This circulation covers all the countries in the region, from the high-tech markets of the Gulf to the mature markets in the Middle East, to the struggling markets in the Maghreb, and to the porous "closed" markets. In the colonial era, two cinema cultures coexisted: the *Gone with the Wind* culture of the picture palaces and the cowboy culture of second- and third-class movie houses. Different audiences were offered different films in clearly separated spaces. Today, audiences experience cinema in different platforms, but they all have access to the same films. The culture of immediacy, visible both in the day-and-date theatrical releases and the quick availability on the pirate DVD markets, enable spectators from the North Africa and Middle East market to watch the same films at the same time as the rest of the world. In that sense, spectators in North Africa and the Middle East can have the feeling of fully participating in a global culture equated to Hollywood programs. This is accentuated by the fact that big and small screens, legal and illegal modes of access have created a continuum in which US films continually circulate. While this imagination is global, with the same heroes and franchises discussed all over the world, consumption remains eminently local.

The fact that the same films circulate over diverse platforms should thus not obfuscate the very diversity of cinema experiences in North Africa and the Middle East. Social classes remain a strong determinant. While middle-class viewers will resort to a wide variety of options, from the multiplex to pirated DVDs, working-class viewers will have more limited options, turning to the small screens and piracy. Films are thus not experienced in the same context, in terms of comfort and technical quality. The great diversity of platforms, both legal and illegal, makes it difficult to actually evaluate and describe the different cinema experiences. Gender also remains crucial. In her study on satellite television in the

Maghreb, Hadj-Moussa notes the separation between men watching sport and political shows on Arab and Western channels, and women watching Arab satellite channels showing Brazilian and Mexican *telenovelas*, and Egyptian, Syrian, and Turkish soap operas and series. She points out, however, that women might very well be watching the sanitized programs of Arabic-speaking channels because they are expected to do so (Hadj-Moussa 2015, 127). The place of women in theater audiences is definitely an issue to be considered. The revival of the movie theaters through multiplexing echoes the development from the nickelodeon to the picture palace in 1920s USA, when exhibitors tried to give more respectability to their theaters by attracting the middle-class family audiences (Mingant 2015a). In a similar way, multiplexes are turning their back on the unruly male-only audiences of older cinemas, trying to attract women and their children. In Saudi Arabia, the issue of female presence will probably continue to be debated and the idea of segregated audiences might reappear. Age, class, gender still determine people's access to and experience of cinema.

That Hollywood films are very much experienced locally—and in fact localized—is visible through issues of languages and censorship. Access to films is determined by language—dubbed French versions in North Africa, English versions with French and Arabic subtitles in Lebanon, English versions with Arabic subtitles in the Gulf. It is also determined by censorship, with different avatars of Hollywood films depending on the strictness and political priorities of the national censorship board. While spectators feel they commune in the global culture, many do not access the original version intended by the filmmakers, and myriad alternative versions circulate. Illegal dubbing practices also participate in the multiplication of versions. Hollywood films are additionally very much localized in the sense that they insert in specific mediascapes. Each market has its own film and media culture, as shown in the difference of audience tastes in the three geographically close markets of Egypt, Lebanon, and Israel. Some markets have their national film champions as in Egypt, Morocco, Lebanon, and the UAE. Each also feels different foreign influences. In North Africa, Hollywood films rub shoulders with French cinema. In the Gulf, the other cinematic reference is Bollywood.

Transnational phenomena are always about the complex dynamics of imagination. Spectators in North Africa and the Middle East do commune with a global culture in which Hollywood films remain the benchmark; but they also insert these films in imaginary landscapes that vary according to one's nationality, age, social class, and gender. To understand these complex cultural landscapes, one should go beyond cinema, as audiences live in a world where films exist in a continuum with TV series and reality TV programs. While spectators might enjoy Hollywood films, they can, at the same time, favor Syrian TV series. Further exploration of the variety of cultural mixes existing locally would reveal the dynamic work of imagination. Hollywood cinema has proved and will continue to be a useful exploratory tool into transnational culture dynamics. When it comes to audiences, Hollywood cinema has a Janus-like quality: on the one hand, it stands as the symbol of a shared global culture; on the other hand, it goes through very concrete processes of localization, adaption, and reappropriation inevitable to local consumption. At the heart of this volume is thus the constant tension between local lives and global imaginations symbolized by Hollywood.

Notes

Introduction

1. "Hollywood's Foreign Business: 1963–1973," *Variety*, May 23, 1974.

Chapter 1

1. For a detailed history of the Hollywood studios, see Finler 2003.

2. Omnia was also in charge of the North and West of France, Corsica, and Switzerland.

3. Pathé, Conseil d'administration, vol. 2, 1908–1913, March14, 1911, and March 19, 1912, Pathé Archives, Fondation Seydoux-Pathé, Paris.

4. US foreign service report, Beirut, December 18, 1924, NARA, RG 59, Country File, Syria/Lebanon, 1910–1929, M722, roll 14. See also *Wid's Year Book* 1920.

5. Pathé Consortium Cinéma, Comité de direction, April 27, 1923; Procès verbaux des délibérations du comité de direction, October 4, 1922–June 11, 1924, Pathé Archives.

6. Letter from Associated First National Pictures Inc. to the US Consul, Beyrouth, October 19, 1923, NARA, RG 59, Country File, Syria/Lebanon, 1910–1929, M722, roll 14.

7. Legation of the USA Teheran, Persia, to Secstate, June 14, 1926, NARA, RG 59, Country File, Persia, 1910–1929, M715, rolle 13.

8. US Department of Commerce 1930; Report from vice-consul Loder Park, Aden, August 25, 1927, NARA RG 59, Country File, Arabia, 1919–1929, box 10076.

9. US foreign service report, Office of Consulate General, Beirut, Syria, December 18, 1924, NARA, RG 59, Country File, Syria, 1919–1929, M722, roll 14.

10. In the early 1930s, Paramount, Artistes Associés, Universal, and MFM were all producing films in France (Garçon 2006, 96).

11. As Guback noted in his study *The International Film Industry: Western Europe and America since 1945*, "membership in a foreign industry association" is a means commonly applied by the US majors to ensure favorable market conditions for their films (Guback 1969, 108).

12. Report from Consul Smith, Tunis, to DOS, April 18, 1926, NARA, RG 59, Country File, Tunisia, 1910–1929, M560, roll 156.

13. Report from Consul Smith, Tunis, to DOS, April 18, 1926, NARA, RG 59, Country File, Tunisia, 1910–1929, M560, roll 156.

14. Report from Consul Smith, Tunis, to DOS, April 18, 1926, NARA, RG 59, Country File, Tunisia, 1910–1929, M560, roll 156.

15. Letter from Consul Smith, Tunis, to DOS, "Institution of a Film Censoring Committee," January 27, 1926, Country File, Tunisia, 1910–1929, M560, roll 156.

16. Pathé Consortium Cinéma, Procès-verbal de la réunion du conseil d'administration, September 10, 1924, Pathé Archives.

17. Procès-verbaux des délibérations du comité de direction, Octobre 4, 1922–June 11, 1924, Pathé Archives.

18. Pathé Consortium Cinéma, Procès verbaux des délibérations du comité de direction, October 4, 1922–June 11, 1924; November 28, 1922; January 15, 1923; March 21, 1923, Pathé Archives.

19. In 1924, Gaumont had branches in Algiers, Bordeaux, Casablanca, Lille, Lyon, Marseille, Nancy, Nantes, Strasbourg, Toulouse, and Tunis (Garçon 2006, 64).

20. Letter from the US Consulate General Beirut to Secstate, May 13, 1929, NARA, RG 59, Country File, Syria, 1910–1929, M722, roll 14.

21. Letter from Geist DOS, July 28, 1942, NARA, RG 59, Country File, Egypt, 1940–1944, box 5781.

22. Letter from Vice Consul Loder Park, Aden, Arabia, August 25, 1927, NARA RG 59, Country File, Arabia, 1910–1929, box 10076.

23. "U.S. Pictures Have Head Start in Favor with Palestine Public," *Motion Picture Herald*, February 2, 1937, MHL.

24. James T. Scott, "Motion Pictures (Syria and the Lebanon)," April 1943, NARA, RG 59, Country File, Lebanon, 1940–1944, T1178, roll 5.

25. "Motion Picture Notes," Cairo to DOC, August 14, 1934, NARA, RG 151, 281, box 1307.

26. Telegram from Tunis to SecState, March 22, 1949, NARA, RG 59, Country File, Tunisia, 1945–1949, box 6325.

27. Letter from Foreign Service of the USA, Baghdad, April 18, 1950, NARA, RG 59, Country File, Iraq, 1950–1954, box 5489.

28. "Motion Picture Notes," Cairo to DOC, August 14, 1934, NARA, RG 151, 281, box 1307.

29. Report from Foreign Service of the USA, Baghdad to DOS, April 20, 1950, NARA, RG 59, Country File, Iraq, 1950–1954, box 5489.

30. Letter from MGM to SecState, November 19, 1942, NARA, RG 59, Country File Algeria, 1940–1944, box 5211; Letter from Division of Commerce,

"Re: North Africa," January 28, 1943, NARA, RG 59, Country File, Algeria, 1940–1944, box 5211; Report from AmConGen, Algiers to DOS, July 24, 1952, NARA, RG 59, Country File, Algeria, 1950–1954, box 5008.

31. Letter from MPPDA to DOS, May 26, 1942, NARA, RG 59, Country File, Morocco, 1940–1944, box 5766.

32. Report from Tunis to DOS, September 1, 1951, NARA, RG 59, Country File, Tunisia, 1950–1954, box 5361.

33. Report from AmConGen, Algiers to DOS, July 24, 1952, NARA, RG 59, Country File, Algeria, 1950–1954, box 5008.

34. Copy of a letter from the Director of Customs, Baghdad, Iraq, November 26, 1949, NARA, RG 59, Country File, Iraq, 1950–1954, box 5489.

35. Lettre de Louis Roché, Ambassadeur de France au Liban, à M. Le Ministre des Affaires étrangères, direction des relations culturelles, Beyrouth, August 29, 1956, Archives diplomatiques de Nantes, 91PO/B 103; Lettre à son excellence monsieur le Minister de France, Beyrouth, April 6, 1951, Archives diplomatiques de Nantes, 91PO/B 103.

36. Annex no. 2 to Report from Foreign Service of the USA, Baghdad, to DOS, April 20, 1950, NARA, RG 59, Country File, Iraq, 1950–1954, box 5489.

37. AmEmbassy Baghdad to DOS, October 13, 1954, NARA RG 59, Country File, Iraq, 1950–1954, box 5489.

38. AmLegation, Tangier, to DOS, August 24, 1951, NARA, RG 50, Country File, Morocco, 1950–1954, box 5354. *Film Daily Year Book 1950*; AmLegation, Tangier, to SecState, June 6, 1944, NARA, RG 59, Country File, Morocco, 1940–1944, box 5766.

39. Aigram from DOS to AmEmbassy Tehran, March 29, 1952, NARA, RG 59, Country File, Iran, 1950–1954, box 5516; Report by Foreign Service of the USA Tehran to DOS, April 14, 1950, NARA, RG 59, Country File, Iran, 1950–1954, box 5516.

40. Report by Clare H. Timberlake, US Consul, Aden, Arabia, July 2, 1943, NARA, RG 59, Country File, Arabia, 1940–1944, box 5796.

41. Letter from Frederick L. Herron, MPPDA to Paul Culberston, DOS, September 12, 1933, NARA, RG 59, Country File, Mesopotamia, 1920–1939, T1180, roll 9.

42. Letter from Legation of the USA, Baghdad, to SecState, December 2, 1933, NARA, RG 59, Country File, Mesopotamia, 1920–1939, T1180, roll 9; *Film Daily Year Book* 1938.

43. Letter from Frederick L. Herron, MPPDA to Paul Culberston, DOS, September 12, 1933, NARA, RG 59, Country File, Mesopotamia, 1920–1939, T1180, roll 9.

44. Letter from AmLegation, Tangier, to SecState, April 2, 1945, NARA RG 59, Country File, Morocco, 1945–1949, box 7130.

45. Letter from AmLegation, Tangier, to SecState, April 2, 1945, NARA RG 59, Country File, Morocco, 1945–1949, box 7130; Letter from Ben Miggins to

Murray Silverstone, March 6, 1945; Letter from AmLegation, Tangier, to SecState, April 2, 1945, NARA, RG 59, Country File, Morocco, 1945–1949, box 7130.

46. Annual Motion Picture Report, Aden, Arabia, to DOS, December 22, 1951, NARA, RG 59, Country File, Yemen, 1950–1954, box 4909.

47. AmEmbassy Tehran to DOS, August 18, 1951, NARA, RG 59, Country File, Iran, 1950–1954, box 5516; AmEmbassy to DOS, September 17, 1952, NARA RG 59, Country File, Iran, 1950–1954, box 5516.

48. Document File Note from Persia, November 15, 1932, NARA, RG 59, 1930–1939, M1202, roll 8.

49. Report from Motion Picture Section, DOC, Electrical Division, to Calcutta Office, April 19, 1937, NARA, RG 151, 281, Box 1312.

50. DOS to AmEmbassy, Tehran, May 18, 1951, NARA RG 59, Country File, Iran, 1950–1954, box 5516.

51. Report from Tunis to DOS, September 1, 1951, NARA, RG 59, Country File, Tunisia, 1950–1954, box 5361.

52. AmEmbassy, Baghdad, to DOS, June 17, 1952, NARA, RG 59, Country File, Iraq, 1950–1954, 5489; Document File Note from Persia, November 15, 1932, NARA, RG 59, Country File, Iran, 1930–1939, M1202, roll 8.

53. Report by Foreign Service of the USA Tehran to DOS, April 14, 1950, NARA, RG 59, Country File, Iran, 1950–1954, box 5516; Letter from Milliken to de Wold, March 9, 1945, NARA RG 59, Country File, Morocco, 1945–1949, box 7130.

54. Letter from W. Murray to F. Herron, September 19, 1933, NARA RG 59, Country File, Iraq, 1920–1939, T1180, roll 9.

55. DOS to AmEmbassy Tehran, March 29, 1952, NARA, RG 59, Country File, Iran, 1950–1954, box 5516.

56. Letter from Frederick L. Herron, MPPDA to Paul Culberston, DOS, September 12, 1933, NARA, RG 59, Country File, Mesopotamia, 1920–1939, T1180, roll 9.

57. Letter from AmLegation, Tangier, to SecState, April 2, 1945, NARA RG 59, Country File, Morocco, 1945–1949, box 7130.

58. Letter from Legation of the USA, Baghdad, to SecState, December 2, 1933, NARA, RG 59, Country File, Mesopotamia, 1920–1939, T1180, roll 9.

Chapter 2

1. Letter from foreign service of the USA, Baghdad, "Motion Pictures—Theatre Equipment, Iraq," April 18, 1950, NARA, RG59, Country File, Iraq, 1950–1954, 887.452, 250, 41, 10 7, box 5489.

2. Report from American Consul Nielsen, Tehran, September 1, 1927, NARA, RG 59, Country File, Persia, M 715, roll 13.

3. Consulate General, Beirut, Syria, to DOS, December 18, 1924, NARA, RG 59, Country File, Syria, M722, roll 14.

4. Report from American Consul Nielsen, Tehran, September 1, 1927, NARA, RG 59, Country File, Persia, M 715, roll 13.

5. American Foreign Service report, Beirut, December 18, 1924, Country File, Syria/Lebanon, 1910–1929, M722, roll 14.

6. Consulate General, Beirut, Syria, to DOS, December 18, 1924, NARA, RG 59, Country File, Syria/Lebanon 1910–1929, M722, roll 14.

7. Consulate General, Beirut, Syria, to DOS, December 18, 1924, NARA, RG 59, Country File, Syria/Lebanon, 1910–1929, M722, roll 14.

8. Consulate General, Beirut, Syria, to DOS, December 18, 1924, NARA, RG 59, Country File, Syria/Lebanon, 1910–1929, M722, roll 14.

9. "Voluntary Economic Data, Motion Pictures," Aden to DOS, January 11, 1950, NARA, RG 59, Country File, Yemen, 1950–1954, box 4909.

10. Traveling cinema initiatives will not be studied here as they responded to noncommercial logics.

11. This chapter will deal only with commercial cinemas. One should not forget, however, the presence of specifically Western film consumption spaces: "oil cinemas," that is, cinemas organized by American oil companies, military cinemas, and private clubs. In Saudi Arabia, the royal family had also created its own film-watching spaces, although cinema was forbidden to the rest of the population.

12. In some countries, the first talking film shown was in fact American such as *Sonny Boy* (1929) in Palestine or *Rio Rita* (1929) in Iran (Leaman 2001, 359; Naficy 2011a, 228).

13. Letter from Chesbrough to Canty, December 23, 1931, NAGRA, RG 151, 281, Egypt File, box 1307.

14. Letter from Richard May to DOC, December 5, 1925, NARA, RG 151, 281, Egypt File, box 1307.

15. Report by James T. Scott, "Motion Pictures (Syria and the Lebanon)," April 1943, NARA, RG 59, Country File, Lebanon, 1940–1944, T1178, roll 5.

16. Algiers to DOS, July 24, 1952, NARA, RG 59, Country File, Algeria, 1950–1954, box 5008.

17. "US Pictures Have Head Start in Favor with Palestine Public," *Motion Picture Herald*, February 2, 1937, MHL.

18. AmEmbassy Baghdad to DOS, June 26, 1952, NARA, RG 59, Country File, Iraq, 1950–1954, box 5489.

19. Aden to DOS, July 8, 1950, NARA, RG 59, Country File, Aden, 1950–1954, box 4909.

20. Aden to DOS, July 8, 1950, NARA, RG 59, Country File, Aden, 1950–1954, box 4909.

21. AmEmbassy Tehran to DOS, August 18, 1951, NARA, RG 59, Country File, Iran, 1950–1954, box 5516.

22. AmEmbassy Tehran to DOS, August 18, 1951, NARA, RG 59, Country File, Iran, 1950–1954, box 5516.

23. Foreign Service of the USA, Aden, to DOS, December 14, 1949, NARA, RG 59, Country File, Aden, 1945–1949, box 6140.

24. Annual Motion Picture Report from Aden, Arabia, to DOS, December 22, 1951, NARA, RG 59, Country File, Yemen, 1950–1954, box 4909.

25. Am Con Gen, Algiers, to DOS, July 24 1952, NARA RG 59, Country File, Algeria, 1950–1954, box 5008.

26. Amlegation Casablanca to DOS, December 28 1951, NARA, RG 59, Country File, Morocco, 1950–1954, box 5354.

27. Amlegation Casablanca to DOS, December 28 1951, NARA, RG 59, Country File, Morocco, 1950–1954, box 5354.

28. "U.S. Pictures Have Head Start in Favor with Palestine Public," *Motion Picture Herald*, February 2, 1937, MHL.

29. Letter from the High Commissioner for Palestine to the Secretary of State of the Colonies, Jerusalem, February 11, 1932, National Archives of Great Britain, Public Records Office, Colonial Office, CO323/1122/3, Colonial Film Committee.

30. "U.S. Pictures Have Head Start in Favor with Palestine Public," *Motion Picture Herald*, February 2, 1937, MHL.

31. C. Timberlake, "Motion Picture," Aden, Arabia, July 2, 1943, NARA, RG 59, 1940–1944, Country File, Arabia, box 5786.

32. C. Timberlake, "Motion Picture," Aden, Arabia, July 2, 1943, NARA, RG 59, 1940–1944, Country File, Arabia, box 5786.

33. Document file note, 890g00 General conditions/59 for 1511, from Iraq, "Modesty in Baghdad movies. Men and women may not sit together as matinee performance," July 25, 1935, NARA, RG 59, Country File, Mesopotamia, 1920–1939, T1180, roll 9.

34. "Annual Report on Entertainment Motion Pictures, 35mm," from Aman to DOS, Feb. 27, 1950, NARA, RG 59, 1950–1954, Country File, Jordan, box 5466.

35. Gender-segregation seems to have continued even after the sartorial legislations on veil (Naficy 2011a, 200).

36. Intersectionality refers to the combination of multiple forms of discriminations based on sex, race, or class. It was theorized by Crenshaw in 1989 as a way to rethink the experience of Black women in the US (Crenshaw 1989).

37. Foreign Service of the USA, Baghdad, to DOS, April 21, 1950, NARA, RG 59, Country File, Iraq, 1950–1954, box 5489.

38. AmEmbassy Tehran to DOS, August 18, 1951, NARA, RG 59, Country File, Iran, 1950–1954, box 5516.

39. C. Timberlake, "Motion Picture," Aden, Arabia, July 2, 1943, NARA, RG 59, 1940–1944, Country File, Arabia, box 5786.

40. Algier to SecState, October 12, 1942, NARA, RG 59, Country File, Algeria, 1940–1944, box 5211.

41. AmEmbassy Tehran to DOS, August 18, 1951, NARA RG 59, Country File, Iran, 1950–1954, box 5516.

42. AmEmbassy Tehran to DOS, August 18, 1951, NARA RG 59, Country File, Iran, 1950–1954, box 5516.

43. Copie d'une lettre adressée aux Affaires étrangères accompagnée d'un rapport relatif au retrait des films américains, September 19, 1942; Note de la Résidence générale de France au Maroc pour DAP2, "Retrait des films américains," September 19, 1942, Archives diplomatiques de Nantes, Fonds Maroc, 1 MA/200/187 (1942–1949).

44. AmEmbassy Baghdad to DOS, June 26, 1952, NARA, RG 59, Country File, Iraq, 1950–1954, box 5489.

45. Semi-annual report, Casablanca to DOS, April 14, 1950, NARA, RG 59, Country File, Morocco, 1950–1954, box 5354.

46. Report from Vice-Consul Park, Aden, Arabia, August 25, 1927, NARA, RG 59, Country File, Arabia, 1919–1929, box 10076.

47. Foreign Service of the USA, Baghdad, To DOS, April 21, 1950, NARA, RG 59, Country File, Iraq, 1950–1954, box 5489.

48. C. Timberlake, "Motion Picture," Aden, Arabia, July 2, 1943, NARA RG 59, 1940–1944, Country File, Arabia, box 5786.

49. Foreign Service of the USA, Tehran, to DOS, April 14, 1950, NARA, RG 50, Country File, Iran, 1950–1954, box 5516.

50. Report from Vice-Consul Park, Aden, Arabia, August 25, 1927, NARA, RG 59, Country File, Arabia, 1919–1929, box 10076.

Chapter 3

1. Letter from Director General of the European Department to MGM, Alexandria, May 2, 1934, NARA, RG 59, Country File, Egypt, 1930–1939, T1251, roll 12.

2. AmConsulate to SecState, December 10, 1932, NARA, RG 59, Country File, Palestine, M1037, roll 13.

3. C. Timberlake, "Motion Picture," Aden, Arabia, July 2, 1943, NARA RG 59, 1940–1944, Country File, Arabia, box 5786.

4. AmConsulate to SecState, December 10, 1932, NARA, RG 59, Country File, Palestine, M1037, roll 13.

5. American Consulate General Beirut to SecState, May 13, 1929, NARA, RG 59, Country File, Syria, 1910–1929, M722, roll 14.

6. American Consulate General, Jerusalem, to SecState, September 7, 1935, NARA, RG 59, Country File, Palestine, M1038, roll 13.

7. AmConsulate to SecState, December 10, 1932, NARA, RG 59, Country File, Palestine, M1037, roll 13.

8. Report from Beirut to DOS, May 10, 1927, NARA, RG 59, Country File, Syria, 1910–1929, M722, roll 14.

9. AmConsulate to SecState, December 10, 1932, NARA, RG 59, Country File, Palestine, M1037, roll 13.

10. Letter from the American Consulate General, Beirut, Syria, to secstate, May 13, 1929, "Prohibition against Showing of Fox Motion Picture Film in Syria," NARA, Country File, Syria, 1910–1929, M722, roll 14.

11. Consul Smith, Tunis, to DOS, March 22, 1926, NARA, RG 59, Country File, Tunisia, 1910–1029, M560, roll 156.

12. AmLegation Cairo to SecState, June 29, 1934, NARA RG 59, Country File, Egypt, 1930–1939, T1251, roll 12.

13. AmLegation Cairo to SecState, June 29, 1934, NARA RG 59, Country File, Egypt, 1930–1939, T1251, roll 12.

14. AmLegation Cairo to SecState, June 29, 1934, NARA RG 59, Country File, Egypt, 1930–1939, T1251, roll 12.

15. Letter from American Consulate General, Beirut, to Michel Amme, May 13, 1929, NARA, RG 59, Country File, Syria, 1910–1929, M722, roll 14.

16. French Residency in Morocco to Ministère des Affaires étrangères, September 19, 1942, Archives diplomatiques de Nantes, Morocco, 1 MA/200/187 (1942–1949).

17. French Residency in Morocco to Ministère des Affaires étrangères, September 19, 1942, Archives diplomatiques de Nantes, Morocco, 1 MA/200/187 (1942–1949).

18. AmLegation, Tangier, to SecState, June 10, 1942, NARA, RG 59, Country File, Morocco, 1940–1944, box 5766.

19. Letter from the American Consulate General, Algiers, "Projected Action, Vichy Action against American Films," July 13, 1942, NARA, RG 59, Country File, Algeria, 1940–1944, box 5211.

20. "Motion Pictures Notes," from Felix Cole, American Consul General, Algiers, Sept 25, 1941, NARA, RG 50, Country File, Algeria, 1940–1944, box 5211; Letter from the American Consulate General, Algiers, "Projected Action, Vichy Action against American Films," July 13, 1942, NARA, RG 59, Country File, Algeria, 1940–1944, box 5211.

21. General Nogues, Morocco, to French State Department, September 17, 1942, Archives diplomatiques de Nantes, Maroc 1MA/200/187 (1942–1949).

22. General Nogues, Morocco, to French State Department, September 17, 1942, Archives diplomatiques de Nantes, Maroc 1MA/200/187 (1942–1949).

23. General Nogues, Morocco, to French State Department, September 17, 1942, Archives diplomatiques de Nantes, Maroc 1MA/200/187 (1942–1949).

24. General Nogues, Morocco, to French State Department, September 17, 1942, Archives diplomatiques de Nantes, Maroc 1MA/200/187 (1942–1949).

25. Telegram From Algeria to Secretary of State, Washington, Sept 12, 1942; Telegram from the DOS to American Consul, Algiers, October 7, 1942; Telegram from Algiers' Cole to Sec of State, October 12, 1942, NARA, RG 59, Country File, Algeria, 1940–1944, box 5211; Telegram from M. Childs, Tangier, to SecState, October 29, 1942, NARA, RG59, Country File, Morocco, 1940–1944, box 5766.

26. Letter from MGM to Secretary of State, November 19, 1942, NARA, RG 59, Country File, Algeria, 1940–1944, box 5211.

27. Letter from Division of Commerce, reNorth Africa, January 28, 1943; Letter from R. Geist to Mr. Gould, February 5, 1943; Letter from Modern film Corporation (NY) to Division of Commercial Affairs, February 8, 1943; from Universal Pictures to Division of Commercial Affairs, February 2, 1943, NARA RG 59, Country File, Algeria, 1940–1944, box 5211.

28. Letter from Thomas Burke, to Mr. Spyros, December 5, 1942, NARA, RG 59, Country File, Algeria, 1940–1944, box 5211.

29. "Red Tape Cut on Pix for Africa," *Hollywood Reporter*, April 8, 1943, MHL.

30. From Universal Pictures to Division of Commercial Affairs, February 2, 1943, NARA RG 59, Country File, Algeria, 1940–1944, box 5211.

31. Foreign Service of the USA, Baghdad, to DOS, April 20, 1950, NARA, RG 59, Country File, Iraq, 1950–1954, box 5489.

32. AmEmbassy, Baghdad, to SecState, April 12, 1949, NARA, RG 59, Country File, Iraq, 1945–1949, box 7220.

33. AmEmbassy, Baghdad, to SecState, February 1, 1949, NARA, RG 59, Country File, Iraq, 1945–1949, box 7220; AmEmbassy, Baghdad, to SecState, April 1, 1949, NARA, RG 59, Country File, Iraq, 1945–1949, box 7220.

34. AmEmbassy, Baghdad, to SecState, February 1, 1949, NARA, RG 59, Country File, Iraq, 1945–1949, box 7220.

35. Foreign Service of the USA, Baghdad, to DOS, August 17, 1950, NARA, RG 59, Country File, Iraq, 1950–1954, box 5489.

36. Foreign Service of the USA, Baghdad, to DOS, August 17, 1950, NARA, RG 59, Country File, Iraq, 1950–1954, box 5489.

37. Letter from M. Healy, MPAA, to Victor von Lossberge, American Embassy, Baghdad, May 9, 1950, NARA, RG 59, Country File, Iraq, 1950–1954, box 5489.

38. Telegram from M. Healy, MPAA, to Abdel Karin Bey El Uzri, Minister of Finance, Baghdad, May 7, 1950, NARA, RG 59 Country File, Iraq, 1950–1954, box 5489.

39. Foreign Service of the USA, Baghdad, to DOS, August 17, 1950, NARA, RG 59, Country File, Iraq, 1950–1954, box 5489.

40. Foreign Service of the USA, Baghdad, to DOS, August 17, 1950, NARA, RG 59, Country File, Iraq, 1950–1954, box 5489.

41. AmEmbassy, Baghdad, to SecState, February 1, 1949, NARA, RG 59, Country File, Iraq, 1945–1949, box 7220.

42. AmEmbassy, Tehran, to DOS, August 18, 1951, NARA, RG 59, Country File, Iran, 1950–1954, box 5516.

43. AmEmbassy, Tehran, to DOS, December 21, 1953, NARA, RG 59, Country File, Iran, 1950–1954, box 5516. Tehran originally agreed to import films only from countries with which it had clearing of barter agreement. It had to withdraw this restriction, however, as the US authorities, in the name of MPAA, argued it was contrary to the 1943 Reciprocal Trade Agreement.

44. Amembassy, Tehran, to DOS, September 17, 1952, NARA, RG 59, Country File, Iran, 1950–1954, box 5516.

45. AmEmbassy, Baghdad, to DOS, February 4, 1955, NARA, RG 59, Country File, Iraq, 1955–1959, box 4962.

46. Comptes-rendu du contrôle cinématographique, Archives diplomatiques de Nantes, Morocco, 1MA/200/187 (1942–1949).

47. Civil Inspector, Oujda to Interior Director, May 20, 1955, Archives diplomatiques de Nantes, Morocco, 1MA/200/191 B.

48. Civil Inspector, Oujda, to Director of the Interior, May 20, 1955, Archives diplomatiques de Nantes, Morocco, 1MA/200/191 B.

49. AmEmbassy, Baghdad, to DOS, February 4, 1955, NARA, RG 59, Country File, Iraq, 1955–1959, box 4962.

50. AmEmbassy, Baghdad, to DOS, NARA, RG 59, Country File, Iraq, 1955–1959, box 4962.

51. AmEmbassy, Baghdad, to DOS, February 4, 1955, NARA, RG 59, Country File, Iraq, 1955–1959, box 4962.

52. AmEmbassy, Baghdad, to DOS, February 15, 1955, NARA, RG 59, Country File, Iraq, 1955–1959, box 4962.

53. AmLegation, Cairo, to SecState, August 1, 1944, NARA, RG 59, Country File, Egypt, 1940–1944, box 5781.

54. AmEmbassy, tehran, to DOS, November 26, 1951, NARA, RG 59, Country File, Iran, 1950–1954, boc 5516.

55. AmEmbassy Tehran to SecState, March 30, 1951, NARA, RG 59, Country File, Iran, 1950–1954, box 5516.

56. Report from American Consulate General, Algiers, to DOS public information, comments on motion pictures in Algeria, May 19, 1960, NARA, RG 59, Country File, Algeria, 1960–1963, box 2570; Report from Tunis to DOS, "Entertainment Motion Pictures, 35mm," September 1, 195, NARA, RG59, Country File, Tunisia, 1950–1954, box 5361; Report from Amlegation, Casablanca, to DOS, December 28, 1951, "Motion Pictures, Year 1951," NARA, RG 59, Country File, Morocco, 1950–1954, box 5354.

Chapter 4

1. "Ban on Pix to Iran, an Economic Issue, Not Politics: Valenti," *Variety*, December 26, 1979.

2. In 1958, for example, as the pro-Western Iraqi monarchy was overthrown by General Abdel Karim Kassem, the US sent troops to protect Lebanon for a few months (Nouailhat 2015, 215).

3. State to Cairo, May 19, 1940, NARA, RG 59, Country File, Egypt, 1940–1944, box 5781; Cairo to State, May 26, 1945, NARA, RG 59, Country File, Egypt, 1945–1949, box 7156.

4. Baghdad to State, November 29, 1939, NARA, RG 59, Country File, Mesopotamia, 1930–1939, T1180, roll 9.

5. Damascus to State, April 21, 1947, NARAn, RG 59, Country File, Syria, 1945–1949, box 7199.

6. Cairo to State, March 2, 1948, NARA, RG 59, Country File, Egypt, 1945–1949, box 7156.

7. Cairo to State, March 8, 1948, NARA, RG 59, Country File, Egypt, 1945–1949, box 7156.

8. Letter from Alexandria to DOS, January 16, 1951, NARA, RG 59, Country File, Egypt, 1950–1954, box 5384; Letter from Amlegation, Damascus, to DOS, "Samson and Syria," August 14, 1952, NARA, RG 59, Country File, Syria, 1950–1954, box 5439; Report from Amlegation, Beirut, to DOS, "Motion pictures, Lebanon, 1950," March 19, 1951, NARA, RG 59, Country File, Lebanon, 1950–1954, box 5448.

9. Airgram from AmEmbassy, Kuwait, to DOS, May 13, 1965, NARA, RG 59, INCO Motion Pictures, 1964–1966, box 1203. Similar references appear in "Annual Report on Entertainment Motion Pictures, 35mm," from Aman to DOS, February 27, 1950, NARA, RG 59, Country File, Jordan, 1950–1954, box 5466; Airgram from AmEmbassy, Beirut, to DOS, October 16, 1972, NARA, INCO, 281, 1970–1973, box 1310; "Syria Bans Seven Films with Links to Jews," *New York Times*, October 20, 1983; Report from Damascus to DOS, "Motion Pictures," May 8, 1950, NARA, RG 59, Country File, Syria, 1950–1954, box 5439; Report from Amlegation, Damascus, to DOS, June 15, 1952, NARA, RG 59, Country File, Syria, 1950–1954, box 5439; Airgram from AmEmbassy, Damascus, to DOS, November 19, 1963, NARA, INCO 281, 1963, box 3545.

10. Airgram from AmEmbassy, Baghdad, to DOS, June 6, 1963, NARA, RG 59, INCO Motion Pictures, 1963, box 3545.

11. Airgram from AmEmbassy, Baghdad, to DOS, June 6, 1963, NARA, RG 59, INCO Motion Pictures, 1963, box 3545.

12. Airgram from AmEmbassy, Baghdad, to DOS, June 6, 1963, NARA, RG 59, INCO Motion Pictures, 1963, box 3545.

13. Airgram from AmEmbassy, Baghdad, to DOS, June 6, 1963, NARA, RG 59, INCO Motion Pictures, 1963, box 3545.

14. Telegram from Cairo to DOS, June 15, 1948. NARA, RG 59, Country file, Egypt, 1945–1949, box 7156.

15. "Arab Film Rally of '64 Reported; UNESCO Volume Replete with Typos, Repeats 'Blacklist' Vis-à-Vis Israel," *Variety*, June 29, 1966.

16. "Arab Film Rally of '64 Reported; UNESCO Volume Replete with Typos, Repeats 'Blacklist' Vis-à-Vis Israel," *Variety*, June 29, 1966.

17. "Arab Film Rally of '64 Reported; UNESCO Volume Replete with Typos, Repeats 'Blacklist' Vis-à-Vis Israel," *Variety*, June 29, 1966.

18. "Iraq Bans Pix on Israel Ties," *Variety*, October 27, 1965; "Kuwait's Pic Blacklist," *Variety*, November 3, 1982; "Syria Bans Seven Films with Links to Jews," *New York Times*, October 20, 1983.

19. "Egypt Ends 'Zionist' Film Boycott," *Los Angeles Times*, September 18, 1979.

20. "After Being Banned from Egypt for 17 Years, Elizabeth Taylor was Welcomed There with Flowers," *Los Angeles Times*, September 17, 1979; "Arabs End Ban of Actors from TV 'Death of Princess,'" *Variety*, May 19, 1982; "Nasser, Sadat, and Now: Yanks' Interest in Egypt Is Varied," *Variety*, May 12, 1982.

21. "Egypt Ends 'Zionist' Film Boycott," *Los Angeles Times*, September 18, 1979.

22. "Arab Film Rally of '64 Reported; UNESCO Volume Replete with Typos, Repeats 'Blacklist' Vis-à-Vis Israel," *Variety*, June 29, 1966.

23. "U.S. Film Biz in Egypt Not Okay," *Variety*, March 21, 1979.

24. "Censorship Gets Tougher in Iraq," *Variety*, December 22, 1977.

25. "Nasser, Sadat, and Now: Yanks' Interest in Egypt Is Varied," *Variety*, May 12, 1982.

26. Letter from AmEmbassy, Cairo, to DOS, "Egyptian Controls Affecting Certain Foreign Motion Pictures," December 20, 1956, NARA, RG 59, Country File, Egypt, 1955–1959, box 4878.

27. Airgram from Caro to DOS, July 26, 1965, NARA, RG 59, Country File, Egypt, 1960–1963, box 2764.

28. Telegram from AmEmbassy, Cairo, to SecState, November 5, 1956, NARA, RG 59, Country File, Egypt, 1955–1959, box 4878.

29. Telegram from AmEmbassy, Cairo, to SecState, November 20, 1956, NARA, RG 59, Country File, Egypt, 1955–1959, box 4878.

30. Letter from AmEmbassy, Cairo, to DOS, December 20, 1956, NARA, RG 59, Country File, Egypt, 1955–1959, box 4878.

31. Telegram from USINT, Cairo, to SecState, April 2, 1970; Telegram from AmEmbassy, London, to SecState, April 19, 1970; Telegram from USINT, Cario, to SecState, May 1970, NARA, RG 59, INCO Motion Pictures, 1970, 1973, box 1309.

32. Airgram from DOC to Amlegation, Damascus, April 21, 1947, NARA, RG 59, Country File, Syria, 1945–1949, box 7199; Airgram from Damascus to DOS, December 15, 1947, NARA, RG 59, Country File, Syria, 1945–1949, box 7199.

33. Report from Damascus to DOS, July 27, 1951, NARA, RG 59, Country File, Syria, 1950–1954, box 5439.

34. Letter from AmEmbassy, Damascus, to DOS, July 15, 1954, NARA, RG 59, Country File, Syria, 1950–1954, box 5439; Letter from DOS to AmEmbassy, Damascus, June 25, 1954, NARA, RG 59, Country File, Syria, 1950–1954, box 5439; Letter from AmEmbassy to DOS, June 30, 1954, NARA, RG 59, Country File, Syria, 1950–1954, box 5439.

35. Airgram from DOS to Amlegation, Damascus, April 21, 1947, NARA, RG 59, Country File, Syria, 1945–1949, box 7199.

36. Letter from AmEmbassy, Damascus, to DOS, July 15, 1954, NARA, RG 59, Country File, Syria, 1950–1954, box 5439; Letter from AmEmbassy to DOS, June 30, 1954, NARA, RG 59, Country File, Syria, 1950–1954, box 5439.

37. "U.S. and Egypt 'Back in business': Aid to Theatres Conditions Pact," *Variety*, June 5, 1968; "Egypt Lifted Its Ban on Hollywood Films," *Variety*, November 29, 1967.

38. *Centre interarabe du cinéma et de la télévision: Informations/News* (Beirut), no. 96–97, June 15, 1971; *Centre interarabe du cinéma et de la télévision: Informations/News* (Beirut), no. 134–35, March 15, 1973.

39. Airgram from AmEmbassy, Algiers, to DOS, "Possibility of Exclusion of Western Films from Algerian Market," June 9, 1969, NARA, INCO, 281, 1967–1969, box 1127.

40. *Centre interarabe du cinéma et de la télévision: Informations/News* (Beirut), no. 122–23, September 15, 1972.

41. *Centre interarabe du cinéma et de la télévision: Informations/News* (Beirut), no. 96–97, June 15, 1971.

42. "US Embassy Sends 6 Films to Syria," *Variety*, July 26, 1972.

43. *Centre interarabe du cinéma et de la télévision: Informations/News* (Beirut), no. 96–97, June 15, 1971.

44. US Department of State, "U.S. Relation with Syria," Bureau of Near Eastern Affairs, Fact Sheet, March 20, 2014, http://www.state.gov/r/pa/ei/bgn/3580.htm.

45. Tehran to State, March 9, 1967, RG 59, INCO, 281, Iran, box 1128.

46. "Frowns on MPAA 'or Else' Motif," *Variety*, October 21, 1975.

47. "Yank Cos. Fly Iranian Flag; Now Eligible to Import Films," *Variety*, May 19, 1976.

48. "Ban on Pix to Iran, an Economic Issue, Not Politics: Valenti," *Variety*, December 26, 1979.

49. Quoted in "MPEA Huddles to Ponder Iran Future for US Film Biz," *Variety*, November 28, 1979.

50. "Ban on Pix to Iran, an Economic Issue, Not Politics: Valenti," *Variety*, December 26, 1979.

51. "MPEA Shuns Cannes for L.A. after Oscars; Libya, Turkey 'in,' Lebanon Still Best in Mid-East," *Variety*, December 19, 1979.

52. Airgram from State/ICA/USIA to International Cooperation Administration, April 1, 1961, NARA, RG 59, Country File, Tunisia, 1960–1963, box 2760.

53. Letter from American Embassy, Tunis, to Department of State, "Discussion of GOT-MPEAA Film Dispute and Other Tunisian Cinema Developments by Information Secretary Masmoudi and MPEAA Vice-President Johnson," February 2, 1961, NARA, RG 59, Country File, Tunisia, 1960–1963, box 2760.

54. Letter from American Embassy, Tunis, to DOS, "Soviet Bloc Interest in Tunisian Film Industry," October 14, 1960, RG 59, Country File, Tunisia, 1960–1963, box 2760; Telegram from American Embassy, Tunis, to Secretary of State, Washington, December 3, 1960, NARA, RG 59, Country File, Tunisia, 1960–1963, box 2760.

55. Letter from Johnson (MPEA) to Martindale (DOS), November 25, 1960, NARA, RG 59, Country File, Tunisia, 1960–1963, box 2760.

56. Letter from AmEmbassy, Rabat, to DOS, "Motion Picture Problems in Morocco," 26 June 1962, NARA, RG 59, Country File, Morocco, 1960–1963, box 2755.

57. Letter from AmEmbassy, Rabat, to DOS, "Motion Picture Problems in Morocco," 26 June 1962, NARA, RG 59, Country File, Morocco, 1960–1063, box 2755.

58. Letter from AmEmbassy, Tunis, to DOS, February 2, 1961, NARA, RG 59, Country File, Tunisia, 1960–1963, box 2760.

59. Airgram from AmEmbassy, Algiers, to DOS, June 9, 1969, NARA, RG 59, INCO Motion Pictures, 1967–1969, box 1127.

60. This series of arguments, revolving around the metaphors of films as "turnips" (in French, *navet*) echoes the Communist condemnation of American films in France immediately after World War II.

61. *Centre Interarabe du cinéma et de la télévision: Informations/News* (Beirut), no. 78–79, October 1, 1970.

62. Organisation internationale de la francophonie, "Hommage à Tahar Cheriaa (1927–2010)," 2011, accessed October 28, 2014, www.francophonie.org/IMG/pdf/Hommage_Tahar_Cheriaa.pdf.

63. Telegram from AmEmbassy, Rabat, to SecState, December 4, 1963, NARA, RG 59, INCO Motion Pictures, 1963, box 3545.

64. Airgram from AmEmbassy, Rabat, to DOS, "'Moroccanization' of Motion Pictures Distribution," December 20, 1963, NARA, RG 59, INCO Motion Pictures, 1963, box 3545.

65. Airgram from AmEmbassy, Rabat, to DOS, commercial program, entertainment motion pictures, September 30, 1972, NARA, RG 59, INCO Motion Pictures, 1970–1973, box 1310.

66. Organisation internationale de la francophonie, "Hommage à Tahar Cheriaa (1927–2010)," 2011, accessed October 28, 2014, www.francophonie.org/IMG/pdf/Hommage_Tahar_Cheriaa.pdf.

67. Department of State Memorandum of Conversation between MPEAA Johnson and DOS Martindale, "Tunisian Film Dispute," February 2, 1961, NARA, RG 59, Country File, Tunisia, 1960–1963, box 2760.

68. Airgram from American Embassy, Tunis, to DOS, "Motion Picture Code," July 10, 1965, NARA, RG 59, INCO Motion Pictures, 1964–1966, box 1203.

69. "Les Tunisiens préfèrent Brigitte, mais . . . ," *Afrique action*, February 12, 1961, NARA, RG 59, Country File, Tunisia, 1960–1963, box 2760; Letter from American Embassy, Tunis, to DOS, "Visit to Tunis of MPEAA Representative," December 8, 1960, NARA, RG 59, Country File, Tunisia, 1960–1963, box 2760.

70. Telegram from American Embassy, Tunis, to Secretary of State, Washington, June 9, 1971, NARA, RG 59, INCO Motion Pictures 1970–1973, box 1310.

71. Letter from AmEmbassy, Rabat, to DOS, April 26, 1962, NARA, RG 59, Country File, Morocco, 1960–1963, box 2755; Telegram from American Embassy, Rabat, to Secretary of State, Washington, June 21, 1962, NARA, RG 59, Country File, Morocco, 1960–1963, box 2755.

72. Letter from American Embassy, Tunis, to Department of State, February 2, 1961, NARA, RG 59, 1960–1963, Country File, Tunisia, box 2760.

73. Telegram from American Embassy, Tunis, to Secretary of State, Washington, December 3, 1960, NARA, RG 59, Country File, Tunisia, 1960–1963, box 2760.

74. Telegram from Tunis to SecState, December 12, 1960, NARA, RG 59, Country File, Tunisia, 1960–1963, box 2760.

75. Airgram from Rabat to DOS, Jan 17, 1964, NARA, RG 59, INCO Motion Pictures, 1964–1966, box 1203.

76. Telegram from American Embassy, Tunis, to Secretary of State, "Motion Picture Export Association Financial Problems in Tunisia," June 9, 1971, NARA, RG59, INCO Motion Pictures, 1970–1973, box 1310.

77. Airgram from AmEmbassy, Algiers to DOS, "Resumption of Film Shipments to Algeria," March 26, 1965, NARA, RG 59, INCO Motion Pictures, 1964–1966, box 1202; Airgram from AmEmbassy, Algiers, to DOS, "Progress on Question of American Films," October 30, 1967, NARA, RG 59, INCO Motion Pictures, 1967–1969, box 1127; Airgram from AmEmbassy, Algiers, to DOS, "Problems of American Films," October 30, 1967, NARA, RG 59, INCO Motion Pictures, 1967–1969, box 1127; Airgram from AmEmbassy, Algiers, to DOS, "American Films in Algeria," February 19, 1968, NARA, RG 59, INCO Motion Pictures, 1967–1969, box 1127.

78. "Algeria Seizes U.S. Distribs: MPEA Caught by Grim Surprise," *Variety*, June 4, 1969.

79. Telegram from AmEmbassy, Algiers, to SecState, "Algerian Films," June 7, 1969, NARA, IRG 59, NCO Motion Pictures, 1967–1969, box 1127.

80. Telegram from USINT Algiers to SecState, 8 April 1974, NARA online archives, document number: 1974ALGIER00726.

81. AmEmbassy, Rabat, to DOS, June 6, 1961, NARA, RG 59, Country File, Morocco, 1960–1963, box 2755.

82. AmEmbassy, Rabat, to DOS, November 17, 1961, NARA, RG 59, Country File, Morocco, 1960–1963, box 2755; AmEmbassy, Rabat, to DOS, April 26, 1962, NARA, RG 59, Country File, Morocco, 1960–1963, box 2755.

83. AmEmbassy, Rabat, to DOS, March 30, 1962, NARA, RG 59, Country File, Morocco, 1960–1963, box 2755.

84. AmEmbassy, Rabat, to DOS, November 17, 1961, NARA, RG 59, Country File, Morocco, 1960–1963, box 2755; Rabat to SecState, July 18, 1962, NARA, RG 59, Country File, Morocco, 1960–1963, box 2755.

85. Letter from American Embassy, Tunis, to DOS, December 8, 1960, NARA, RG 59, Country File, Tunisia, 1960–1963, box 2760.

86. Telegram from DOS to American Embassy, Tunis, December 9, 1960, NARA, RG 59, Country File, Tunisia, 1960–1963, box 2760.

87. Airgram from AmEmbassy, Algiers, to DOS, March 26, 1965, NARA, RG 59, INCO Motion Pictures, 1964–1966, box 1202; AmEmbassy, Algiers, to DOS, October 30, 1967, NARA, RG 59, INCO Motion Pictures, 1967–1969, box 1127.

88. Letter from MPEA to Martindale, DOS, November 25, 1960, NARA, RG 59, Country File, Tunisia, 1960–1963, box 2760.

89. Letter from MPEA to Martindale, DOS, November 25, 1960, NARA, RG 59, Country File, Tunisia, 1960–1963, box 2760.

Chapter 5

1. "TV Tops Arab Terrorists as Threat to Israeli Exhibitors; Biz Off 50%," *Variety*, October 9, 1986; "Israeli Theaters Report Business Boom Continues," *Box Office*, June 14, 1976.

2. "'Macho' Films Show Muscle at Lebanese B. O.," *Hollywood Reporter*, July 19, 1988.

3. "The Show Goes On—under the Gun," *Los Angeles Times*, July 15, 1984; "Showbiz as Usual in Lebanon," *Daily Variety*, December 26, 1989.

4. "The Show Goes On—under the Gun," *Los Angeles Times*, July 15, 1984.

5. "The Battle for Algiers: Filmmakers Risk It All," *Variety*, April 8, 1996.

6. "Video Pirates Storm Egyptian Market," *Screen International*, March 4, 1989.

7. "The Threat of Video Piracy," *Hollywood Reporter*, August 28, 1984.

8. SecState to AmEmbassy, Abu Dhabi, October 5, 1976, NARA, RG 59, NARA archives online, document number: 1976STATE247962.

9. "Globus Sez Pic Piracy Costing US $5-Mil a Year," *Variety*, October 30, 1985.

10. "Showbiz as Usual in Lebanon," *Daily Variety*, December 26, 1989.

11. "Videocassette Piracy Slowed in Israel, but Will It Last?," *Variety*, May 7, 1980; "The Threat of Video Piracy," *Hollywood Reporter*, August 28, 1984.

12. "'Macho' Films Show Muscle at Lebanese B. O.," *Hollywood Reporter*, July 19, 1988.

13. "Admissions Falter in Israel, but 1981 Not as Bad as '80," *Variety*, October 19, 1981.

14. "Videocassette Piracy Slowed in Israel, but Will It Last?," *Variety*, May 7, 1980; "The Threat of Video Piracy," *Hollywood Reporter*, August 28, 1984.

15. "The Threat of Video Piracy," *Hollywood Reporter*, August 28, 1984.

16. "Video Pirates Storm Egyptian Market," *Screen International*, March 4, 1989.

17. "The Threat of Video Piracy," *Hollywood Reporter*, August 28, 1984.

18. "Videocassette Piracy Slowed in Israel, but Will It Last?," *Variety*, May 7, 1980.

19. "Admission Price Increase, TV Affect Israel Market," *Hollywood Reporter*, August 31, 1976.

20. "Problems Facing Israeli Cinemas," *Variety*, January 9, 1980.

21. "Israeli Theaters and Attendances," *Variety*, October 24, 1984.

22. "Nasser, Sadat, and Now: Yanks' Interest in Egypt Is Varied," *Variety*, May 12, 1982.

23. "Lebanon's Warfare Cripples Filmgoing, Production Efforts," *Hollywood Reporter*, January 17, 1984.

24. "Tunis Distrib H. Q. Is Right in the Middle of Things," *Variety*, May 9, 1990.

25. "State Controls State of Algerian Exhib/Distrib," *Variety*, May 9, 1990.

26. "Showbiz as Usual in Lebanon," *Daily Variety*, December 26, 1989; "Morocco's Exhibs: We Can't Make a Dirham," *Variety*, May 9, 1990.

27. "Morocco's Exhibs: We Can't Make a Dirham," *Variety*, May 9, 1990; "At Iraqi Cinema, a Flashback to Better Times," *Los Angeles Times*, May 7, 2009.

28. "Nasser, Sadat, and now: Yanks' interest in Egypt is varied," *Variety*, May 12, 1982.

29. "State Controls State of Algerian Exhib/Distrib," *Variety*, May 9, 1990.

30. "State Controls State of Algerian Exhib/Distrib," *Variety*, May 9, 1990.

31. "Morocco's Exhibs: We Can't Make a Dirham," *Variety*, May 9, 1990.

32. "'Macho' Films Show Muscle at Lebanese B. O.," *Hollywood Reporter*, July 19, 1988.

33. "Soaring Inflation, Leveling Off of Attendance Marking Israeli Pix Biz a Market of Extreme," *Variety*, January 9, 1980.

34. "20th-Fox Leads Yank B. O. Take in Israeli Market," *Variety*, January 10, 1979.

35. "Soaring Inflation, Leveling Off of Attendance Marking Israeli Pix Biz a Market of Extreme," *Variety*, January 9, 1980.

36. "UA Ankles Israel Distribery; Down B. O. Screens Cited," *Variety*, May 7, 1980; "Israeli Screens in Distributor Hands: Lockup Leaves Indies Extinct," *Variety*, December 28, 1983.

37. "Cannon's Dimnort App'td Top at UIP Israel as GG Expands," *Hollywood Reporter*, December 29, 1983.

38. "Israeli Trade Smiles, Hesitantly, on Its Former Peck's Bad Boys," *Variety*, February 29, 1984: "Gilad Is Major and Indie," *Variety*, October 24, 1984.

39. "Israeli Distributor Hands: Lockup Leaves Indies Extinct," *Variety*, December 28, 1983.

40. "Soaring Inflation, Leveling Off of Attendance Marking Israeli Pix Biz a Market of Extreme," *Variety*, January 9, 1980.

41. "CIC Drops Freundlich in Israel, Surkis to Helm UIP Transition," *Variety*, April 13, 1983.

42. "Cannon's Dimnort App'td Top at UIP Israel as GG Expands," *Hollywood Reporter*, December 29, 1983.

43. "Inflation, Devaluation Sparking Fears among Distribs in Israel," *Daily Variety*, October 31, 1983; "Israeli Distrib, in Coin Panic, Beg Licensors to Cut Demands," *Variety*, November 2, 1983; "Israeli Distribs Win Eased Rental Terms," *Variety*, November 30, 1983.

44. "UA Ankles Israel Distriberry; Down B. O. Screens Cited," *Variety*, May 7, 1980; "Israeli Screens in Distributor Hands: Lockup Leaves Indies Extinct," *Variety*, December 28, 1983.

45. "You Snatch My Pack, I'll Snatch Theirs," *Screen International*, June 9, 1990; "Intrigue, Secrecy Surrounded UIP's Israel Deal with Cannon," *Variety*, February 29, 1984.

46. "You Snatch My Pack, I'll Snatch Theirs," *Screen International*, June 9, 1990.

47. "You Snatch My Pack, I'll Snatch Theirs," *Screen International*, June 9, 1990.

48. "Egypt Seeing Fewer Yank Films," *Hollywood Reporter*, December 13, 1983.

49. "Egypt Says 'Sadat's Enough; Boots Col Films, Productions," *Hollwyood Reporter*, January 30, 1984.

50. "Egyptian Judge Waives Fines on 'Sadat' Trial, Oks Boycott," *Hollywood Reporter*, March 29, 1984; "Fox Signs with Egyptian Distrib," *Hollywood Reporter*, March 22, 1988.

51. "Nasser, Sadat, and Now; Yanks' Interest in Egypt Is Varied," *Variety*, May 12, 1982.

52. "Nasser, Sadat, and Now; Yanks' Interest in Egypt Is Varied," *Variety*, May 12, 1982.

53. "Col and Valenti react to 'Sadat' Furor in Egypt," *Daily Variety*, February 4, 1984.

54. "Fox Signs with Egyptian Distrib," *Hollywood Reporter*, March 22, 1988.

55. "Special Report: Egypt," *Hollywood Reporter*, January 27, 1984.

56. "Fox Signs with Egyptian Distrib," *Hollywood Reporter*, March 22, 1988.

57. "Fox Signs with Egyptian Distrib," *Hollywood Reporter*, March 22, 1988.

58. "Cairo New Film Base in Mideast as Beirut Fades," *Variety*, September 1, 1976.

59. "Lebanon," *Hollywood Reporter*, May 8, 1984.

60. Empire, "Abou Us," *empire.com.lb*.

61. "The Show Goes On—under the Gun," *Los Angeles Times*, July 15, 1984.

62. "The Show Goes On—under the Gun," *Los Angeles Times*, July 15, 1984.

63. "The Show Goes On—under the Gun," *Los Angeles Times*, July 15, 1984.

64. "The Show Goes On—under the Gun," *Los Angeles Times*, July 15, 1984.

65. "The Show Goes On—under the Gun," *Los Angeles Times*, July 15, 1984.

66. "Live from Beirut," *Hollywood Reporter*, August 28, 1984; "West Invades Lebanon Multis,"*Variety*, November 18, 1996.

67. "The Show Goes On—under the Gun," *Los Angeles Times*, July 15, 1984.

68. "Israeli Exhibs to Maintain Support of Export Assn.'s Antipiracy Plan," *Variety*, June 14, 1989.

69. "U.S. Warns Arabs to Get It Together on Film/Vid Piracy," *Variety*, December 28, 1988.

70. "U.S. Warns Arabs to Get It Together on Film/Vid Piracy," *Variety*, December 28, 1988.

71. USTR, Special 301 fact sheet on intellectual property, May 25, 1989. USTR, "Hills Announces Results of Special 301 Review," April 27, 1990; USTR, Special 301 fact sheet on intellectual property, April 26, 1991.

72. "Egypt Is Warned about Piracy," *Screen International*, March 3, 1990.

73. "Egypt to Lay Down Copyright Law," *Variety*, March 9, 1992; "Egypt's New Copyright Law Lacks Teeth," *Variety*, June 22, 1992.

74. USTR, "USTR Announces Special 301, Title VII Reviews," April 29, 1992; USTR, "USTR Announces Three Decisions," April 30, 1993.

75. "Iranians Just Wanna Have Fun," *Variety*, February 14, 1990.

76. "Iranian Film Biz Revisited; Lots US Cassettes, Pictrues Backlog," *Variety*, June 6, 1984.

77. "Iranian Film Biz Revisited; Lots US Cassettes, Pictrues Backlog," *Variety*, June 6, 1984.

78. "Iranian Film Biz Revisited; Lots US Cassettes, Pictrues Backlog," *Variety*, June 6, 1984. "Iranians Just Wanna Have Fun," *Variety*, February 14, 1990.

79. "State Monopoly of Algerian Pic Prod Being Discontinued," *Variety*, October 3, 1984.

80. "State Controls State of Algerian Exhib/Distrib," *Variety*, May 9, 1990.

81. "At Iraqi Cinema, a Flashback to Better Times," *Los Angeles Times*, May 7, 2009.

82. "Tunisia—an Oasis of Western Culture," *Los Angeles Times*, 1982.

83. "Tunis Distrib H. Q. Is Right in the Middle of Things," *Variety*, May 9, 1990.

Chapter 6

1. "Why 'Titanic' Conquered the World," *New York Times*, April 26, 1998.

2. "Why 'Titanic' Conquered the World," *New York Times*, April 26, 1998.

3. Robert W. Welkos and Yehia Ranwa, "Death to U.S. but Not Films," *Los Angeles Times*, October 31, 2001.

4. "Why 'Titanic' Conquered the World," *New York Times*, April 26, 1998; Williams, Michael, "'Titanic' Runs Afoul of Algerian Pirates," *Variety*, February 1, 1999.

5. *Variety Arabia*, February 2012, 23.

6. "A Naplouse, les Palestiniens retournent au cinéma," *L'Orient-Le Jour*, June 25, 2009, https://www.lorientlejour.com/article/622875/A_Naplouse%252C_les_Palestiniens_retournent_au_cinema.html.

7. Sarah Levy, "Cinema under Siege," *Hollywood Reporter*, November 19–25, 2002.

8. Al-Kasaba Theatre and Cinematheque, "About Us," 2018 http://alkasaba.org/details.php?id=nhk4w9a1463yho9leoo23.

9. Jillian Kestler-D'Amours, "East Jerusalem Cinema Reopens after 25 Years," *Electronic Intifada*, February 20, 2012, https://electronicintifada.net/

content/east-jerusalem-cinema-reopens-after-25-years/10969; "Jerusalem Cinema Reopens after 26 Years," *Ma'an News.com*, March 2, 2012, http://www.maannews.com/Content.aspx?id=463853; Yabous Cultural Centre, "List of Donors," 2018, accessed October 18, 2018, http://yabous.org/en/?page_id=2214.

10. "Jenin Cinema Opens to Fanfare," *Ma'an News.com*, August 7, 2010, http://www.maannews.com/Content.aspx?id=305420; AFP, "Le cinéma des célébrités en Cisjordanie ferme ses portes," November 30, 2016, https://www.la-croix.com/Culture/Le-cinema-celebrites-Cisjordanie-ferme-portes-2016-11-30-1300807156; Ahmad Al-Bazz, "Palestine's Disappearing Cinemas," *Electronic Intifada*, October 9, 2017, https://electronicintifada.net/content/palestines-disappearing-cinemas/21876.

11. "A New Beginning: First Movie Theatre in 22 Years Opens in Nablus," *Ma'an News.com*, July 17, 2009, http://www.maannews.com/Content.aspx?id=211444.

12. "Signs of Economic Life Return to West Bank City," NPR, July 10, 2009, https://www.npr.org/templates/story/story.php?storyId=106406800&ft=1&f=3.

13. "A New Beginning: First Movie Theatre in 22 Years Opens in Nablus," *Ma'an News.com*, July 17, 2009, http://www.maannews.com/Content.aspx?id=211444.

14. "Palestine's Disappearing Cinemas," *Electronic Intifada*, October 9, 2017, https://electronicintifada.net/content/palestines-disappearing-cinemas/21876.

15. Palestine Trade Tower official website, http://www.palestinetradetower.com/.

16. Palestine Tower Cinemas, Genfk page, accessed October 19, 2018, https://www.genfk.com/user.php?id=649374795133313.

17. "Iraq Aims to Revive Cinema!," *Baghdad Invest*, April 28, 2011, https://archive.is/20130118013702/http://www.baghdadinvest.com/Cinema_Iraq_Films.html.

18. "Baghdad Film Fest Aims to Break Cultural Isolation," AFP, October 5, 2011, http://www.yourmiddleeast.com/features/baghdad-film-fest-aims-to-break-cultural-isolation_1944.

19. "At Iraqi Cinema, a Flashback to Better Times," *Los Angeles Times*, May 7, 2009.

20. "At Iraqi Cinema, a Flashback to Better Times," *Los Angeles Times*, May 7, 2009.

21. "At Iraqi Cinema, a Flashback to Better Times," *Los Angeles Times*, May 7. 2009; "Culture in Post-Saddam Iraq," *Middle East Quarterly*, Summer 2007, 33–42, http://www.meforum.org/1707/culture-in-post-saddam-iraq.

22. "Iraq, US Film Industries Struggle with War," *Monsters and Critics*, August 19, 2010, http://www.monstersandcritics.com/news/middleeast/features/article_1578557.php/Iraq-US-film-industries-struggle-with-war-Feature; "Baghdad Film Fest Aims to Break Cultural Isolation," AFP, October 5, 2011, http://www.yourmiddleeast.com/features/baghdad-film-fest-aims-to-break-cultural-isolation_1944.

23. "Iraq, US Film Industries Struggle with War," *Monsters and Critics*, August 19, 2010, http://www.monstersandcritics.com/news/middleeast/features/article_1578557.php/Iraq-US-film-industries-struggle-with-war-Feature.

24. "Iraq Aims to Revive Cinema!," *Baghdad Invest*, April 28, 2011, https://archive.is/20130118013702/http://www.baghdadinvest.com/Cinema_Iraq_Films.html#selection-469.0-469.238.

25. "Iraq Aims to Revive Cinema!," *Baghdad Invest*, April 28, 2011, https://archive.is/20130118013702/http://www.baghdadinvest.com/Cinema_Iraq_Films.html#selection-469.0-469.238.

26. "Empire Cinema, Now Open in Erbil," *Empire.com*, June 12, 2013, http://www.circuit-empire.com/newsDetails.asp?newstype=2&isgulg=1.

27. "Le groupe Empire va exploiter 14 salles de cinéma à Erbil, en Irak," *Le commerce du Levant*, March 8, 2011, https://www.lecommercedulevant.com/article/18298-le-groupe-empire-va-exploiter-14-salles-de-cinma-erbil-en-irak-.

28. "Mario G. Haddad, Empire International," December 12, 2014, https://www.screendaily.com/interviews/mario-g-haddad-empire-international-/5081057.article.

29. "Le groupe Empire va exploiter 14 salles de cinéma à Erbil, en Irak," *Le commerce du Levant*, March 8, 2011, https://www.lecommercedulevant.com/article/18298-le-groupe-empire-va-exploiter-14-salles-de-cinma-erbil-en-irak-.

30. "New 14-Screen Multiplex Cinema for Erbil," *Iraq Business News*, February 2011, http://www.iraq-businessnews.com/2011/02/22/new-14-screen-multiplex-cinema-for-erbil/.

31. "How Two Brits in a Pub Launched a Film Festival in a War Zone," *Hollywood Reporter.com*, November 30, 2011, http://www.hollywoodreporter.com/news/how-two-brits-a-pub-267522.

32. Empire Cinema Erbil Facebook page, accessed October 19, 2018, https://www.facebook.com/pg/empirecinemaskurdistan/reviews/.

33. "A New Beginning: First Movie Theatre in 22 Years Opens in Nablus," *Ma'an News*, July 17, 2009, http://www.maannews.com/Content.aspx?id=211444.

34. "Tim Riordan Reveals His Secrets to Maintaining Good Studio Relationships," *Variety Arabia*, December 2011.

35. "Tim Riordan Reveals His Secrets to Maintaining Good Studio Relationships," *Variety Arabia*, December 2011.

36. "Tim Riordan Reveals His Secrets to Maintaining Good Studio Relationships," *Variety Arabia*, December 2011.

37. "Tim Riordan Reveals His Secrets to Maintaining Good Studio Relationships," *Variety Arabia*, December 2011.

38. "News Corp Snaps Up $70m Rotana Stake," *Arabian Business*, February 23, 2010, https://www.arabianbusiness.com/news-corp-snaps-up-70m-rotana-stake-65967.html.

39. "LBC, Rotana Merger Details Vague," *Variety*, November 16, 2007, https://variety.com/2007/tv/news/lbc-rotana-merger-details-vague-1117976176/#!.

40. "Rotana and Fox Sign $26.7m deal with Disney," *Digital Studiome.com*, December 14, 2009, https://www.digitalstudiome.com/article-2098-rotana-and-fox-sign-267m-deal-with-disney.

41. "News Corp Ups Stake in Alwaleed's Rotana," *Arabian Business*, May 16, 2012, https://www.arabianbusiness.com/news-corp-ups-stake-in-alwaleed-s-rotana-458084.html?utm_source=Jarvis&utm_medium=arabianbusiness.com&utm_campaign=recommended.

42. "Timeline," *beinmediagroup.com*, 2018, accessed November 7, 2018, https://www.beinmediagroup.com/the-group/.

43. "Qatar's beIN Strikes Deal with Middle East Distributor to Expand Pay-TV Offering," *Hollywood Reporter*, November 18, 2015, https://www.hollywoodreporter.com/news/qatars-bein-strikes-deal-middle-841795; "beIN Media Group Seals Deal with Italia Film International," December 15, 2015, https://www.beinmediagroup.com/article/bein-media-group-seals-deal-with-italia-film-international/.

44. "Miramax Acquired by Qatar-Based beIN Media Group," *Deadline Hollywood*, March 2, 2016, https://deadline.com/2016/03/bein-media-group-acquires-miramax-1201713199/.

45. "Qatar's beIN Inks Turner Deal to Expand Entertainment Channels," *Arabian Business*, January 8, 2016, https://www.arabianbusiness.com/qatar-s-bein-inks-turner-deal-expand-entertainment-channels-616715.html#.Vo8FcvkrLIU.

46. "AMC Networks Launches Five Channels on Miramax Owner beIN in Middle East, North Africa," *Variety*, July 26, 2016, https://variety.com/2016/tv/global/amc-networks-miramax-bein-1201823090/.

47. "beIN Expands Its Entertainment Portfolio," *beinmediagroup.com*, February 28, 2017, https://www.beinmediagroup.com/article/bein-expands-entertainment-portfolio-launch-demand-services-seven-new-channels/.

48. "beIN MENA Signs Acquisition Deal with Warner Bros.," *beinmediagroup.com*, October 18, 2016, https://www.beinmediagroup.com/article/bein-mena-signs-acquisition-deal-warner-bros/.

49. "Satellite Censorship Arab League Style," *Arab Media and Society*, March 14, 2008 https://www.arabmediasociety.com/satellite-censorship-arab-league-style/.

50. "TV Censorship . . . a Dying Art?," *Variety Arabia*, April 2012.

51. "TV Censorship . . . a Dying Art?," *Variety Arabia*, April 2012.

52. "TV Censorship . . . a Dying Art?," *Variety Arabia*, April 2012.

53. "TV Censorship . . . a Dying Art?," *Variety Arabia*, April 2012.

54. "TV Censorship . . . a Dying Art?," *Variety Arabia*, April 2012.

55. "MBC Bollywood," 2018, accessed November 8, 2018, http://www.mbc.net/en/corporate/channels/mbc-bollywood.html.

56. "To Pay or Not to Pay," *Variety Arabia*, April 2012.

57. "TV Channels Should Consider Being Number Two, Says Advertising Expert," *Variety Arabia*, May 2012.

58. "Iran's Shadowy Tape Man, Spreading What's Forbidden," *New York Times*, October 5, 2000, https://www.nytimes.com/2000/10/05/movies/the-pop-life-iran-s-shadowy-tape-man-spreading-what-s-forbidden.html.

59. Quoted in "Iran Destroys 100,000 Satellite Dishes to Stop Citizens Watching 'Morally Damaging Television That Corrupts Islamic Values," *Mail Online*, July 25, 2016, https://www.dailymail.co.uk/news/article-3706645/Iran-

destroys-100-000-satellite-dishes-stop-citizens-watching-morally-damaging-television-corrupts-Islamic-values.html.

60. "MBC Persia Hits the Airwaves," *Digital Studio me.com*, October 4, 2018, https://www.digitalstudiome.com/broadcast/broadcast-business/30701-mbc-persia-hits-the-airwaves.

61. "Declaring War against Piracy," *Variety Arabia*, April 2012.

62. "Regional Distributors Struggle against Illegal TV Movie Channels," *Variety Arabia*, February 2012.

63. "Ali Jaber Talks about His New Role," *Variety Arabia*, December 2011.

64. "Iran's Shadowy Tape Man, Spreading What's Forbidden," *New York Times*, October 5, 2000,https://www.nytimes.com/2000/10/05/movies/the-pop-life-iran-s-shadowy-tape-man-spreading-what-s-forbidden.html.

65. "Watching Shrek in Tehran," *Believer*, March 1, 2010, https://believer-mag.com/watching-shrek-in-tehran/.

66. "Iran Film Industry Struggling under Censorship, Piracy," *arabian business.com*, June 8, 2008, http://www.arabianbusiness.com/iran-film-industry-struggling-under-censorship-piracy-48666.html.

67. "Censorship in the UAE," *TimeOutDubai.com*, April 20, 2010; "Muslim Countries Vary Greatly in Censorship of Hollywood Films," *FoxNews.com*, October 21, 2010, http://www.foxnews.com/entertainment/2010/10/19/muslim-countries-vary-greatly-censorship-hollywood-films/#ixzz1sx4ySkGQ.

68. "Hollywood veut empêcher les soldats de pirater des films en Irak," *Numerama*, May 15, 2010, https://www.numerama.com/magazine/15731-hollywood-veut-empecher-les-soldats-de-pirater-des-films-en-irak.html.

69. "The Migrant Pirates," *Mail Online*, March 4, 2016, https://www.daily mail.co.uk/news/article-3476365/The-migrant-pirates-Refugees-running-huge-fines-illegally-downloading-thousands-films.html.

Chapter 7

1. The issue of production stands outside the limits of this study but is a key element in the collapse of the film markets in North Africa. While Morocco has managed to produce a number of films, holding about 20% of its national market share in the 2010s (Ali 2012b, 124), most of the films from North Africa are coproduced with Europe, and made with the European film festival circuit in mind (Benchenna, Caillé, Mingant 2016, 209). The link between North African films and their national audiences is a different area of exploration.

2. "Salles de cinéma: Les recettes n'ont pas dépassé 41MDH à fin août," *Aujourd'hui le Maroc*, October 5, 2018, http://aujourdhui.ma/culture/cinema/salles-de-cinema-les-recettes-nont-pas-depasse-41-mdh-a-fin-aout.

3. "Le déclin des salles de cinéma en Tunisie," *Euro-Méditerranée*, January 17, 2008, http://euro-mediterranee.blogspot.com/2008/01/le-dclin-des-salles-de-cinma-en-tunisie.html.

4. Many US films are now dubbed in "international French" in Canada, thus eliminating that issue (Ali-Yahia interview).

5. "Coopération Kabylie-Québec dans le domaine du doublage des films," *Siwel*, October 5, 2012, https://www.siwel.info/coorperation-kabylie-quebec-dans-le-domaine-du-doublage-des-films_3011.html.

6. Karim Kherbouche, Pucci sur toutes les lèvres," *La Dépêche de Kabylie*, March 31, 2009, https://www.depechedekabylie.com/culture/68671-pucci-sur-toutes-les-levres/.

7. *Le Monde*, "Canal+ se retire des marchés algérien et marocain," *Le Monde. fr*, March 1, 2011, https://www.lemonde.fr/actualite-medias/article/2011/03/01/canal-se-retire-des-marches-algerien-et-marocain_1486969_3236.html.

8. Mégarama Maroc, http://megarama.ma/index-maroc.html.

9. Morocco Mall, "A propos," 2018, https://www.moroccomall.ma/qui-sommes-nous; "Imax's International Expansion at Tipping Point," *Hollywood Reporter*, January 23, 2013, https://www.hollywoodreporter.com/news/imaxs-international-expansion-at-tipping-414859.

10. "L'ancien cinéma Colisée devient le premier multiplex de Rabat," *Tel Quel*, July 19, 2018, https://telquel.ma/2018/07/19/lancien-cinema-colisee-devient-le-premier-multiplex-a-rabat_1603857; "Au Maroc, le cinéma 'premium' à la conquête des spectateurs," *Capital*, July 25, 2018, https://www.capital.fr/lifestyle/au-maroc-le-cinema-premium-a-la-conquete-des-spectateurs-1299863.

11. "Un multiplexe Pathé en Tunisie en 2018," *ecrannoir.fr*, October 17, 2016, http://ecrannoir.fr/blog/blog/2016/10/17/un-multiplexe-pathe-en-tunisie-en-2018/; "Tunisie: Gaumont Pathé lance à Tunis les travaux du premier cinéma multiplexe du pays," Agence Ecofin, July 11, 2017, https://www.agenceecofin.com/audiovisuel/1107-48761-tunisie-gaumont-pathe-lance-a-tunis-les-travaux-du-premier-cinema-multiplexe-du-pays.

12. "En marge du Festival de Marrakech, des cinémas à l'abandon," *Le Monde.fr*, November 12, 2014, https://www.lemonde.fr/cinema/article/2014/12/11/en-marge-du-festival-de-marrakech-des-cinemas-a-l-abandon_4539265_3476.html.

13. "Save Cinemas in Morocco: Founder Tarik Mounim on the Fight to Preserve Public Art in Morocco," *Morocco World News*, March 25, 2014, https://www.moroccoworldnews.com/2014/03/126390/save-cinemas-in-morocco-founder-tarik-mounim-on-the-fight-to-preserve-public-art-in-morocco/.

14. "En marge du Festival de Marrakech, des cinemas à l'abandon," *Le Monde.fr*, November 12, 2014, https://www.lemonde.fr/cinema/article/2014/12/11/en-marge-du-festival-de-marrakech-des-cinemas-a-l-abandon_4539265_3476.html.

15. "Cinemadrasa, un projet pour promouvoir les salles de cinéma," Festival International du Film de Marrakech, October 18, 2018, accessed October 24, 2018, https://www.festivalmarrakech.info/cinemadrasa-maroc-un-projet-pour-promouvoir-les-salles-de-cinema/.

16. "Le marché du cinéma en Algérie: Interview de Malek Ali Yahia (MD Ciné)," *Algeria Global Markets.net*, January 2, 2016, https://www.agm.net/news/le-marche-du-cinema-en-algerie-interview-de-malek-ali-yahia-md-cine.

17. "Le marché du cinéma en Algérie: interview de Malek Ali Yahia (MD Ciné)," *Algeria Global Markets.net*, January 2, 2016, https://www.agm.net/news/le-marche-du-cinema-en-algerie-interview-de-malek-ali-yahia-md-cine.

18. "Le marché du cinéma en Algérie: interview de Malek Ali Yahia (MD Ciné)," *Algeria Global Markets.net*, January 2, 2016, https://www.agm.net/news/le-marche-du-cinema-en-algerie-interview-de-malek-ali-yahia-md-cine.

19. "Les stars d'Hollywood à la rescousse des cinémas d'Alger," *Le Monde. fr*, March 8, 2018, https://www.lemonde.fr/afrique/article/2018/08/03/les-stars-d-hollywood-a-la-rescousse-des-cinemas-d-alger_5339235_3212.html.

20. "MEDIS, le premier réseau de distributeurs Sud-Méditerranée, lancé à Dubaï," *Euro-Méditerranée*, December 31, 2012, http://euro-mediterranee.blogspot.com/2012/12/medis-le-premier-reseau-de.html.; "Nouvelle rencontre MEDIS à Cannes," *Euro-Méditerranée*, May 27, 2014, http://euro-mediterranee.blogspot.com/2014/05/nouvelle-rencontre-de-medis-cannes.html.

Chapter 8

1. "Empire Building on the Back of the Multiplex," *Screen International*, March 19, 2004; "16-Screen Movie Theater to Open in Jerusalem on Shabbat Too," *Times of Israel*, April 30, 2014, https://www.timesofisrael.com/yes-planet-ups-the-shabbat-ante-in-jerusalem/.

2. "Carry on Regardless," *Screen International*, September 2, 2005.

3. "Cinema City Opens in Rishon LeZion, Israel," *Global City Holdings*, July 19, 2014, http://globalcityholdings.com/a/1186,cinema-city-opens-in-rishon-lezion-israel.

4. "16-Screen Movie Theater to Open in Jerusalem on Shabbat Too," *Times of Israel*, April 30, 2014, https://www.timesofisrael.com/yes-planet-ups-the-shabbat-ante-in-jerusalem/.

5. International Union of Cinemas, *Annual Report, 2012–2013*, 19; International Union of Cinemas, *Annual Report, 2018*, 13.

6. "Multiplex Thrives amid Strife," *Variety*, Jan 5, 2004.

7. "What's Borat Really Saying? Ask an Israeli," *Los Angeles Times*, December 22, 2006, http://articles.latimes.com/2006/dec/22/entertainment/et-borat22.

8. "Distributors: Screen Battles," *Screen Daily*, December 12, 2013, https://www.screendaily.com/features/distributors-screen-battle.

9. Renaissance, "Our Cinemas," 2018, accessed November 14, 2018, http://rnscinemas.net/Cinemas.php.

10. Misr International Films, "Cinemas," 2018, accessed November 14, 2018, http://misrinternationalfilms.com/cinemas.

11. Misr International Films, "Distribution," 2018, accessed November 14, 2018, http://misrinternationalfilms.com/distribution.

12. "Distributors: Screen Battles," *Screen Daily*, December 12, 2013, https://www.screendaily.com/features/distributors-screen-battle.

13. "Prints of a Guy," *Hollywood Reporter*, April 26–May 2, 2005.

14. "Mideast Eager for Hollywood Business: Money Currently Flowing from U.S. to Emirates," *Variety.com*, May 9, 2008.

15. "The Fruits of Revolution Leave Bitter Taste on Egyptian Cinema," *Variety Arabia*, January 30, 2012.

16. Quoted in "Egypt's 'Matrix' Ban Sparking Backlash," *Variety*, June 22, 2003, https://variety.com/2003/biz/news/egypt-s-matrix-ban-sparking-backlash-1117888313/.

17. Quoted in "Egypt's 'Matrix' Ban Sparking Backlash," *Variety*, June 22, 2003, https://variety.com/2003/biz/news/egypt-s-matrix-ban-sparking-backlash-1117888313/.

18. Quoted in "Egypt Bans 'Zionist' Film Exodus and Cites 'Historical Inaccuracies,'" *Guardian*, December 26, 2014, https://www.theguardian.com/film/2014/dec/26/egypt-bans-hollywood-exodus-christian-bale.

19. Quoted in "Egypt Bans 'Zionist' Film Exodus and Cites 'Historical Inaccuracies,'" *Guardian*, December 26, 2014, https://www.theguardian.com/film/2014/dec/26/egypt-bans-hollywood-exodus-christian-bale.

20. "Adam Sandler Faces Middle East Movie Ban," *Telegraph*, August 19, 2008, https://www.telegraph.co.uk/news/celebritynews/2585850/Adam-Sandler-faces-Middle-East-movie-ban.html.

21. "Egypt's 'Matrix' Ban Sparking Backlash," *Variety*, June 22, 2003, https://variety.com/2003/biz/news/egypt-s-matrix-ban-sparking-backlash-1117888313/.

22. "Regional Distributors Struggle against Illegal TV Movie Channels," *Variety Arabia*, February 2012; "Declaring War against Piracy," *Variety Arabia*, April 2012.

23. "Hardtops Renaissance: Egypt Outfit Pegs 100 New Screens for Country," *Daily Variety*, March 12, 1998.

24. "U.S. Pix Sizzling as B. O. Heats Up," *Variety*, February 11, 2002.

25. "Prints of a Guy," *Hollywood Reporter*, April 26–May 2, 2005.

26. "Prints of a Guy," *Hollywood Reporter*, April 26–May 2, 2005.

27. "Prints of a Guy," *Hollywood Reporter*, April 26–May 2, 2005.

28. "Mideast Finds Film Oasis," *Daily Variety*, November 21, 2001.

29. Misr International Films, "Cinemas," 2018, accessed November 14, 2018, http://misrinternationalfilms.com/cinemas.

30. VOX Cinemas, "About Us," 2018, accessed November 15, 2018, https://egy.voxcinemas.com/about.

31. "The Fruits of Revolution Leave Bitter Taste on Egyptian Cinema," *Variety Arabia*, January, 30, 2012; "Egyptian Turmoil Puts Showbiz at a Standstill," *Hollywood Reporter*, February 10, 2011.

32. "The Fruits of Revolution Leave Bitter Taste on Egyptian Cinema," *Variety Arabia*, January 30, 2012.

33. "Censorship Craze Continues in New Egypt," *Variety Arabia*, April 2012; "A Cultural Standoff," *Los Angeles Times*, April 22, 2012.

34. "The Fruits of Revolution Leave Bitter Taste on Egyptian Cinema," *Variety Arabia*, January 30, 2012.

35. "The Fruits of Revolution Leave Bitter Taste on Egyptian Cinema," *Variety Arabia*, January 30, 2012.

36. "West Invades Lebanon Multis," *Variety*, November 18, 1996.

37. "Lebanon," *Screen International*, September 21, 2007; Selim Ramia and Co., "Grand Cinemas," 2018, accessed November 16, 2018, http://srndco.com/grand-cinemas#whoweare.

38. VOX Cinemas, "About Us," 2018, accessed November 15, 2018, https://egy.voxcinemas.com/about.

39. CineKlik, "Experience," 2018, accessed November 15, 2018, https://lb.cineklik.com/cinemas.

40. "West Invades Lebanon Multis," *Variety*, November 18, 1996.

41. "The Human Rights Cost of a Parliament Extension in Lebanon," *Human Rights Watch*, May 31, 2017, https://www.hrw.org/news/2017/05/31/human-rights-cost-parliament-extension-lebanon.

42. Quoted in "Conflict Chills Lebanese Biz," *Variety*, August 21, 2006.

43. "Conflict Chills Lebanese Biz," *Variety*, August 21, 2006.

44. "Steven Spielberg's 'The Post' Gets Banned in Lebanon," *Hollywood Reporter*, January 14, 2018, https://www.hollywoodreporter.com/news/steven-spielbergs-post-gets-banned-lebanon-1074587.

45. "Wonder Woman Kindles Controversy in the Arab World," *France 24*, June 20, 2017, https://www.france24.com/en/20170617-wonder-woman-kindles-controversy-arab-world.

46. "Steven Spielberg's 'The Post' Gets Banned in Lebanon," *Hollywood Reporter*, January 14, 2018, https://www.hollywoodreporter.com/news/steven-spielbergs-post-gets-banned-lebanon-1074587; "Wonder Woman and a Dangerous Precedent for Censorship in Lebanon," *Independent*, June 2, 2017, https://www.independent.co.uk/news/world/middle-east/wonder-woman-banned-israel-lebanon-beirut-censorship-accusations-a7770146.html.

47. "Lebanon Bans Screening of The Nun on Religious Grounds," *New Arab*, September 17, 2018, https://www.alaraby.co.uk/english/society/2018/9/17/lebanon-bans-screening-of-the-nun-on-religious-grounds.

Chapter 9

1. "Grand Ambitions, Interview," *Business Year*, 2014, https://www.thebusinessyear.com/lebanon-2014/grand-ambitions/interview.

2. Selim Ramia and Co. Holding, "A Story of Success," 2018, http://srndco.com/srndco#storyofsuccess.

3. "Grand Ambitions, Interview," *Business Year*, 2014, https://www.thebusinessyear.com/lebanon-2014/grand-ambitions/interview.

4. "Grand Ambitions, Interview," *Business Year*, 2014, https://www.the businessyear.com/lebanon-2014/grand-ambitions/interview.

5. "Grand Ambitions, Interview," *Business Year*, 2014, https://www.the businessyear.com/lebanon-2014/grand-ambitions/interview.

6. "Middle East Cinemas Proliferate," *Hollywood Reporter*, September 7, 2004.

7. "The One to Watch," *Screen International*, November 2011.

8. "Grand Cinemas," 2018, accessed November 21, 2018, https://lb.grand-cinemasme.com/en/aboutus.

9. VOX Cinemas, "About Us," 2018, accessed November 15, 2018, https://egy.voxcinemas.com/about.

10. City Cinema, "About Us," 2018, accessed November 22, 2018, https://citycinemaoman.net/aboutus.html.

11. "Jordan's Film Distributors: Stuck in a Film Reel," *Variety Arabia*, February 26, 2012; Taj Cinemas, "About Us," 2018, accessed November 22, 2018, http://tajcinemas.com/about-us/; Al-Taher Group, "Al-Taher Group," 2018, accessed November 22, 2018, http://www.altaher.com/index.htm.

12. Italia Films, "About Us," 2018, accessed November 22, 2018, http://www.italiafilm.com.lb/Component/Static/About.asp.

13. Shooting Stars, "About Us," 2018, accessed November 22, 2018, http://shootingstarsuae.com/about.php.

14. "Distributors: Screen Battles," *Screen Daily*, December 12, 2013.

15. Front Row Entertainment, "About Us," 2018, accessed November 22, 2018, https://frontrowent.com/en/about-us/company-profile.

16. "Disney Expands into Middle East," *Variety*, October 8, 2008.

17. "The One to Watch," *Screen International*, November 2011.

18. "13 Hot Emerging Markets," *Hollywood Reporter.com*, September 5, 2013, http://www.hollywoodreporter.com/news/iron-man-3-internat.

19. "Owner of the Last Mile," *Variety Arabia*, December 2011.

20. "AMC to Open Saudi Arabia's First Movie Theatre," *Variety*, April 4, 2018, https://variety.com/2018/film/news/amc-movie-theaters-saudi-arabia-1202743116/.

21. "AMC to Open Saudi Arabia's First Movie Theatre," *Variety*, April 4, 2018, https://variety.com/2018/film/news/amc-movie-theaters-saudi-arabia-1202743116/.

22. "Kuwait Looking Large with 2 IMAX Screens," *Variety*, January 19, 2005.

23. IMAX, "IMAX Eyes Expansion in Saudi Arabia; Signs Multi Theatre Deal with VOX Cinemas," May 15, 2018, https://www.imax.com/content/imax-eyes-expansion-saudi-arabia-signs-multi-theatre-deal-vox-cinemas; "IMAX Partners with Vox Cinemas on Screens in Saudi Arabia," *Variety*, May 15, 2018, https://variety.com/2018/biz/news/imax-saudi-arabia-vox-cinemas-screens-1202810945/.

24. "AMC to Open Saudi Arabia's First Movie Theater," *Variety*, April 4, 2018, https://variety.com/2018/film/news/amc-movie-theaters-saudi-arabia-1202743116/.

25. Sony Pictures, "Sony Pictures Television Expands Middle East Distribution with Nex Deals in Egypt, Qatar and Dubai," May 22, 2012, http://www.sonypictures.com/corp/press_releases/2012/05_12/05222012_middleast.html; "Fox Boosts Abu Dhabi Biz," *Variety*, March 9, 2010.

26. Front Row Entertainment, "About Us," 2018, accessed November 22, 2018, https://frontrowent.com/en/about-us/company-profile.

27. Novo Cinemas, 2018, accessed November 23, 2018, https://uae.novocinemas.com/uae.

28. Novo Cinemas, "Cinema experience," 2018, accessed November 23, 2018, https://uae.novocinemas.com/uae/experience.

29. Meraas, "Attractions," 2018, accessed November 23, 2018, https://www.meraas.com/en/leisure/.

30. Emaar Properties, "Emaar Entertainment," 2018, accessed November 23, 2018, https://www.emaar.com/en/what-we-do/entertainment/.

31. Novo Cinemas, "Raising Your Cinema Experience to the 7-Star Level," 2018, accessed November 23, 2018, https://uae.novocinemas.com/uae/experience/7-star.

32. Roxy Cinemas, "A Boutique Ambiance," 2018, accessed November 23, 2018, https://www.theroxycinemas.com/Experience/the-roxy.

33. Roxy Cinemas, "Roxy Mamas," 2018, November 27, 2018, https://www.theroxycinemas.com/events-cinemas/Roxy-Mamas/3.

34. "Jordan's Film Distributors: Stuck in a Film Reel," *Variety Arabia*, February 26, 2012.

35. "Age Classification System," National Media Council website, February 19, 2018, http://nmc.gov.ae/en-us/Media-Center/Events/Pages/Age-Classification-System.aspx.

36. "Censorship Great for Pirates, Bad for Business," *Variety Arabia*, February 16, 2012.

37. "Regional Distributor Struggle against Illegal TV Movie Channels," *Variety Arabia*, April 2012.

38. "Censorship Great for Pirates, Bad for Business," *Variety Arabia*, February 16, 2012.

39. "Censorship Great for Pirates, Bad for Business," *Variety Arabia*, February 16, 2012.

40. "Qatar Bans the Girl on the Train from Cinemas," *Doha News*, October 9, 2016, https://dohanews.co/qatar-bans-the-girl-on-the-train-from-cinemas/.

41. "Artistic Freedom Gets Royal Backing," *Variety Arabia*, February 2012.

42. "Kuwait Bans 'Fahrenheit 9/11,'" *usatoday.com*, August 1, 2004.

43. "Censorship Great for Pirates, Bad for Business," *Variety Arabia*, February 16, 2012.

44. "Jordan Will Not Ban Wonder Woman," *Arutz Sheva*, June 14, 2017, http://www.israelnationalnews.com/News/News.aspx/231061; "The New Wonder Woman Movie Is Banned in Qatar," *Doha News*, June 30, 2017, https://dohanews.co/the-new-wonder-woman-movie-is-banned-in-qatar/; "Wonder Woman Is Officially Banned in Qatar," *StepFeed*, June 30, 2017, https://stepfeed.com/wonder-woman-is-officially-banned-in-qatar-7863.

45. "The One to Watch," *Screen International*, November 2011.

46. "Jordan's Film Distributors: Stuck in a Film Reel," *Variety Arabia*, February 26, 2012.

47. Founded in 1981, the GCC, or Gulf Cooperation Council, is a regional intergovernmental union between the Arab states of the Persian Gulf. It includes Bahrain, Kuwait, Oman, Qatar, Saudi Arabia, and the United Arab Emirates.

48. "Jordan's Film Distributors: Stuck in a Film Reel," *Variety Arabia*, February 26, 2012.

49. "The One to Watch," *Screen International*, November 2011.

50. Box Office Mojo, "United Arab Emirates Box Office November 15–18, 2018," https://www.boxofficemojo.com/intl/uae/?yr=2018&wk=46&p=.htm.

51. "'Black Panther,' to Break Saudi Arabia's 35-Year Cinema Ban," *Variety*, April 5, 2018, https://variety.com/2018/film/global/black-panther-to-break-saudi-arabias-35-year-cinema-ban-1202744703/; "'Sicario: Day of the Soldado' to Be First US Indie Title Released in Saudi Arabia," *Variety*, June 22, 2018, https://variety.com/2018/film/news/sicario-day-of-the-soldado-saudi-arabia-first-u-s-indie-1202854378/; "'Hotel Transylvania 3: Summer Vacation' Is First Arabic-Dubbed Film Released in Saudi Arabia," *Cartoon Brew*, July 18, 2018, https://www.cartoonbrew.com/feature-film/hotel-transylvania-3-summer-vacation-is-first-arabic-dubbed-film-released-in-saudi-arabia-162027.html; "'Kaala' Becomes First Indian Film to Be Released in Saudi Arabia," *Hollywood Reporter*, June 8, 2018, https://www.hollywoodreporter.com/news/kaala-becomes-first-indian-film-be-released-saudi-arabia-1118363; "Hosny's El Badla Marks a First for Egyptian Cinema in Saudi Arabia," *Arab News*, September 20, 2018, http://www.arabnews.com/node/1375141/lifestyle.

52. "The One to Watch," *Screen International*, November 2011.

53. "The One to Watch," *Screen International*, November 2011.

References

Aït Belhoucine, Mariam, and Claude Forest. 2019. "Le Maroc." In *Pratiques et usages du film en Afriques francophones: Maroc, Tchad, Togo, Tunisie*, edited by Patricia Caillé and Claude Forest, 101–68. Villeneuve d'Ascq: Presses universitaires du Septentrion.

Ali, Mahmoud. 2004. *Al-sinema wa al-raqabah fi misr (1896–1952)* [Cinema and Censorship in Egypt, 1896–1952]. Cairo: General Organization of Cultural Palaces.

Ali, Sahar. 2012a. *Project of Statistical Data Collection in Film and Audiovisual Markets in 9 Mediterranean Countries*. Country profile 1, *Egypt*. Tunis: Euromed Audiovisual III.

———. 2012b. *Project of Statistical Data Collection in Film and Audiovisual Markets in 9 Mediterranean Countries*. Country profile 2, *Morocco*. Tunis: Euromed Audiovisual III.

———. 2013a. *Project of Statistical Data Collection in Film and Audiovisual Markets in 9 Mediterranean Countries*. Country profile 3, *Lebanon*. Tunis: Euromed Audiovisual III.

———. 2013b. *Project of Statistical Data Collection in Film and Audiovisual Markets in 9 Mediterranean Countries*. Country profile 4, *Jordan*. Tunis: Euromed Audiovisual III.

———. 2013c. *Project of Statistical Data Collection in Film and Audiovisual Markets in 9 Mediterranean Countries*. Country profile 5, *Palestine*. Tunis: Euromed Audiovisual III.

———. 2014. *Project of Statistical Data Collection in Film and Audiovisual Markets in 9 Mediterranean Countries*. Country profile 6, *Algeria*. Tunis: Euromed Audiovisual III.

Amin, Hussein. 1998. "American Programs on Egyptian Television." In *Images of the U.S. around the World: A Multicultural Perspective*, edited by Yahya Kamalipour, 319–34. Albany: State University of New York Press.

Annuaire du cinéma pour le Moyen-Orient et l'Afrique du Nord, 1951–1952. 1952. Cairo: Éditions Jacques Pascal.

Armes, Roy. 2001. "Cinema in the Maghreb." In *Companion Encyclopedia of Middle Eastern and North African Film*, edited by Oliver Leaman, 420–517. New York: Routledge.

———. 2006. *African Filmmaking: North and South of the Sahara*. Edinburgh: Edinburgh University Press.

———. 2011. "From State Production to *Cinéma d'auteur* in Algeria." In *Film in the Middle East and North Africa: Creative Dissidence*, edited by Josef Gugler, 294–306. Austin: University of Texas Press.

Arora, Poonam. 1995. "'Imperilling the Prestige of the White Woman': Colonial Anxiety and Film Censorship in British India." *Visual Anthropology Review* 11 (2): 36–50.

Askari, Kaveh. 2014. "An Afterlife for Junk Prints: Serials and Other 'Classics' in Late-1920s Tehran." In *Silent Cinema and the Politics of Space*, edited by Jennifer M. Bean, Anupama Kapse, and Laura Horak, 99–120. Bloomington: Indiana University Press.

———. 2016. "Relaying American Film in Iran after World War II." Paper presented at the Society for Cinema and Media Studies conference, Atlanta, March.

———. Forthcoming. *Relaying Cinema in Midcentury Iran: Material Cultures in Transit*. University of California Press.

Augros, Joël, and Kira Kitsopanidou. 2009. *L'economie du cinéma américain: Histoire d'une industrie culturelle et de ses stratégies*. Paris: Armand Colin.

Bachy, Victor. 1978. *Le cinéma de Tunisie*. Tunis: Société tunisienne de diffusion.

Balanche, Fabrice. 2014. *Géopolitique du Moyen-Orient*. Documentation photographique, no. 8102. Paris: La documentation française.

Baliot, Tino, ed. 1985. *The American Film Industry*. London: University of Wisconsin Press.

Benamor, Karim. 2017. "Etat des lieux du cinéma en Tunisie avec M. Lassad Goubantini." *Autour de midi* (radio program), RTCI, March 5. http://www.rtci.tn/etat-lieux-du-cinema-en-tunisie-m-lassaad-goubantini/.

Benchenna, Abdelfettah. 2011. "Les produits culturels issus de la contrefaçon au Maroc: Outils de renforcement de la dépendance culturelle?" In *Piratages audiovisuels: Les voies souterraines de la mondialisation culturelle*, edited by Tristan Mattelart, 101–22. Brussels: de Boeck,

———. 2016. "L'exploitation des films au Maroc à l'ère des multiplexes: La double domination?" *Africultures*, no. 101–2, 214–33.

Benchenna Abdelfettah, Patricia Caillé, and Nolwenn Mingant, eds. 2016. "La circulation des films: Afrique du Nord et Moyen-Orient." Special issue, *Africultures*, no. 101–2.

Bouquet, Olivier, Philippe Pétriat, and Pierre Vermeren. 2016. *Histoire du Moyen-Orient de l'Empire Ottoman à nos jours*. Paris: Publications de la Sorbonne.

Bouzar, Yassine, and Rafik Zénine. 2015. "L'Algérie à la recherche de son cinéma." *Sur les docks* (radio program), France Culture, May 19.

Brahimi, Denise. 2009. *50 ans de cinéma maghrébin*. Paris: Minerve.

Brannon Donaghue, Courtney. 2017. *Localising Hollywood*. London: Palgrave.

Bullich, Vincent. 2011. "Le dispositif diplomatique des Etats-Unis contre le piratage de biens culturels." In *Piratages audiovisuels: Les voies souterraines de la mondialisation culturelle*, edited by Tristan Mattelart, 53–73. Brussels: de Boeck.

Centre cinématographique marocain. 2017. *Bilan cinématographique 2017*.

Caillé, Patricia. 2016. "Researching Film Spectatorship in North Africa." Paper presented at the Society for Cinema and Media Studies conference, Atlanta, April.

Caillé, Patricia, and Alia Arasoughly. 2016. "Qu'est-ce que le cinéma, à qui est-il destiné?" *Africultures*, no. 101–2, 272–93.

Caillé, Patricia, and Claude Forest, eds. 2017. *Regarder des films en Afriques*. Villeneuve d'Ascq: Presses universitaires du Septentrion

———, eds. 2019. *Pratiques et usages du film en Afriques francophones: Maroc, Tchad, Togo, Tunisie*. Villeneuve-d'Ascq: Presses universitaires du Septentrion.

Caillé, Patricia, and Lamia Guiga. 2019. "Pratique des films au regard de l'offre et de la demande en Tunisie urbaine." In *Pratiques et usages du film en Afriques francophones: Maroc, Tchad, Togo, Tunisie*, edited by Patricia Caillé and Claude Forest, 35–100. Villeneuve d'Ascq: Presses universitaires du Septentrion.

Caillé, Patricia, and Zeina Sfeir. 2016. "Au Liban, le cinéma du monde, les classiques, les films d'art et d'essai sont presque totalement absents." *Africultures*, no. 101–2, 178–85.

Caillé, Patricia, and Maher Slouma. 2016. "Portrait d'un entrepreneur: Najeh Slouma, propriétaire d'un vidéo-club en Tunisie." *Africultures*, no. 101–2, 248–53.

Carroll, John. 2001. "Intellectual Property Rights in the Middle East: A Cultural Perspective." *Fordham Intellectual Property, Media and Entertainment Law Journal* 11 (3): 555–600.

Carter, Sandra Gayle. 2009. *What Moroccan Cinema? A Historical and Critical Study, 1956–2006*. Lanham, MD: Lexington Books.

Cheriaa, Tahar. 1978. *Ecrans d'abondance . . . ou cinémas de la libération en Afrique? A propos de l'importation-distribution des films en Afrique (et dans le monde arabe) et de la nécessité de sa nationalisation*. Tunis: SATPEC.

Chevalier, Louis. 1947. *Le problème démographique nord-africain: Travaux et documents*. Cahier no. 6. Paris: Institut national d'etudes démographiques.

Cloarec, Vincent, and Henry Laurens. 2007. *Le Moyen-Orient au 20e siècle*. Paris: Armand Colin.

Cluny, Claude Michel. 1978. *Dictionnaire des nouveaux cinémas arabes*. Paris: Sinbad.

Corm, Georges. 2007. *Le Proche-Orient éclaté, 1956–2007*. Paris: Gallimard.

Cornu, Jean-François. 2014. *Le doublage et le sous-titrage: Histoire et esthétique*. Rennes: Presses universitaires de Rennes.

Corriou, Morgan. 2011. "Un nouveau loisir en situation coloniale: Le cinéma dans la Tunisie du Protectorat (1896–1956)." PhD diss., Université Paris-Diderot.

Crenshaw, Kimberle. 1989. "Demarginalizing the Intersection of Race and Sex: A Black Feminist Critique of Antidiscrimination Doctrine, Feminist Theory and Antiracist Politics." *University of Chicago Legal Forum*, no. 1, 139–67.

Danan, Martine. 1991. "Dubbing as an Expression of Nationalism." *Meta* 36 (4): 606–14.

Decherney, Peter. 2012. *Hollywood's Copyright Wars: From Edison to the Internet*. New York: Columbia University Press.

De Usabel, Gaizka. 1982. *The High Noon of American Films in Latin America*. Ann Arbor, MI: UMI Research Press.

Devictor, Agnès. 2004. *Politique du cinéma iranien: De l'âyatollâh Khomeyni au président Khâtami*. Paris: CNRS Éditions.

D'Hugues, Philippe, and Dominique Muller. 1986. *Gaumont, 90 ans de cinéma*. Paris: Ramsay.

Douin, Jean-Luc. 2001. *Dictionnaire de la censure au cinéma: Images interdites*. Paris: Presses universitaires de France.

———. 2015. *120 ans de cinéma Gaumont*. Paris: Éditions de La Martelière.

Dönmez-Colin, Gönül, ed. 2007. *The Cinema of North Africa and the Middle East*. London: Wallflower.

Dubai Press Club. 2012. *Arab Media Outlook, 2011–2015*. Dubai: Dubai Press Club.

Dwyer, Kevin. 2004. *Beyond Casablanca: M. A. Tazi and the adventure of Moroccan Cinema*. Bloomington: Indiana University Press.

———. 2011. "Morocco: A National Cinema with Large Ambitions" In *Film in the Middle East and North Africa: Creative Dissidence*, edited by Josef Gugler, 325–38. Austin: University of Texas Press.

El Aoufi, Noureddine, and Michel Hollard. 2011. "Politique de la concurrence et spécificités économiques." In *Questions d'économie marocaine*, edited by Azeddine Aksebi et al., 59–84. Rabat: Presses universitaires du Maroc.

EuroMed Audiovisuel II. 2008a. *Paysage audiovisuel méditerranéen: Algérie*.

———. 2008b. *Paysage audiovisuel méditerranéen: Tunisie*.

Ferjani, Riadh. 2011. "L'économie informelle de la communication en Tunisie: De la résistance à la marchandisation." In *Piratages audiovisuels: Les voies souterraines de la mondialisation culturelle*, edited by Tristan Mattelart, 76–99. Brussels: de Boeck.

Ferro, Marc. 1994. *Histoire des colonisations: Des conquêtes aux indépendances, XIIIe–XXe siècle*. Paris: Editions du Seuil.

Film Daily Year Book. 1922–1970. New York: Wid's Films and Film Folks.

Finler, Joel. 2003. *The Hollywood Story*. London: Wallflower.

Forest, Claude. 2018. *Produire des films: Afriques et Moyen Orient*. Villeneuve d'Ascq: Presses universitaires du Septentrion.

Gamal, Muhammad Y. 2008. "Egypt's Audiovisual Translation Scene." *Arab Media and Society*, May.

———. 2009. "Foreign Movies in Egypt: Subtitling, Dubbing and Adaptation." In *Foreign Language Movies: Dubbing vs. Subtitling*, edited by Angelika Goldstein and Biljana Golubović. Hamburg: Verlag Dr. Kovać.

Garçon, François. 2006. *La Distribution cinématographique en France, 1907–1957*. Paris: CNRS Éditions.

Gertz, Nurith, and George Khleifi. 2011. "A Chronicle of Palestinian Cinema." In *Film in the Middle East and North Africa: Creative Dissidence*, edited by Josef Gugler, 187–98. Austin: University of Texas Press.

Ginsberg, Terry, and Chris Lippard. 2010. *Historical Dictionary of Middle Eastern Cinema*. Lanham, MD: Scarecrow.

———, eds. 2020. *Cinema of the Arab World: Contemporary Directions in Theory and Practice*. Cham, Switzerland: Palgrave Macmillan.

Goerg, Odile. 2015. *Fantômas sous les tropiques: Aller au cinéma en Afrique coloniale*. Paris: Vendémiaire.

Gonzalez-Quijano, Yves. 2012. "LBC et Rotana: Passage de la Méditerranée au Golfe." *Culture et politique arabe*, January. https://cpa.hypotheses.org/3213."

Grouix, Pierre, and Rachid Haloui. 2013. *Ciné Fès: La ville, le cinéma, 1896–1963*. Cordes sur Ciel, France: R. de Surtis.

Guback, Thomas. 1969. *The International Film Industry: Western Europe and America since 1945*. Bloomington: Indiana University Press.

Gugler, Josef, ed. 2011. *Film in the Middle East and North Africa: Creative Dissidence*. Austin: University of Texas Press.

Gyory, Michel. 2007. *Questions juridiques relatives à l'industrie du cinéma et de l'audiovisuel dans les pays du Sud de la Méditerrannée*. Euromed Audiovisuel II.

Hadj-Moussa, Ratiba. 2015. *La télévision par satellite au Maghreb et ses publics: Espaces de résistance, espaces critiques*. Grenoble: Presses universitaires de Grenoble.

Hammond, Andrew. 2007. *Popular Culture in the Arab World*. Cairo: American University in Cairo Press.

Hart, Keith. 1992. "Market and State after the Cold War: The Informal Economy Reconsidered." In *Contesting Markets: Analyses of Ideology, Discourse and Practice*, edited by Roy Dilley, 214–27. Edinburgh: Edinburgh University Press.

International Motion Picture Almanac. 1964–2014. Chicago: Quigley.

Issari, Mohammad Ali. 1989. *Cinema in Iran, 1900–1979*. Metuchen: Scarecrow.

Jaidi, Moulay Driss. 1995. *Cinématographiques*. Rabat: Al Majal.

———. 2001. *Histoire du cinéma au Maroc: Le cinéma colonial*. Rabat: Al Majal.

Jaikumar, Priya. 2006. *Cinema at the End of Empire: A Politics of Transition in Britain and India*. Durham, NC: Duke University Press.

Jarvie, Ian. 1992. *Hollywood's Overseas Campaign: The North Atlantic Movie Trade, 1920–1950*. Cambridge: Cambridge University Press.

Kamalipour, Yahya, and Hamid Mowlana, eds. 1994. *Mass Media in the Middle East: A Comprehensive Handbook*. Westport, CT: Greenwood.

Katan Bensamoun, Yvette, and Rama Chalak. 2007. *Le Maghreb: De l'empire ottoman à la fin de la colonisation française*. Paris: Belin.

Kennedy-Day, Kiki. 2001. "Cinema in Lebanon, Syria, Iraq and Kuwait" In *Companion Encyclopedia of Middle Eastern and North African Film*, edited by Oliver Leaman, 364–406. New York: Routledge.

Kerr, Paul, ed. 1986. *The Hollywood Film Industry*. New York: Routledge.

Khamarou, Samir. [c. 1987]. *Le cinéma en Irak*. Master's thesis, Université Paris I Panthéon-Sorbonne.

Khatib, Lina. 2006. *Filming the Modern Middle East: Politics in the Cinemas of Hollywood and the Arab World*. London: I. B. Tauris.

———. 2008. *Lebanese Cinema: Imagining the Civil War and Beyond*. London: I. B. Tauris.

Klinger, Barbara. 2010. "Contraband Cinema: Piracy, *Titanic*, and Central Asia." *Cinema Journal*, 49 (2), 106–24.

Kraidy, Marwan, and Joe Khalil. 2009. *Arab Television Industries*. New York: Palgrave Macmillan.

Labandji, Linda. 2011. "Les biens culturels piratés en Algérie: une fenêtre sur l'ailleurs." In *Piratages audiovisuels: Les voies souterraines de la mondialisation culturelle*, edited by Tristan Mattelart, 123–38. Brussels: de Boeck.

Layadi, Mohamed. 2013. *Etude sur la distribution des films dans les pays du Sud de la Méditerrannée*. Euromed Audiovisuel III.

Leaman, Oliver, ed. 2001. *Companion Encyclopedia of Middle Eastern and North African Film*. New York: Routledge.

León y Barella, Alicia. 2012. *Sauver l'écran en danger: Le cinéma américain en France, 1926–1936*. Thesis for the archivist-paleograph diploma, Ecole nationale des chartes, Paris.

Leonardi, Francesca. 2013. "Les films du débarquement: Etude du lot de 40 longs métrages hollywoodiens sélectionnés par l'Office of War Information pour l'Europe: Genèse, analyse et diffusion en Italie et en France (1943–1945)." PhD diss., Université Sorbonne Nouvelle-Paris 3.

Little, Douglas. 2008. *American Orientalism: The United States and the Middle East since 1945*. Chapel Hill: University of North Carolina Press.

Lobato, Ramon. 2012. *Shadow Economies of Cinema: Mapping Informal Film Distribution*. London: Palgrave Macmillan.

Mahajan, Vijay. 2012. *The Arab World Unbound: Tapping into the Power of 350 Million Consumers*. San Francisco: Jossey-Bass.

Mansour, Dina. 2012. "Egyptian Film Censorship: Safeguarding Society, Upholding Taboos." *Alphaville: Journal of Film and Screen Media*, no. 4. http://www.alphavillejournal.com/Issue%204/PDFs/ArticleMansour.pdf.

Martel, Frédéric. 2010. *Mainstream: Enquête sur cette culture qui plaît à tout le monde*. Paris: Flammarion.

Martin, Florence. 2011. "Cinema and State in Tunisia." In *Film in the Middle East and North Africa: Creative Dissidence*, edited by Josef Gugler, 271–85. Austin: University of Texas Press.

Mattelart, Tristan. 2011. "Piratages audiovisuels et réseaux de la mondialisation par le bas." In *Piratages audiovisuels: Les voies souterraines de la mondialisation culturelle*, edited by Tristan Mattelart, 5–26. Brussels: de Boeck.

Megherbi, Abdelghani. 1985. *Le miroir aux alouettes: Lumière sur les ombres hollywoodiennes en Algérie et dans le monde*. Algiers: ENAL.

Meusy, Jean-Jacques. 2009. *Cinémas de France, 1894–1918: Une histoire en images.* Paris: Arcadia.

Middle East Motion Picture Almanac, 1946–1947. 1947. Cairo: Éditions Jacques Pascal.

Miller, Tobby, Nitin Govil, John McMurria, and Richard Maxwell. 2001. *Global Hollywood.* London: British Film Institute.

Mingant, Nolwenn. 2002. *La pénétration du cinéma américain en France (1944–1958).* Master's thesis, *Université Rennes 2.*

———. 2010. *Hollywood à la conquête du monde: Marchés, stratégies, influences.* Paris: CNRS Éditions.

———. 2012. "No Sex in This City: Hollywood face à la censure au Moyen-Orient." Paper presented at the fifth Droit et Cinema conference, La Rochelle, France, June.

———. 2015a. "Cinema and Social Structures: Hollywood Films and Female Spectators in North Africa and the Middle East." Paper presented at the SERCIA conference, Université d'Arras, September.

———. 2015b. "A Peripheral Market? Hollywood Majors in the Middle East/North Africa Market." *Velvet Light Trap,* no. 75, 73–87.

———. 2016a. "Cinéma hollywoodien en Afrique du Nord et au Moyen-Orient: Une cartographie du marché." *Africultures,* no. 101–2, 128–51.

———. 2016b. "Algérie: Une filière cinématographqiue en lambeaux—témoignages croisés." *Africultures,* no. 101–2, 202–13.

———. 2017. "Un public aux mille visages: Identifier l'expérience des spectateurs du cinéma américain dans le Maghreb de l'ère coloniale." In *Regarder des films en Afriques,* edited by Patricia Caillé and Claude Forest, 63–78. Villeneuve d'Ascq: Presses universitaires du Septentrion.

———. 2018. "Entrer dans le monde du cinéma au XXIe siècle/ Image Nation Abu Dhabi." In *Produire des films: Afriques et Moyen Orient,* edited by Claude Forest, 169–80. Villeneuve d'Ascq: Presses universitaires du Septentrion.

———. 2019. "When the *Thief of Baghdad* Tried to Steal the Show: The Short-Lived Dubbing of Hollywood Films into Arabic in the 1940s." In *Reassessing Dubbing: Historical Approaches and Current Trends,* edited by Irene Ranzato and Serenella Zanotti, 41–62. Amsterdam: John Benjamins.

Mingant, Nolwenn, and Gianluca Chakra. 2016. "Croissance exponentielle au Moyen-Orient." *Africultures,* no. 101–2, 190–201.

Mingant, Nolwenn, and Efi Lifshitz. 2016. "Aperçu du marché cinématographique en Israël." *Africultures,* no. 101–2, 186–89.

Mingant, Nolwenn, Gilles Renouard, and Jean-Christophe Baubiat. 2016. "Promouvoir la circulation du film français en Afrique du Nord et au Moyen-Orient: Le rôle d'UniFrance films." *Africultures,* no. 101–2, 160–69.

Mingant, Nolwenn, and Cecilia Tirtaine. 2018. *Reconceptualising Film Policies.* New York: Routledge.

Moine, Caroline. 2013. "La Fédération internationale des associations de pro-
ducteurs de films: un acteur controversé de la promotion du cinéma après
1945." *Le mouvement social* 2 (243): 91–103.

Naficy, Hamid. 2011a. *A Social History of Iranian Cinema.* Vol. 1, *The Artisanal
Era, 1897–1941.* Durham, NC: Duke University Press.

———. 2011b. *A Social History of Iranian Cinema.* Vol. 2, *The Industrializing Years,
1941–1979.* Durham, NC: Duke University Press.

———. 2012a. *A Social History of Iranian Cinema.* Vol. 3, *The Islamicate Period,
1978–1984.* Durham, NC: Duke University Press.

———. 2012b. *A Social History of Iranian Cinema.* Vol. 4, *The Globalizing Era,
1984–2010.* Durham, NC: Duke University Press.

Newman, David. 2013. "Resisting Hollywood? A Comparative Study of British
Colonial Screen Policies in the Interwar Pacific: Hong Kong, Singapore
and New Zealand." PhD diss., Simon Fraser University, Burnaby, BC.

Nouailhat, Yves-Henri. 2015. *Les Etats-Unis et le monde de 1898 à nos jours.* Paris:
Armand Colin.

Nouri, Shakir. 1986. *A la recherche du cinéma irakien, 1945–1985.* Paris: L'Harmattan.

Orlando, Valerie. 2011. *Screening Morocco: Contemporary Depictions in Film of a
Changing Society.* Athens: Ohio University Press.

Oruc, Firat. 2020. "Petrocolonial Circulations and Cinema's Arrival in the Gulf."
Film History 32 (3):10–42.

Pardo, Alejandro. 2007. *The Europe-Hollywood Coopetition: Cooperation and Competition
in the Global Film Industry.* Pamplona: Ediciones Universidad de Navarra.

Perren, Alisa. 2013. "Rethinking Distribution for the Future of Media Industry
Studies." *Cinema Journal* 52 (3): 165–71.

Perrin, Dominique. 2000. *Palestine: Une terre, deux peuples.* Strasbourg: Septentrion.

Piquet, Caroline. 2013. *Les pays du Golfe de la perle à l'économie de la connaissance:
Les nouvelles terres du libéralisme.* Paris: Armand Colin.

Puttnam, David. 1997. *The Undeclared War: The Struggle for Control of the World's
Film Industry.* London: Harper Collins.

Rouissi, Moncer. 1983. *Population et société au Maghreb.* Horizon maghrébin 1.
Tunis: Cérès.,

Rugh, William. 2004. *Arab Mass Media.* Westport, CT: Praeger.

Sadoul, Georges. 1962. *Histoire du cinéma mondial des origines à nos jours.* Paris:
Flammarion.

———, ed. 1966. *Les cinémas des pays arabes.* Beirut: Centre interarabe du cinéma
et de la télévision.

Sadr, Hamid Reza. 2006. *Iranian Cinema: A Political History.* London: I. B. Tauris.

Sakr, Naomi. 2001. *Satellite Realms: Transnational Television, Globalization and the
Middle East.* London: I. B. Taurus.

———. 2007. *Arab Television Today.* London: I. B. Taurus.

Salmon, Stéphanie. 2014. *Pathé: A la conquête du cinéma, 1896–1929.* Paris: Tallandier.

Segrave, Kerry. 1997. *American Films Abroad: Hollywood's Domination of the World's
Movie Screens from the 1890s to the Present.* Jefferson, NC: McFarland.

———. 2003. *Piracy in the Motion Picture Industry.* Jefferson, NC: McFarland.

Sela, Avraham, ed. 2002. *The Continuum Political Encyclopedia of the Middle East.* New York: Continuum.

Shafik, Viola. 2001. "Cinema in Palestine." In *Companion Encyclopedia of Middle Eastern and North African Film*, edited by Oliver Leaman, 518–32. New York: Routledge.

———. 2007. *Arab Cinema: History and Cultural Identity.* New rev. ed. Cairo: American University in Cairo Press.

Shaheen, Jack. 2008. *Guilty: Hollywood's Verdict on Arabs after 9/11.* Northampton, MA: Olive Branch.

———. 2009. *Reel Bad Arabs: How Hollywood Vilifies a People.* Rev. ed. Northampton, MA: Olive Branch.

Shawky, Ahmed. 2016. "Aperçu du marché égyptien." *Africultures*, no. 101–2, 170–75.

Shohat, Ella. 1989. *Israeli Cinema: East/West and the Politics of Representation.* Austin: University of Texas Press.

Shohat, Ella, and Robert Stam. 1994. *Unthinking Eurocentrism: Multiculturalism and the Media.* London: Routledge.

Simsi, Simon. 2000. *Ciné-passions.* Paris: Dixit.

Smyth, Rosaleen. 1979. "The Development of British Colonial Film Policy, 1927–1939, with Special Reference to East and Central Africa." *Journal of African History* 20 (3): 437–50.

Sohrabi, Hadi, and Behzad Dowran. 2016. "Iran: A Friction between State Ideology and Network Society." In *Geoblocking and Global Video Culture*, edited by Ramon Lobato and James Meese, 168–77. Theory on Demand 18. Amsterdam: Institute of Network Cultures.

Srour, Némésis. 2018. "Bollywood film traffic: Circulation des films hindi au Moyen-Orient (1954–2014)." PhD diss., Ecole des hautes etudes en sciences sociales.

Srour, Némésis, and Antoine Zeind. 2016. "Pourquoi devrais-je prendre des risques et [distribuer] un film Bollywood?" *Africultures*, no. 101–2, 152–59.

Stora, Benjamin. 2012. "Le cinéma algérien, entre deux guerres." *Confluences Méditerranée* 2 (81): 181–88.

Tav-Nof, Zeev. 1974. "Israel." *International Film Guide 1974.* London: Tàntivy.

Thiollet, Hélène. 2009. *Le Moyen-Orient: 50 cartes et fiches.* Paris: Ellipses.

Thompson, Kristin. 1985. *Exporting Entertainment: America in the World Film Market, 1907–1934.* London: British Film Institute.

Thompson, Elizabeth. 2000. *Colonial Citizens: Republican Rights, Paternal Privilege, and Gender in French Syria and Lebanon.* New York: Columbia University Press.

———. 2010. "Scarlett O'Hara in Damascus: Hollywood, Colonial Politics, and Arab Spectatorship during World War II." In *Globalizing American Studies*, edited by Brian T. Edwards and Dilip Parameshwar Gaonkar, 184–208. Chicago: University of Chicago Press.

Thoraval, Yves. 1996. *Regards sur le cinéma égyptien.* 2nd ed. Paris: Harmattan.

———. 2000. *Les cinémas du Moyen-Orient: Iran, Egypte, Turquie, 1896–2000.* Paris: Séguier.

————. 2003. *Les ecrans du croissant fertile: Irak, Liban, Palestine, Syrie*. Biarritz, France: Atlantica.

Trumpbour, John. 2002. *Selling Hollywood to the World: U.S. and European Struggles for Mastery of the Global Film Industry, 1920–1959*. New York: Cambridge University Press.

Ulf-Møller, Jens. 2001. *Hollywood's Film Wars with France: Film Trade Diplomacy and the Emergence of the French Film Quota Policy*. Rochester, NY: University of Rochester Press.

UNESCO Institute for Statistics (UIS). 2021. "Egypt, Cinema infrastructure." http://uis.unesco.org/en/country/eg?theme=culture.

UNESCO. 1949. *Rapport de la commission des besoins techniques: Presse, film, radio— après enquête dans quatorze pays et territoires*. Paris: UNESCO.

Union Internationale des Cinémas (UNIC). 2017. *Annual Report*.

Union Internationale des Cinémas (UNIC). 2018. *Annual Report*.

United States Trade Representative (USTR). 1988–2018. Special 301 reports.

US Department of Commerce. [c. 1928]. *Short-Subject Film Market in Latin America, Canada, the Far East, Africa and the Near East*. Trade Information Bulletin no. 544.

————. 1930. *Market for US Motion Picture Equipment in Asia, Africa and Oceania*. Trade Information Bulletin no. 701.

————. 1949a. *Digest of International Developments: Iraq*. World Trade in Commodities, September.

————. 1949b. *Motion Picture Digest of International Development: Egypt*.

Vasey, Ruth. 1997. *The World According to Hollywood, 1918–1939*. Madison: University of Wisconsin Press.

Vitalis, Robert. 2000. "American Ambassador in Technicolor and Cinemascope: Hollywood and Revolution on the Nile." In *Mass Mediations: New Approaches to Popular Culture in the Middle East and Beyond*, edited by Walter Armbrust, 269–91. Berkeley: University of California Press.

Weiss, Martin. 2017. "Arab League Boycott of Israel." Congressional Research Service, August 25, 2017. https://sgp.fas.org/crs/mideast/RL33961.pdf.

Wid's Year Book. 1920–1921. New York: Wid's Films and Film Folks.

Willems, Gilles. 1997. "Aux origines du groupe Pathé-Nathan." In *Une histoire économique du cinéma français (1895–1995)*, edited by Pierre-Jean Benghozi and Christian Delage, 93–110. Paris: Harmattan.

Yunis, Alia. 2014. "Red Carpet Education: The Persian Gulf Approach to Film Festivals." In *Film Festival Yearbook 6: Film Festivals and the Middle East*, edited by Dina Iordanova, and Stefanie Van de Peer, 270–83. St. Andrews, Scotland: St. Andrews Film Studies.

Archives

Bibliothèque du film, Cinémathèque française, Paris, France.

Centre des archives diplomatiques de Nantes, France.
    Beirut (92PO/B, 91PO/B/212, 91PO/B 103).
    Morocco (1MA/200/187, 1MA/200/190, 1MA/200/191 A, 1MA/200/191 B).
    Syria/Lebanon (1SL/250/1-83).
National Archives at College Park, Maryland (NARA), USA.
    Record Group 59, General Records of the Department of State, Country
        Files, 1910–1963.
    Record Group 59, General Records of the Department of State, INCO
        Motion Pictures, 1963–1973.
    Record Group 151, Records of the Bureau of Foreign and Domestic
        Commerce, 281 Motion Pictures General.
    Online archives of the National Archives, RG 59, 1973–1977. https://www.
        archives.gov/.
Margaret Herrick Library (MHL), Los Angeles, USA.
    Clipping files.
Pathé Archives, Fondation Seydoux-Pathé, Paris, France.

Interviews

I am deeply indebted to the film professionals in North Africa, the Middle East, France, and the US who accepted an invitation to share their insights with me. Two dozen interviews were led with film distributors. The book also benefited from discussions with other interlocutors as diverse as the Oman embassy staff and the European Motion Picture Association managing director. Some of the interviewees agreed to appear in the book and are listed below. Given the sensitive nature of the information shared, some preferred to remain anonymous. The interviews were led by the author, mostly by Skype or on the phone, and were occasionally complemented by email exchanges. Mohamed Layadi's remarks were part of a discussion held at a MENA Cinema seminar, at the Maison des sciences de l'homme Paris-Nord.

Ali-Yahia, Malek. MD Ciné, Algeria. Conducted in 2013.
Awad, Sherif. Former UIP manager, Egypt. Conducted in 2013.
Benkiran, Najib. Former president of the Moroccan Chamber of Film Distributors.
    Conducted in 2013 and 2017.
Chakra, Gianluca. Front Row Entertainment, Dubai. Conducted in 2013.
Cripps, Andrew. Former president and COO of UIP. Conducted in 2013.
El-Azar, Selim. Gulf Film, UAE. Conducted in 2014.
Fahim, Joseph. Chief programmer, Cairo International Film Festival, Egypt.
    Conducted in 2013.
Hachemi, Zertal. Cirta Films, Algeria. Conducted in 2013.
Haddad, Mario, Sr. CEO Empire and Empire International, Beirut. Conducted
    in 2014.

Marrakchi, Hamid. Former president of the Moroccan Chamber of Exhibitors. Conducted in 2013.

Mekary, Pierre. Operations manager, Iraqi Cinema, Baghdad. Conducted in 2018.

Layadi, Mohamed. Exhibitor, le Colisée, Marrakech. Conducted in 2015.

Marcich, Chris. President and managing director of MPA EMEA office, Brussels. Conducted in 2014.

Mounim, Tarik. Save Cinemas in Morocco, Casablanca. Conducted in 2018.

Saliby, Hyam. Italia Film International, Beirut. Conducted in 2014.

Salem, Badar. Former *Variety Arabia* journalist. Conducted in 2013.

Sigaro, Alina. Universal Pictures International. Conducted in 2013.

Viane, Mark. Former distribution executive, UIP. Conducted in 2013.

Zeind, Antoine. United Motion Pictures, Egypt. Conducted in 2013 and 2018.

Index

THE SUNY SERIES

HORIZONS of CINEMA

MURRAY POMERANCE | EDITOR

Nenad Jovanovic, *Brechtian Cinemas*

Will Scheibel, *American Stranger*

Amy Rust, *Passionate Detachments*

Steven Rybin, *Gestures of Love*

Seth Friedman, *Are You Watching Closely?*

Roger Rawlings, *Ripping England!*

Michael DeAngelis, *Rx Hollywood*

Ricardo E. Zulueta, *Queer Art Camp Superstar*

John Caruana and Mark Cauchi, editors, *Immanent Frames*

Nathan Holmes, *Welcome to Fear City*

Homer B. Pettey and R. Barton Palmer, editors, *Rule, Britannia!*

Milo Sweedler, *Rumble and Crash*

Ken Windrum, *From El Dorado to Lost Horizons*

Matthew Lau, *Sounds Like Helicopters*

Dominic Lennard, *Brute Force*

William Rothman, *Tuitions and Intuitions*

Michael Hammond, *The Great War in Hollywood Memory, 1918–1939*

Burke Hilsabeck, *The Slapstick Camera*

Niels Niessen, *Miraculous Realism*

Alex Clayton, *Funny How?*

Bill Krohn, *Letters from Hollywood*

Alexia Kannas, *Giallo!*

Homer B. Pettey, editor, *Mind Reeling*

Matthew Leggatt, editor, *Was It Yesterday?*

Merrill Schleier, editor, *Race and the Suburbs in American Film*

Neil Badmington, *Perpetual Movement*

George Toles, *Curtains of Light*

Erica Stein, *Seeing Symphonically*

Alexander Sergeant, *Encountering the Impossible*

Brendan Hennessey, *Luchino Visconti and the Alchemy of Adaptation*

William Rothman, *The Holiday in His Eye*

Jason Sperb, *The Hard Sell of Paradise*

†Charles Warren, edited by William Rothman and Joshua Schulze, *Writ on Water*

CPSIA information can be obtained
at www.ICGtesting.com
Printed in the USA
LVHW012140121022
730573LV00003B/168